IRON MAN
LEGACY OF DOOM

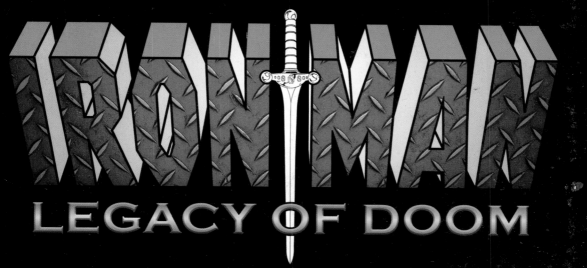

IRON MAN
LEGACY OF DOOM

Plot: David Michelinie & Bob Layton
Script: David Michelinie
Pencils: Ron Lim
Inks: Bob Layton
Colors: Chris Sotomayor & Moose Baumann (Issue #1)
Letters: Artmonkeys Studios

Editors: Molly Lazer with Alejandro Arbona

Collection Editor: Cory Levine

Assistant Editor: John Denning

Editors, Special Projects: Jennifer Grünwald & Mark D. Beazley

Senior Editor, Special Projects: Jeff Youngquist

Senior Vice President of Sales: David Gabriel

Book Design: Carrie Beadle

Special Thanks to Stuart Vandal

Editor in Chief: Joe Quesada
Publisher: Dan Buckley

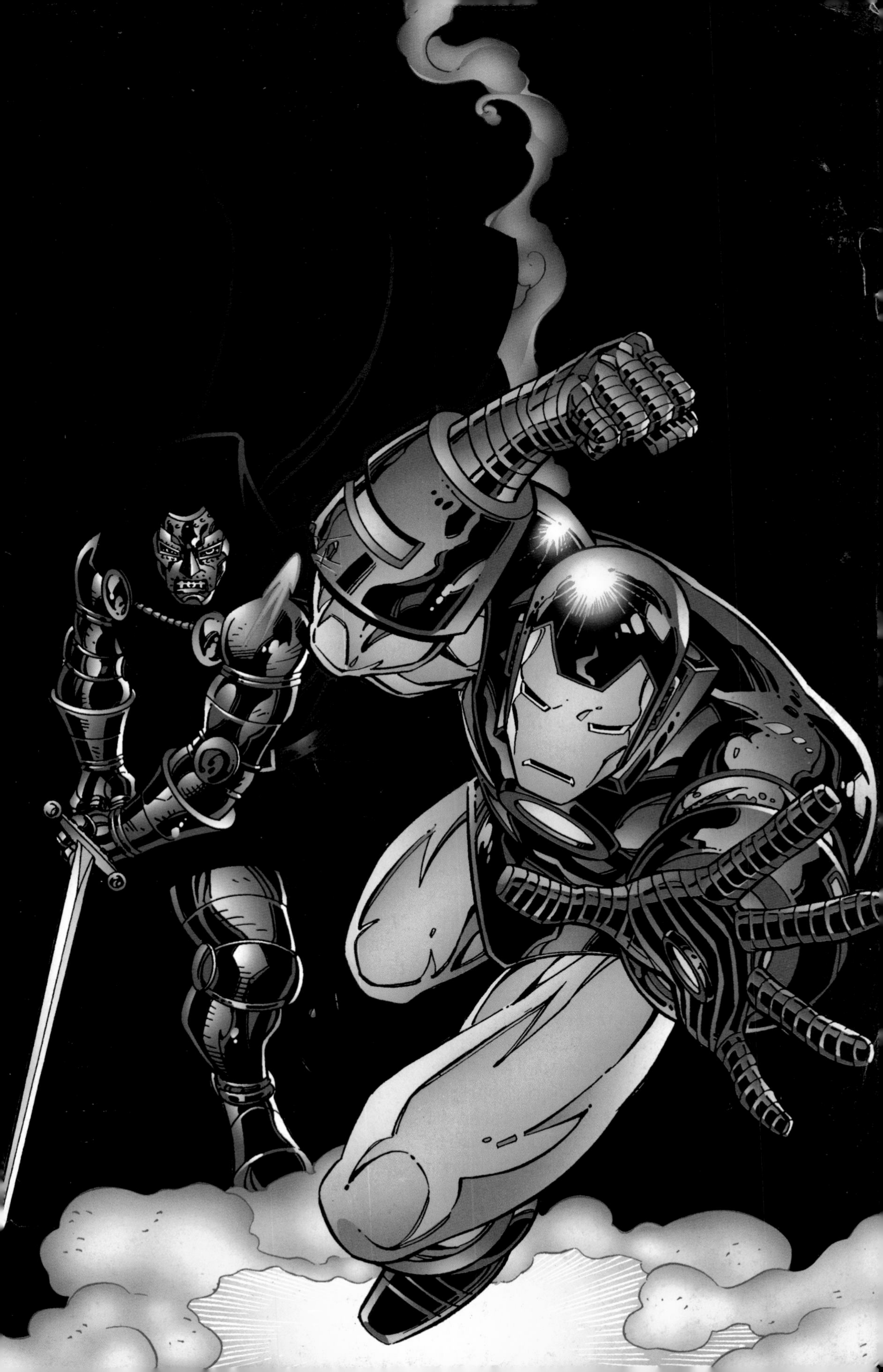

Previously in "Doomquest" (*Iron Man #149-150* and *#249-250*)

With his sorceress mother long trapped in Mephisto's realm, once a year on mid-summer's eve Latverian tyrant Victor von Doom would have a window of opportunity to free her. Having found his science insufficient to defeat the demons guarding her, Doctor Doom turned to sorcery, using his time machine to study under the greatest mages of history. Seeking the tutelage of King Arthur's evil half-sister, the witch Morgan Le Fay, Doom discovered his time machine needed booster circuits, which he elected to steal from Stark International. The company's owner, Tony Stark, a.k.a. the armored Avenger Iron Man, tracked Doom back to his castle, breached its defenses and confronted Doom. The two men ended up grappling atop Doom's time machine, when Doom's servant Dr. Gert Hauptmann seized the opportunity to avenge his brother Gustav, casually murdered by Doom years earlier. Triggering the time machine, Hauptmann flung both men into the distant past, then destroyed the device to trap them there!

Ironically the two foes found themselves exactly where Doom had been trying to reach, rematerializing in 6th century Britain just outside of Camelot, late in Arthur's reign. Merlin's spells had trapped Morgan in her castle in the Valley of Wailing Mists after her repeated attempts to slay Arthur, and Merlin himself had been laid to rest by the sorceress Nimue, to sleep until his country and king most needed him again. Suspicious that the new arrivals' "magic" was related to Morgan, Arthur's knights brought the pair before the king. Arthur bid them each stay the night while he deliberated their conflicting stories. Absconding as soon as he learned Morgan's whereabouts, Doom visited the imprisoned enchantress, who agreed to teach him if he first slew Arthur for her. Using a metal chip taken from Arthur's sword Excalibur, Morgan raised an undead army, which Doom then led in battle against Arthur's knights and Iron Man. With Arthur's forces losing to opponents who continued to fight even after being hacked to pieces, Iron Man realized the only chance to win was to stop the person animating them, and he fled the field, racing to Morgan's castle. Morgan watched him easily best her stronghold's defenses, and she fled into another dimension, her legions of the damned collapsing like puppets with their strings cut. Doom rushed to the castle, fearing that his bargain could not now be fulfilled, and angrily confronted Iron Man, promising to slay him...one day. For with no reason now to stay, Doom sought to return home, and he recognized it would take the circuitry in both their armors to have a chance of constructing a device to do so. Agreeing to a temporary truce and working together, the two scientists succeeded, returning to their own era, but before they went their separate ways, Doom promised they would meet again...

As prophecy dictated, in 2093 A.D. Merlin awoke after centuries of slumber as the time of Britain's greatest need approached. Prophecy also stated King Arthur would be reborn to defend his country, but Merlin discovered modern technology had interfered; Arthur had been due to be born seventeen years before Merlin awoke, thus ensuring he would be of age when the crisis ensued, but Arthur's parents had chosen to pursue their careers before having children, and had the embryo frozen for more than a decade. Though possessed of his former life's memories, Arthur was a child in form, too young and frail for the trials ahead. Meanwhile the threat revealed itself, as an elderly Doctor Doom, kept alive beyond his allotted span through a combination of sorcery and science allied himself with Andros Stark, descendent of Arno Stark the Iron Man of 2020, to usurp control of ancient but lethal defense satellites orbiting the Earth. Informed by Arthur about Tony Stark and Doom's visit to Camelot, Merlin summoned the two of them to 2093 and asked for their assistance during the current crisis. Tony found himself outmatched by his successor and was forced to flee from combat, while Doom refused to help, instead intending to return home with purloined future weapons. However, after discovering that only Merlin's magic could return him home, and only if he returned as he had come, in the company of Iron Man, Doom acquiesced. Armed with Excalibur, Iron Man had a rematch with Andros, this time soundly defeating him, while Doom destroyed his future self as an abomination lacking dignity. With their mission completed Merlin returned the two men home. As they were about to depart, Doom taunted Iron Man with the revelation that he had learned Stark's dual identity from 2093's history books and would use that knowledge against him. However, Merlin's spell did not permit either man to return with anything they had not brought with them, and they reappeared in the present with their memories of the future taken from them. Exchanging harsh words but unsure what had happened, the two men parted company once more.

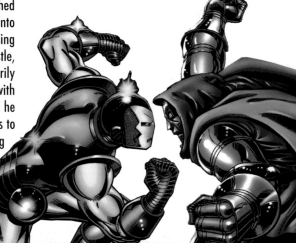

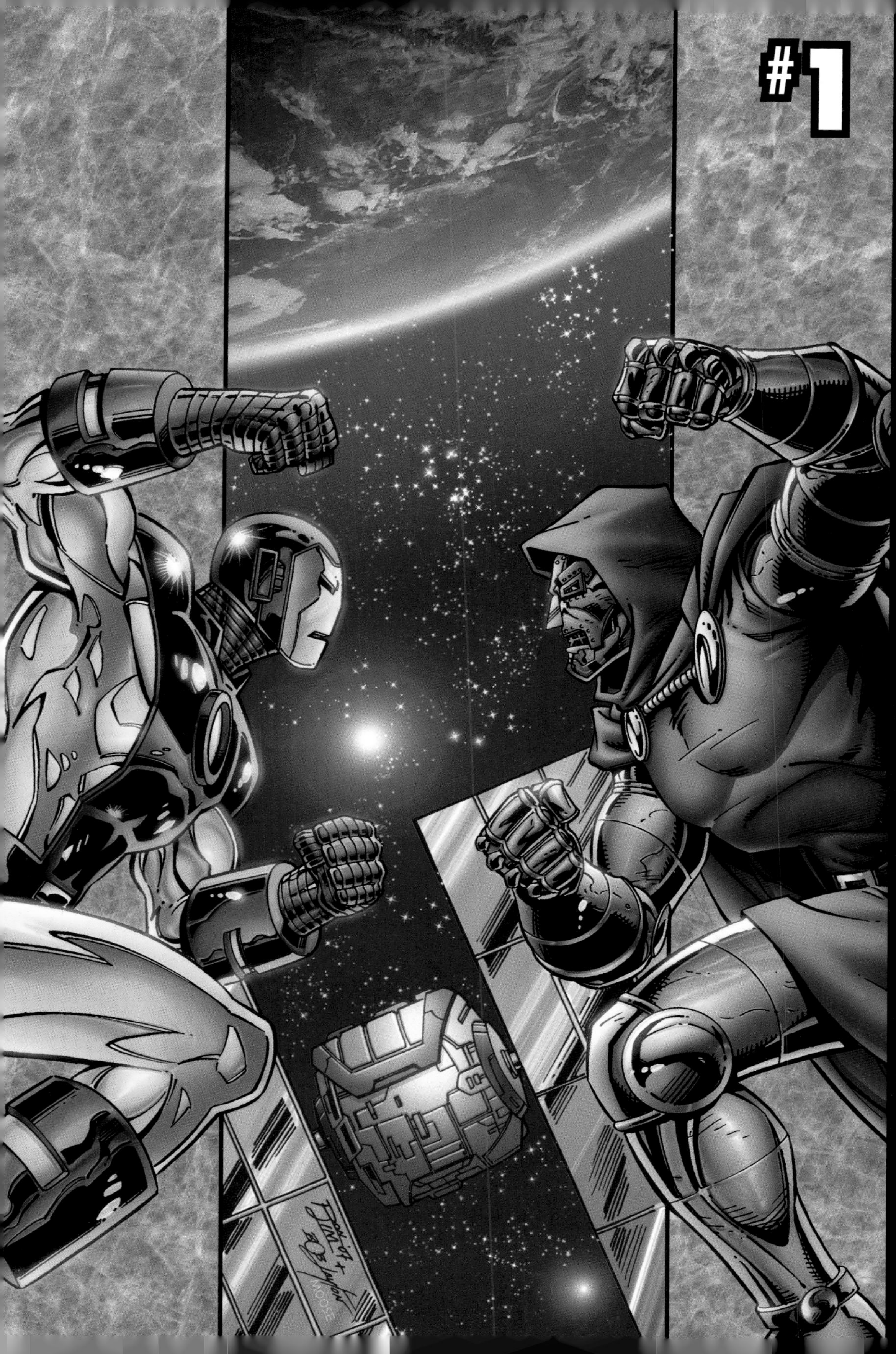
#1

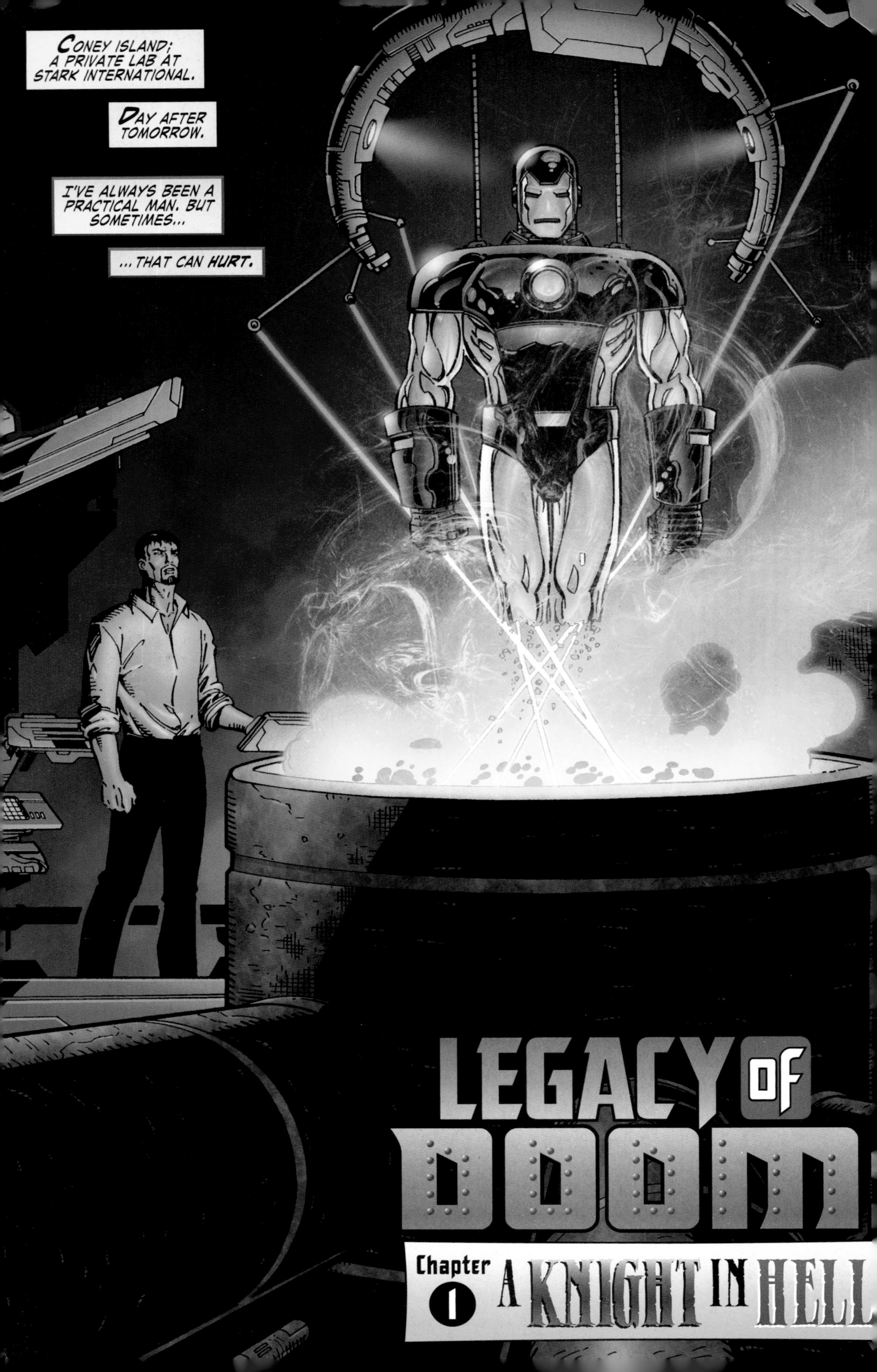
CONEY ISLAND; A PRIVATE LAB AT STARK INTERNATIONAL.
DAY AFTER TOMORROW.
I'VE ALWAYS BEEN A PRACTICAL MAN. BUT SOMETIMES...
...THAT CAN HURT.
LEGACY OF DOOM
Chapter 1 A KNIGHT IN HELL

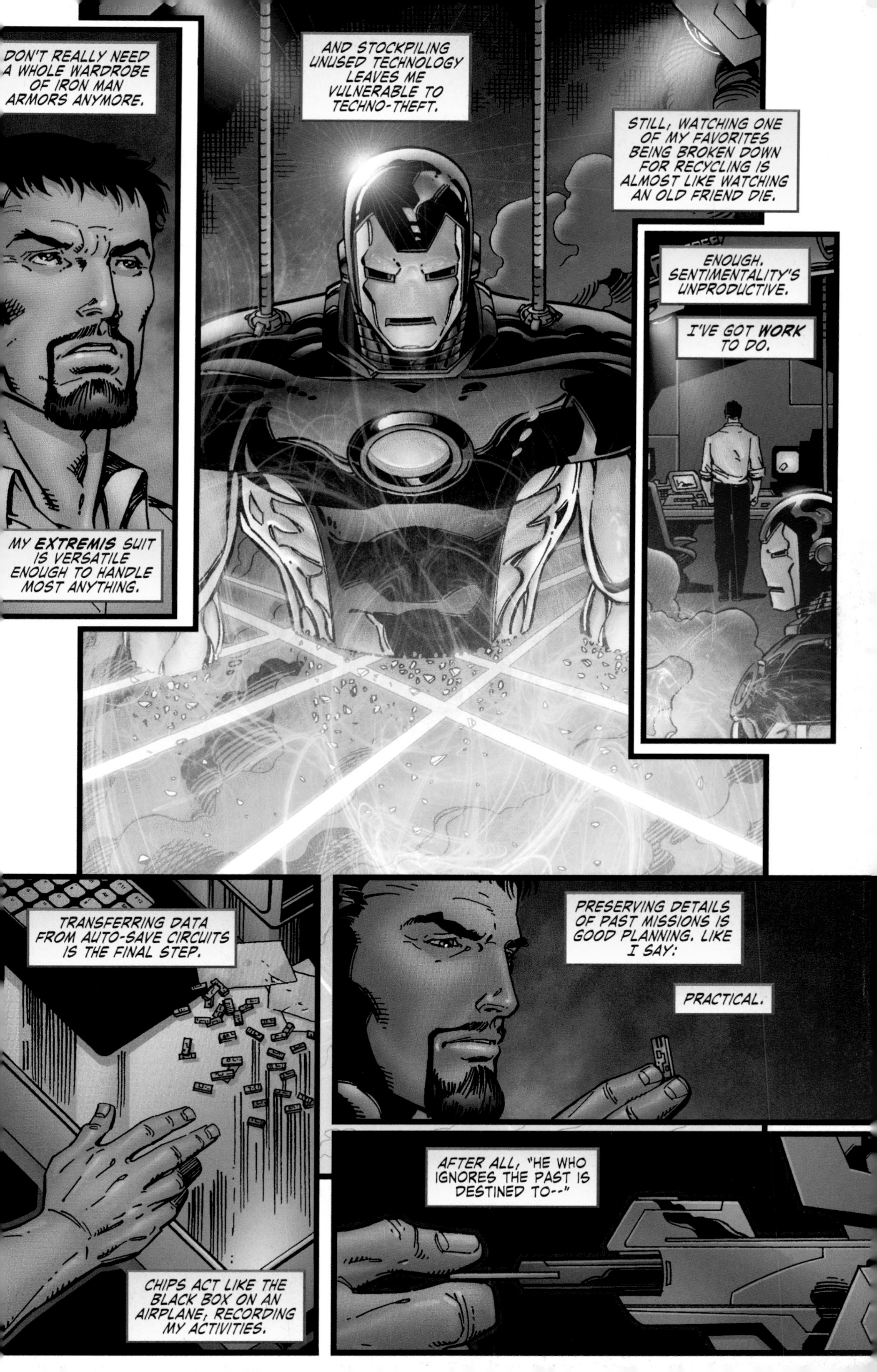
DON'T REALLY NEED A WHOLE WARDROBE OF IRON MAN ARMORS ANYMORE.
MY **EXTREMIS** SUIT IS VERSATILE ENOUGH TO HANDLE MOST ANYTHING.
AND STOCKPILING UNUSED TECHNOLOGY LEAVES ME VULNERABLE TO TECHNO-THEFT.
STILL, WATCHING ONE OF MY FAVORITES BEING BROKEN DOWN FOR RECYCLING IS ALMOST LIKE WATCHING AN OLD FRIEND DIE.
ENOUGH. SENTIMENTALITY'S UNPRODUCTIVE.
I'VE GOT **WORK** TO DO.
TRANSFERRING DATA FROM AUTO-SAVE CIRCUITS IS THE FINAL STEP.
CHIPS ACT LIKE THE BLACK BOX ON AN AIRPLANE, RECORDING MY ACTIVITIES.
PRESERVING DETAILS OF PAST MISSIONS IS GOOD PLANNING. LIKE I SAY:
PRACTICAL.
AFTER ALL, "HE WHO IGNORES THE PAST IS DESTINED TO--"

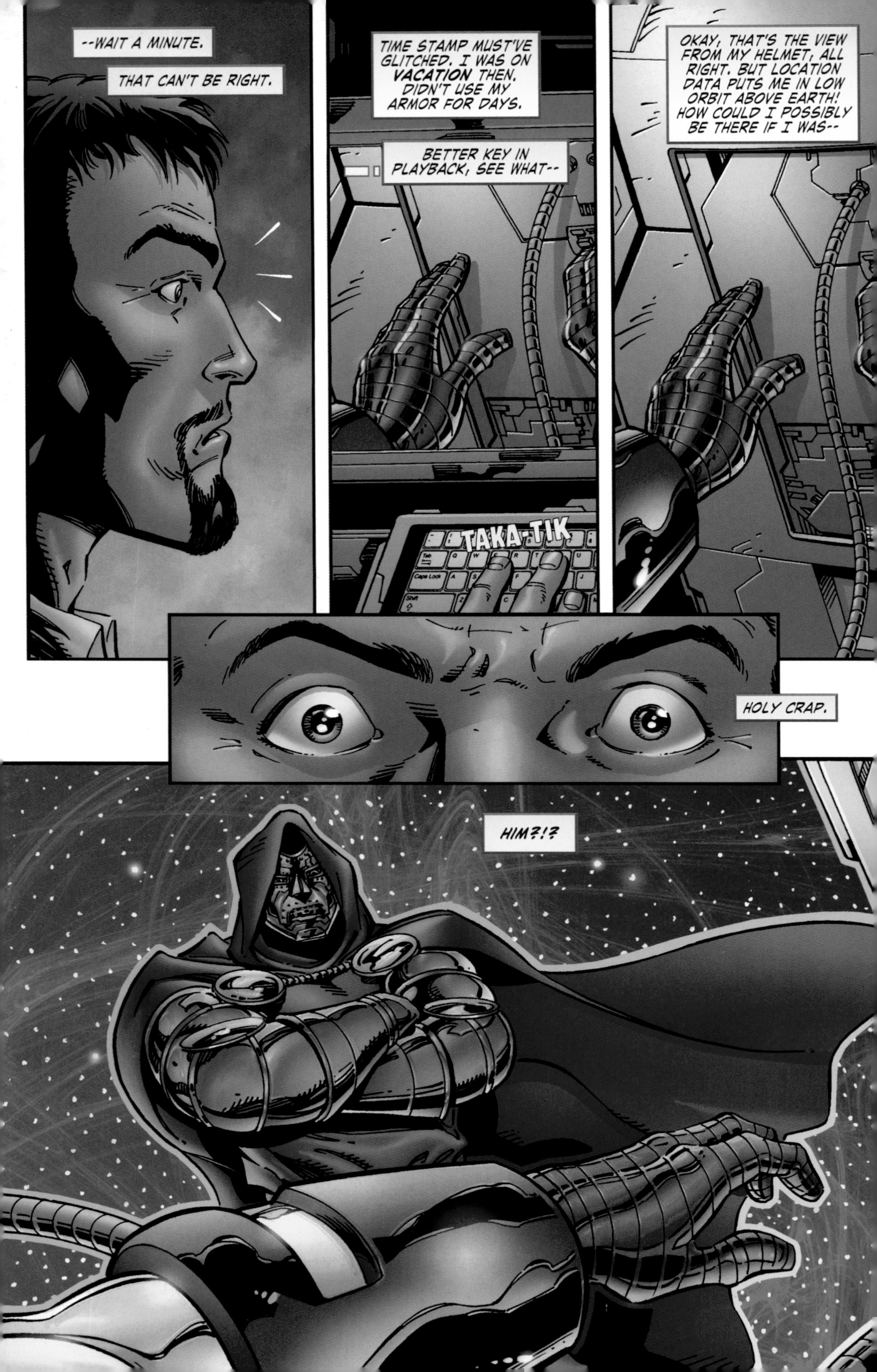
--WAIT A MINUTE.
THAT CAN'T BE RIGHT.
TIME STAMP MUST'VE GLITCHED. I WAS ON VACATION THEN. DIDN'T USE MY ARMOR FOR DAYS.
BETTER KEY IN PLAYBACK, SEE WHAT--
TAKA-TIK
OKAY, THAT'S THE VIEW FROM MY HELMET, ALL RIGHT. BUT LOCATION DATA PUTS ME IN LOW ORBIT ABOVE EARTH! HOW COULD I POSSIBLY BE THERE IF I WAS--
HOLY CRAP.
HIM?!?

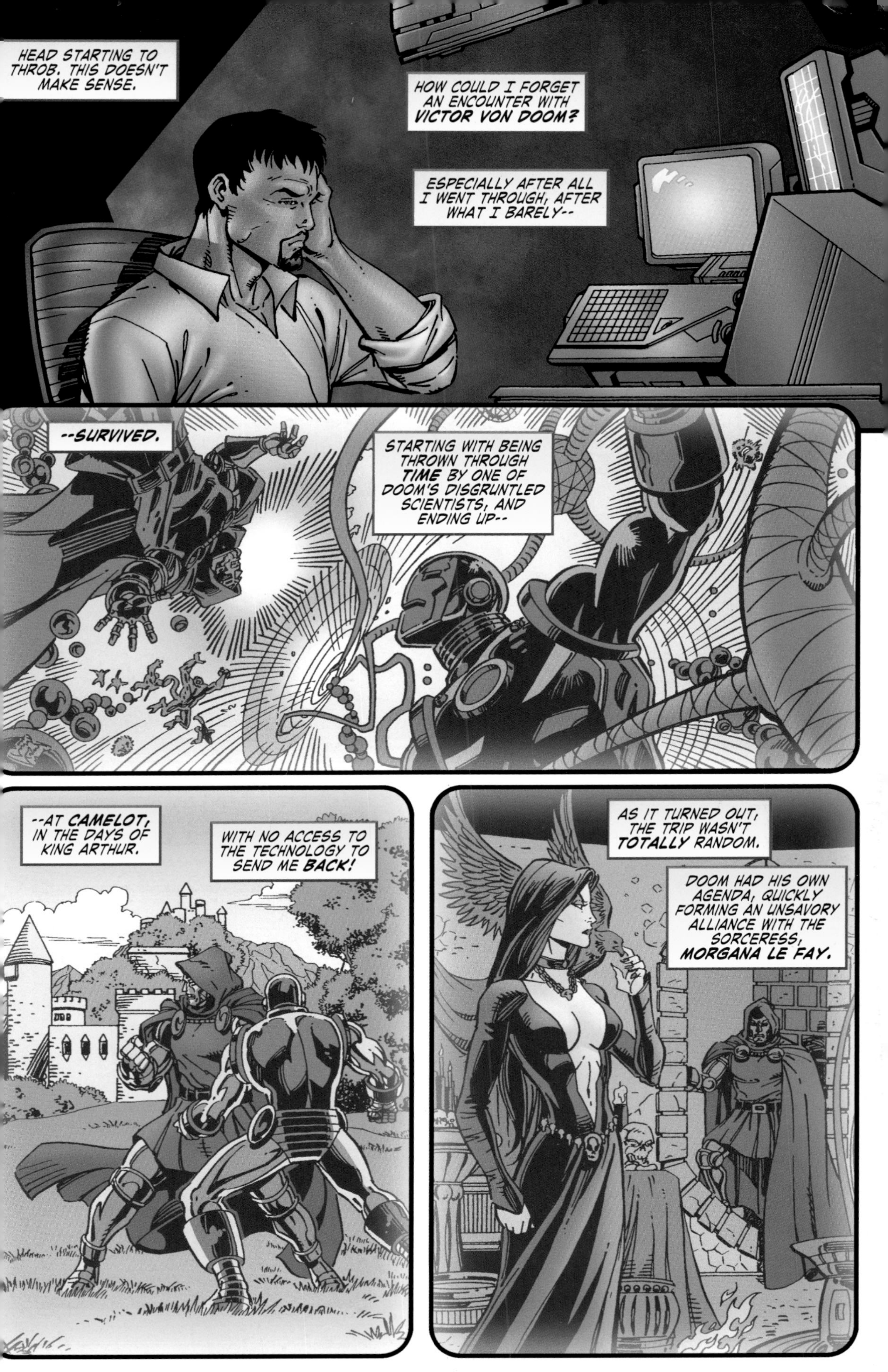
HEAD STARTING TO THROB. THIS DOESN'T MAKE SENSE.
HOW COULD I FORGET AN ENCOUNTER WITH VICTOR VON DOOM?
ESPECIALLY AFTER ALL I WENT THROUGH, AFTER WHAT I BARELY--
--SURVIVED.
STARTING WITH BEING THROWN THROUGH TIME BY ONE OF DOOM'S DISGRUNTLED SCIENTISTS, AND ENDING UP--
--AT CAMELOT, IN THE DAYS OF KING ARTHUR.
WITH NO ACCESS TO THE TECHNOLOGY TO SEND ME BACK!
AS IT TURNED OUT, THE TRIP WASN'T TOTALLY RANDOM.
DOOM HAD HIS OWN AGENDA, QUICKLY FORMING AN UNSAVORY ALLIANCE WITH THE SORCERESS, MORGANA LE FAY.

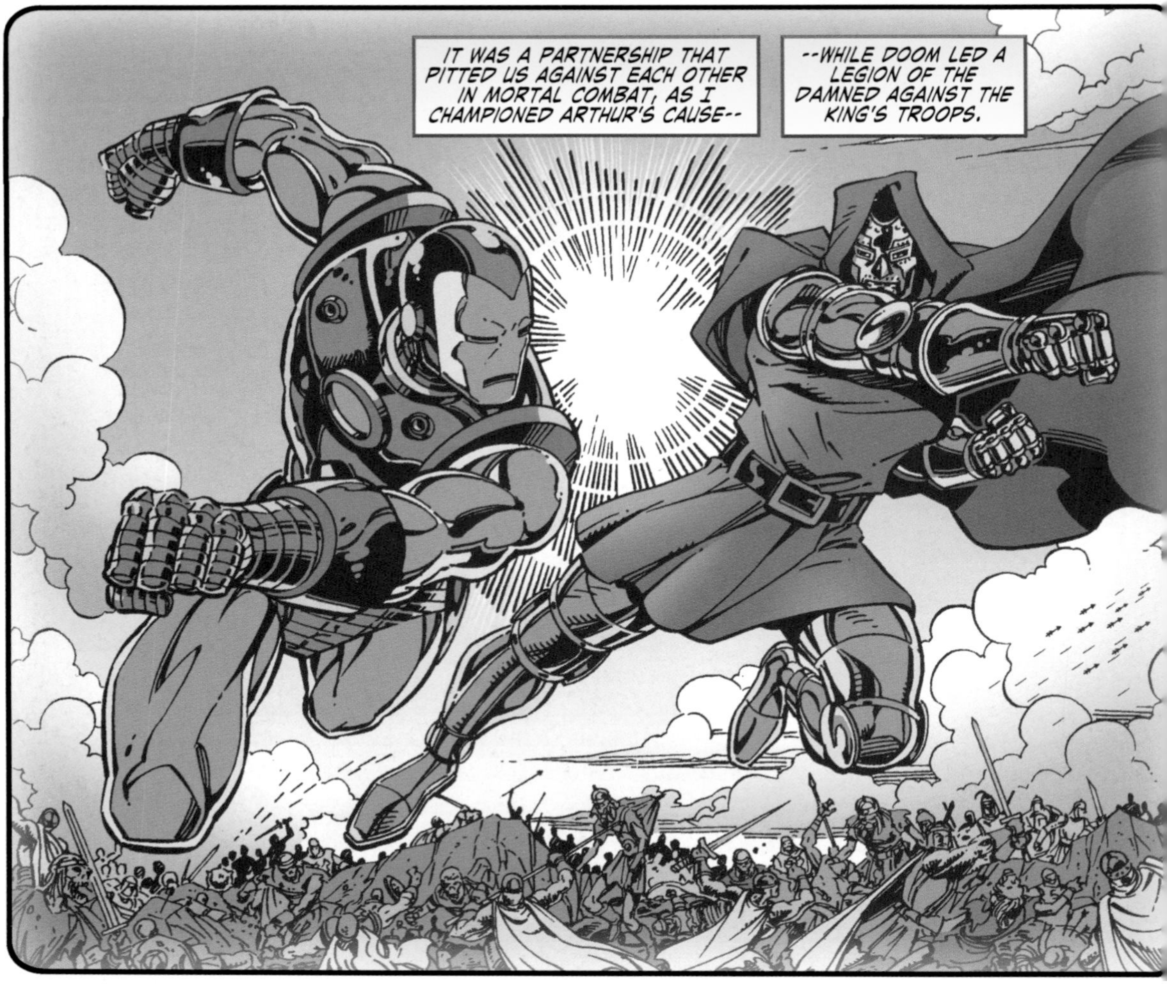
IT WAS A PARTNERSHIP THAT PITTED US AGAINST EACH OTHER IN MORTAL COMBAT, AS I CHAMPIONED ARTHUR'S CAUSE--
--WHILE DOOM LED A LEGION OF THE DAMNED AGAINST THE KING'S TROOPS.
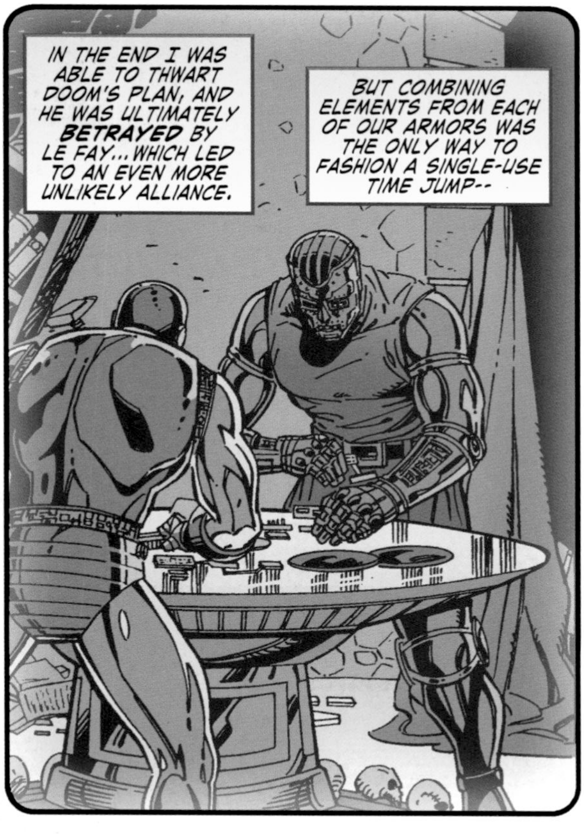
IN THE END I WAS ABLE TO THWART DOOM'S PLAN, AND HE WAS ULTIMATELY **BETRAYED** BY LE FAY...WHICH LED TO AN EVEN MORE UNLIKELY ALLIANCE.
BUT COMBINING ELEMENTS FROM EACH OF OUR ARMORS WAS THE ONLY WAY TO FASHION A SINGLE-USE TIME JUMP--
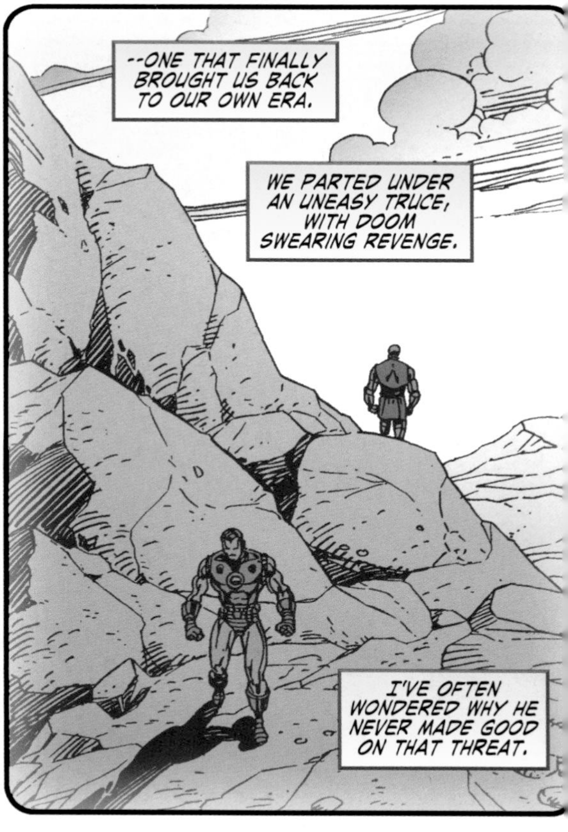
--ONE THAT FINALLY BROUGHT US BACK TO OUR OWN ERA.
WE PARTED UNDER AN UNEASY TRUCE, WITH DOOM SWEARING REVENGE.
I'VE OFTEN WONDERED WHY HE NEVER MADE GOOD ON THAT THREAT.

WHICH STILL DOESN'T EXPLAIN--

--AGH! HEAD FEELS LIKE IT'S BEING RIPPED APART!

ONE IMAGE TRIGGERING ANOTHER, LIKE A DAM BURSTING! IT'S TOO MUCH!

I...I-I...

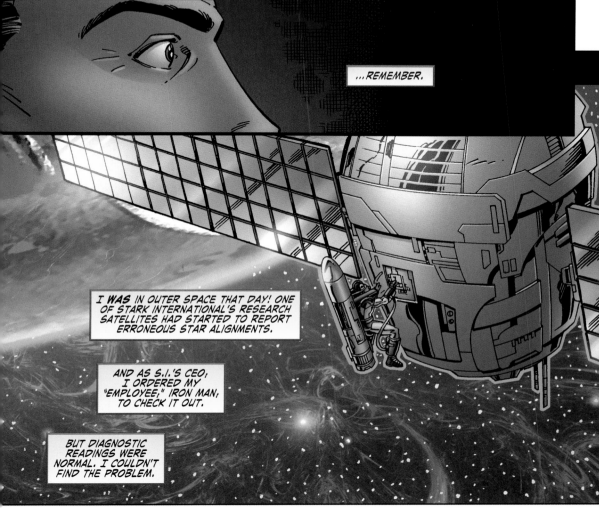

...REMEMBER.

I *WAS* IN OUTER SPACE THAT DAY! ONE OF STARK INTERNATIONAL'S RESEARCH SATELLITES HAD STARTED TO REPORT ERRONEOUS STAR ALIGNMENTS.

AND AS S.I.'S CEO, I ORDERED MY "EMPLOYEE," IRON MAN, TO CHECK IT OUT.

BUT DIAGNOSTIC READINGS WERE NORMAL. I COULDN'T FIND THE PROBLEM.

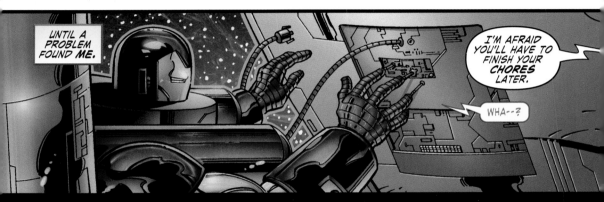

UNTIL A PROBLEM FOUND ME.

I'M AFRAID YOU'LL HAVE TO FINISH YOUR CHORES LATER.

WHA--?

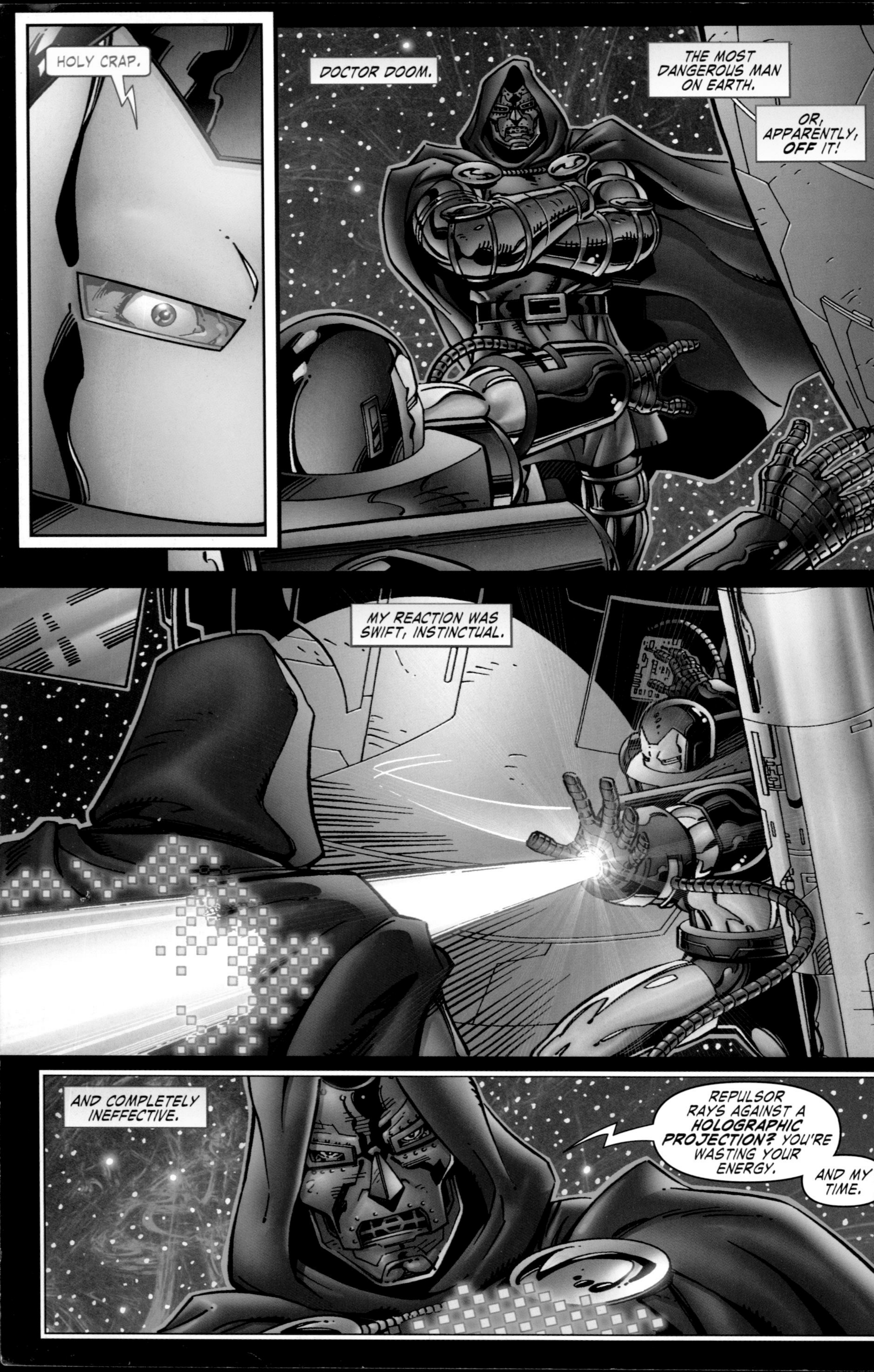
HOLY CRAP.
DOCTOR DOOM.
THE MOST DANGEROUS MAN ON EARTH.
OR, APPARENTLY, OFF IT!
MY REACTION WAS SWIFT, INSTINCTUAL.
AND COMPLETELY INEFFECTIVE.
REPULSOR RAYS AGAINST A HOLOGRAPHIC PROJECTION? YOU'RE WASTING YOUR ENERGY.
AND MY TIME.

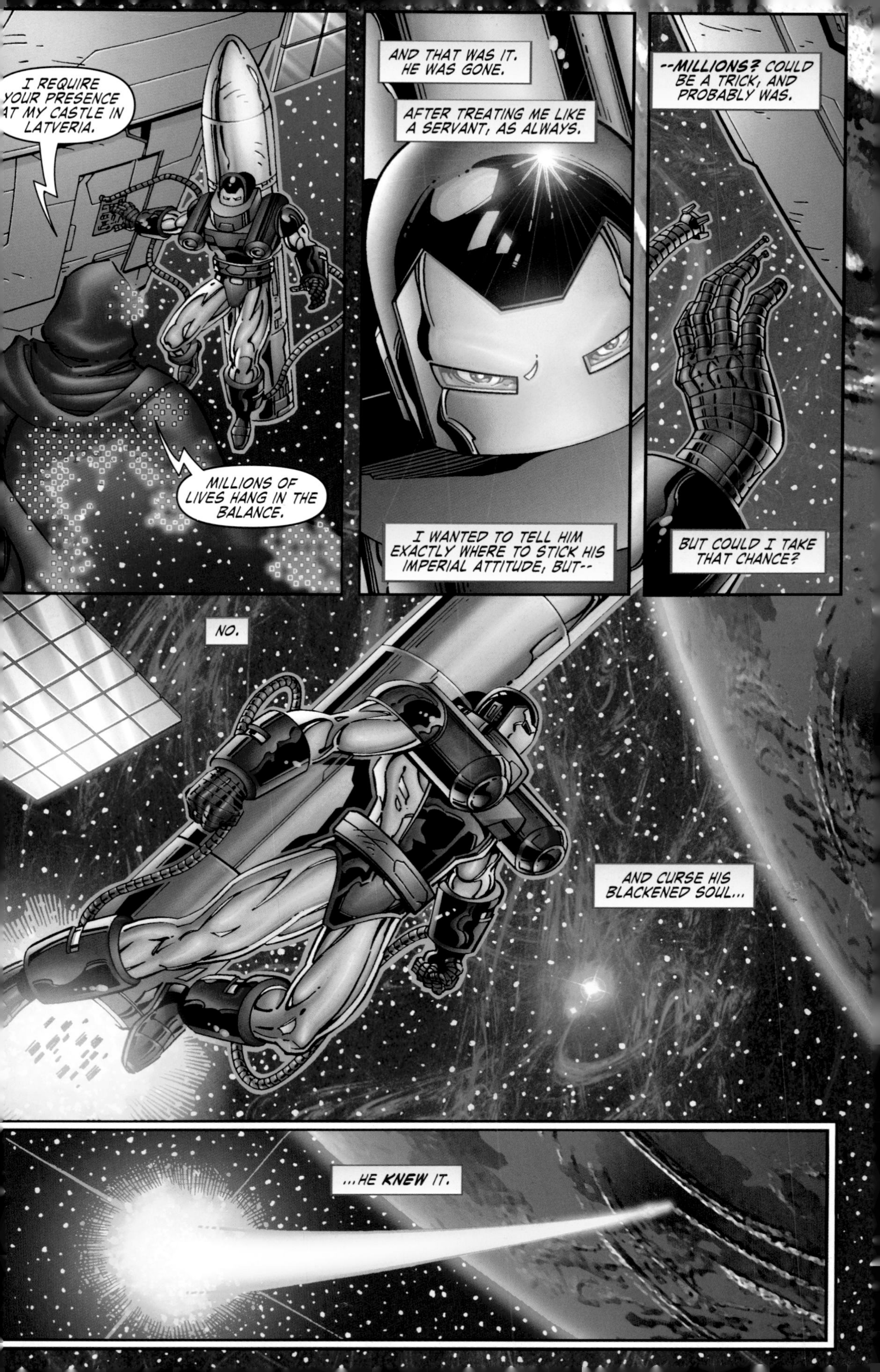

I REQUIRE YOUR PRESENCE AT MY CASTLE IN LATVERIA.
MILLIONS OF LIVES HANG IN THE BALANCE.
AND THAT WAS IT. HE WAS GONE.
AFTER TREATING ME LIKE A SERVANT, AS ALWAYS.
I WANTED TO TELL HIM EXACTLY WHERE TO STICK HIS IMPERIAL ATTITUDE, BUT--
--MILLIONS? COULD BE A TRICK, AND PROBABLY WAS.
BUT COULD I TAKE THAT CHANCE?
NO.
AND CURSE HIS BLACKENED SOUL...
...HE KNEW IT.

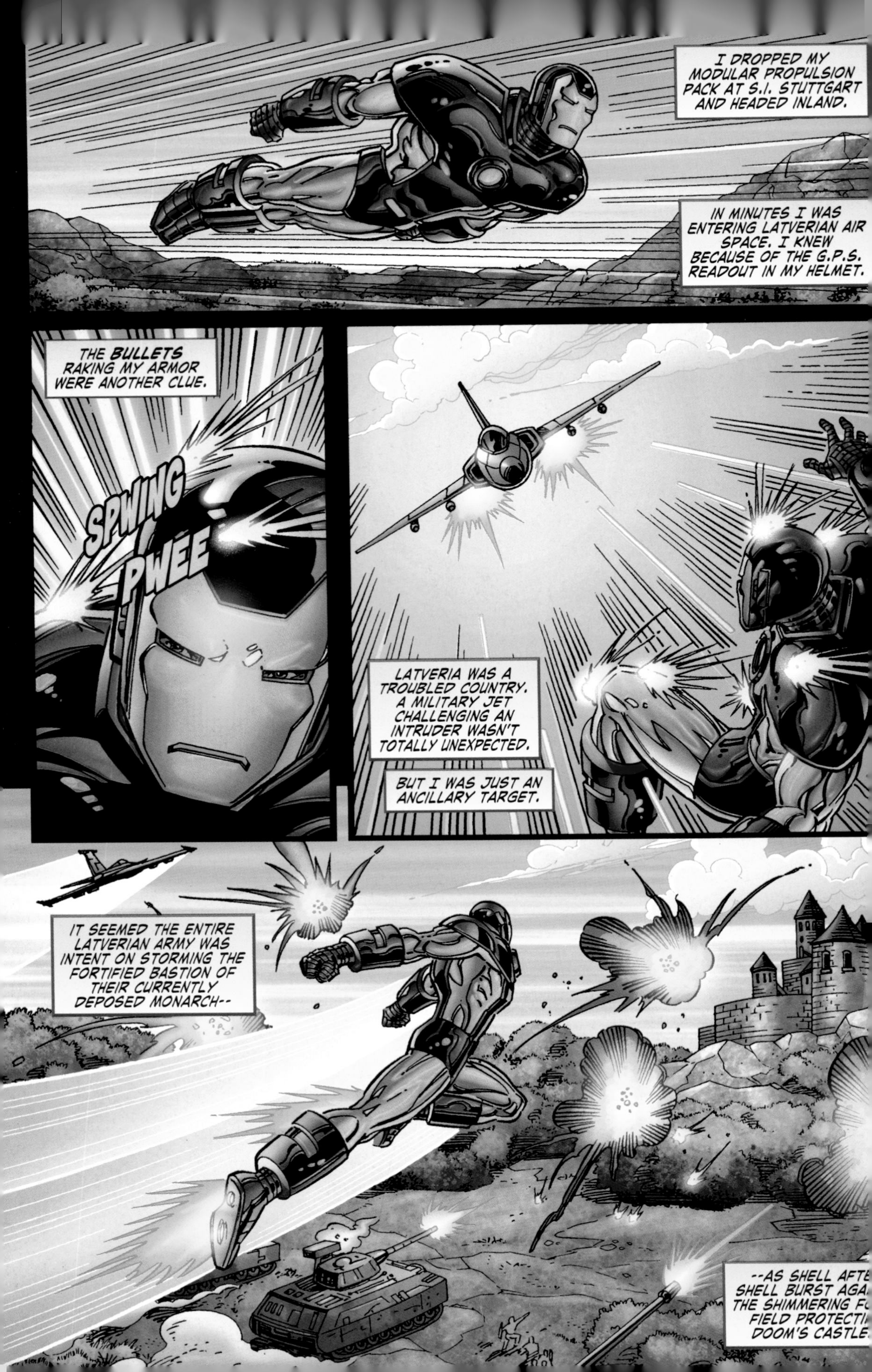
I DROPPED MY MODULAR PROPULSION PACK AT S.I. STUTTGART AND HEADED INLAND.
IN MINUTES I WAS ENTERING LATVERIAN AIR SPACE. I KNEW BECAUSE OF THE G.P.S. READOUT IN MY HELMET.
THE BULLETS RAKING MY ARMOR WERE ANOTHER CLUE.
SPWING
PWEE
LATVERIA WAS A TROUBLED COUNTRY. A MILITARY JET CHALLENGING AN INTRUDER WASN'T TOTALLY UNEXPECTED.
BUT I WAS JUST AN ANCILLARY TARGET.
IT SEEMED THE ENTIRE LATVERIAN ARMY WAS INTENT ON STORMING THE FORTIFIED BASTION OF THEIR CURRENTLY DEPOSED MONARCH--
--AS SHELL AFTE
SHELL BURST AGA
THE SHIMMERING F
FIELD PROTECTI
DOOM'S CASTLE

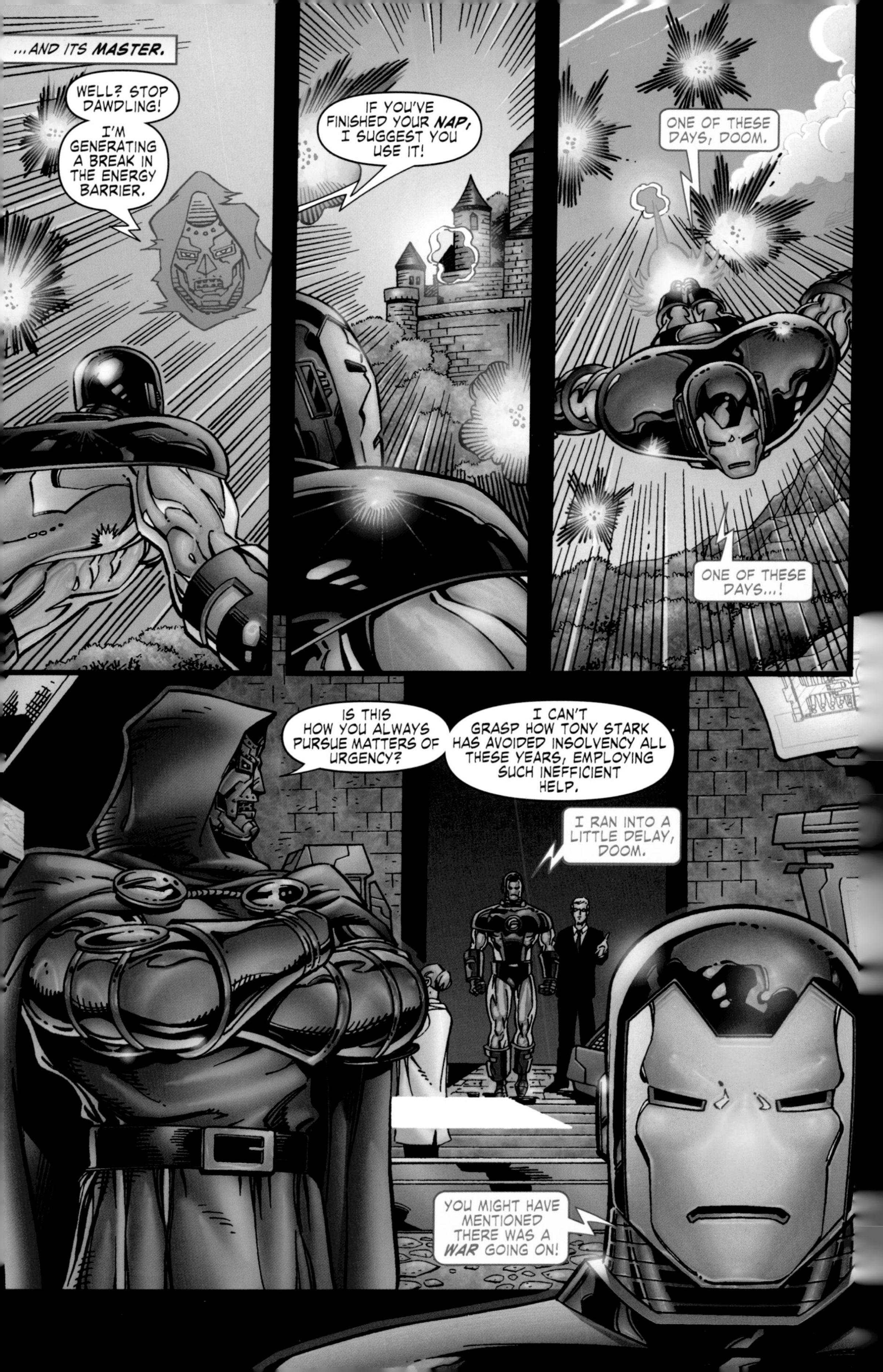
...AND ITS MASTER.
WELL? STOP DAWDLING!
I'M GENERATING A BREAK IN THE ENERGY BARRIER.
IF YOU'VE FINISHED YOUR NAP, I SUGGEST YOU USE IT!
ONE OF THESE DAYS, DOOM.
ONE OF THESE DAYS...!
IS THIS HOW YOU ALWAYS PURSUE MATTERS OF URGENCY?
I CAN'T GRASP HOW TONY STARK HAS AVOIDED INSOLVENCY ALL THESE YEARS, EMPLOYING SUCH INEFFICIENT HELP.
I RAN INTO A LITTLE DELAY, DOOM.
YOU MIGHT HAVE MENTIONED THERE WAS A WAR GOING ON!

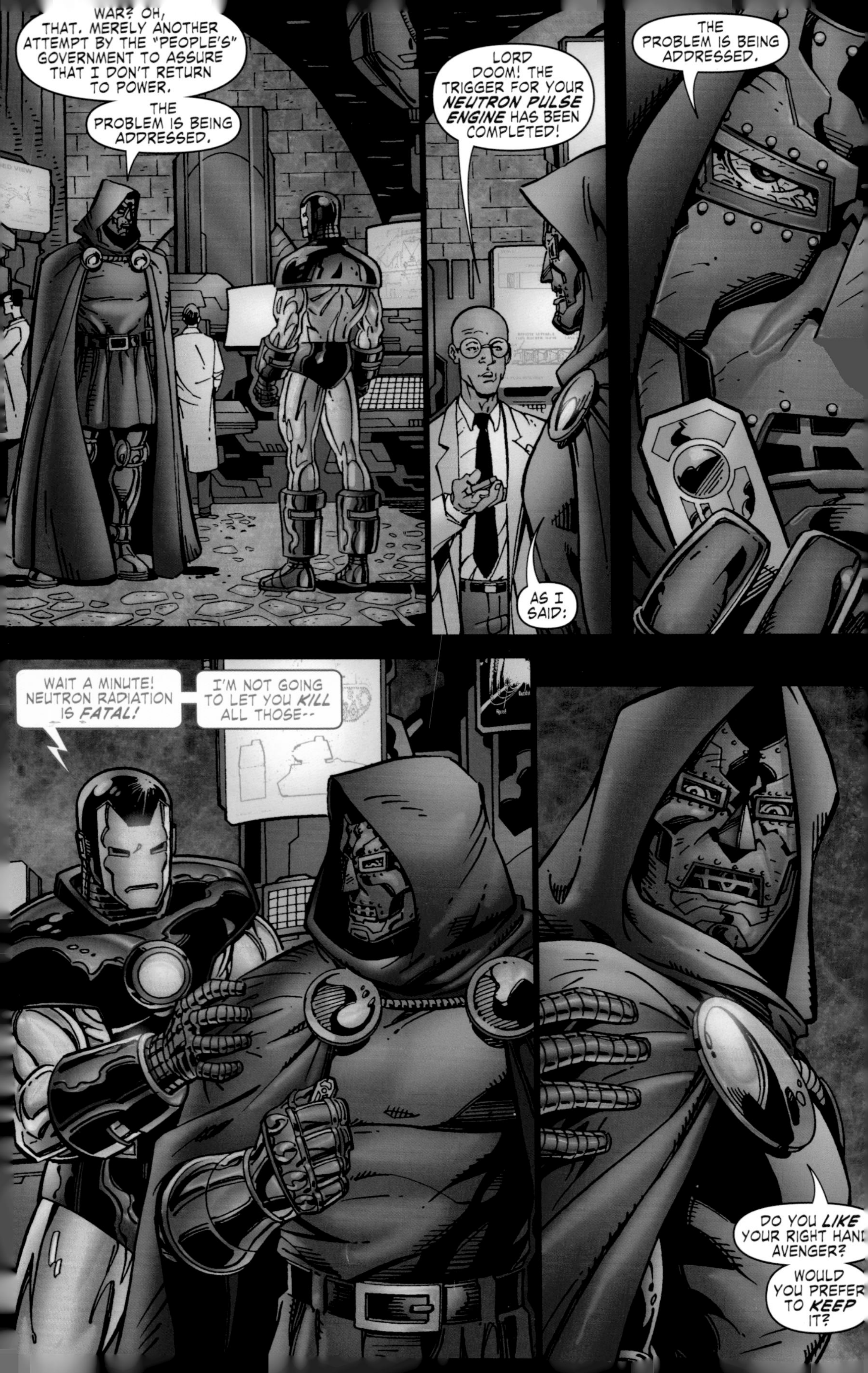
WAR? OH, THAT. MERELY ANOTHER ATTEMPT BY THE "PEOPLE'S" GOVERNMENT TO ASSURE THAT I DON'T RETURN TO POWER.
THE PROBLEM IS BEING ADDRESSED.
LORD DOOM! THE TRIGGER FOR YOUR NEUTRON PULSE ENGINE HAS BEEN COMPLETED!
AS I SAID:
THE PROBLEM IS BEING ADDRESSED.
WAIT A MINUTE! NEUTRON RADIATION IS FATAL!
I'M NOT GOING TO LET YOU KILL ALL THOSE--
DO YOU LIKE YOUR RIGHT HAND AVENGER?
WOULD YOU PREFER TO KEEP IT?

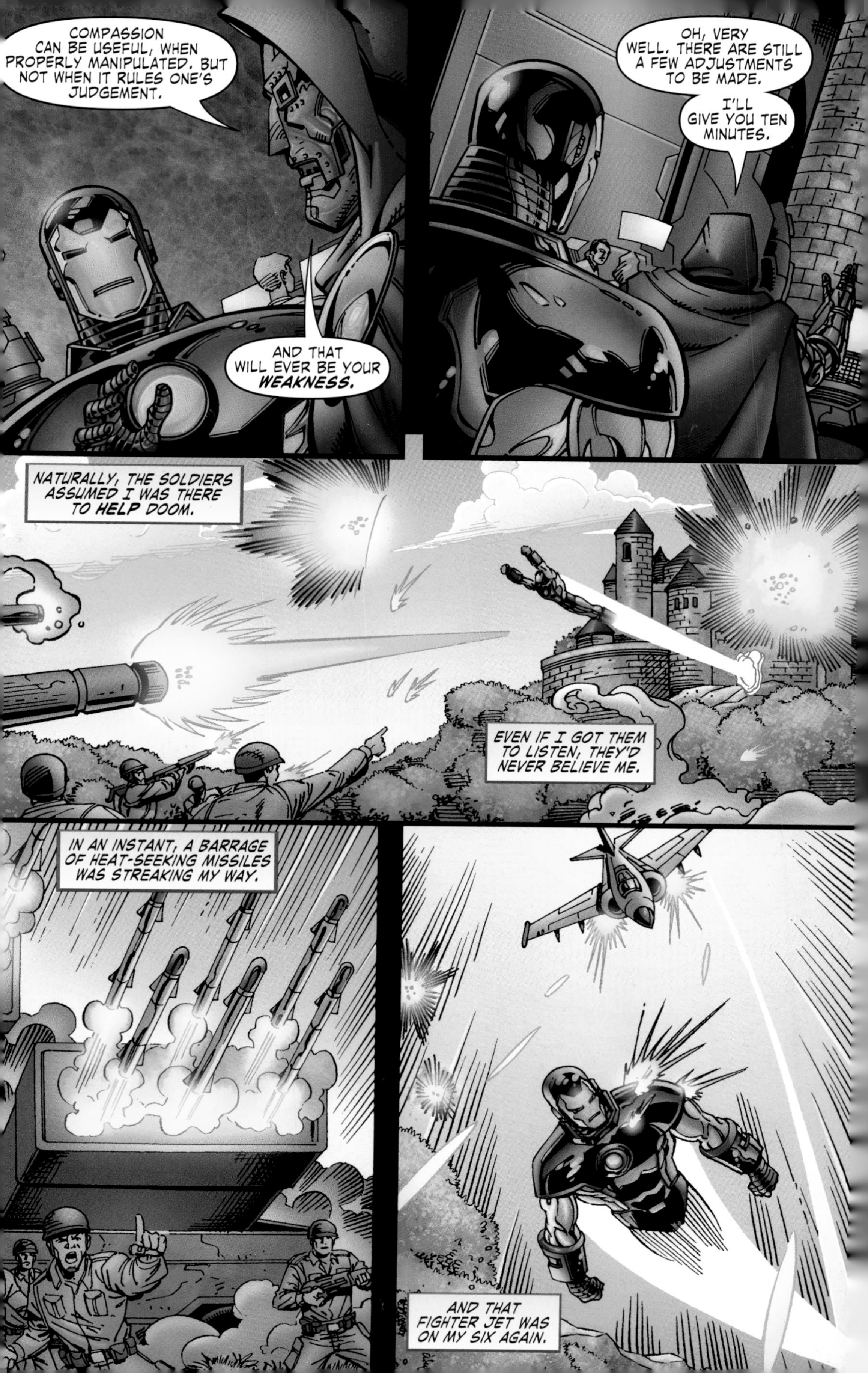
COMPASSION CAN BE USEFUL, WHEN PROPERLY MANIPULATED. BUT NOT WHEN IT RULES ONE'S JUDGEMENT.
AND THAT WILL EVER BE YOUR WEAKNESS.
OH, VERY WELL. THERE ARE STILL A FEW ADJUSTMENTS TO BE MADE.
I'LL GIVE YOU TEN MINUTES.
NATURALLY, THE SOLDIERS ASSUMED I WAS THERE TO HELP DOOM.
EVEN IF I GOT THEM TO LISTEN, THEY'D NEVER BELIEVE ME.
IN AN INSTANT, A BARRAGE OF HEAT-SEEKING MISSILES WAS STREAKING MY WAY.
AND THAT FIGHTER JET WAS ON MY SIX AGAIN.

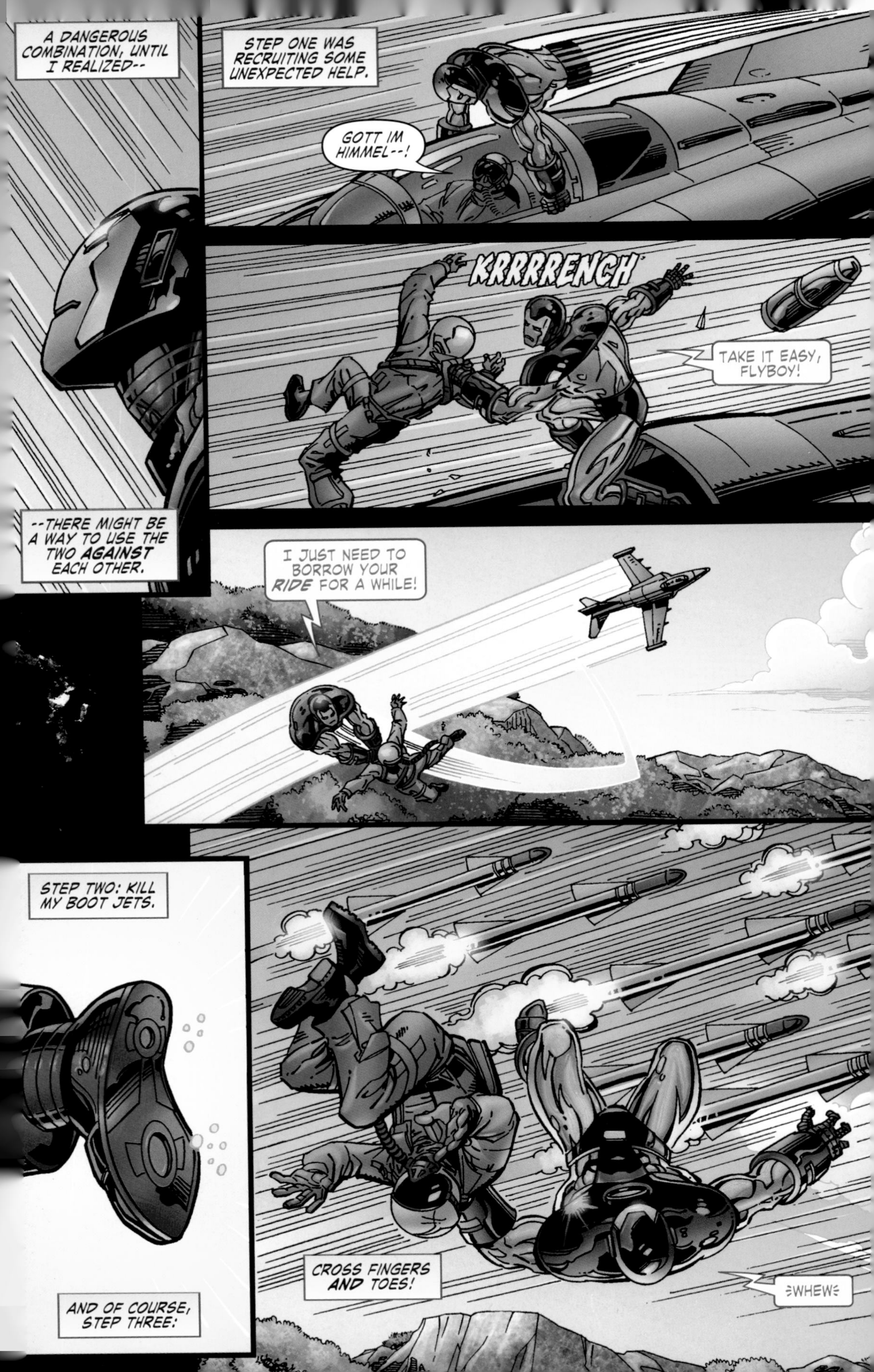
A DANGEROUS COMBINATION, UNTIL I REALIZED--
STEP ONE WAS RECRUITING SOME UNEXPECTED HELP.
GOTT IM HIMMEL--!
KRRRRENCH
TAKE IT EASY, FLYBOY!
--THERE MIGHT BE A WAY TO USE THE TWO AGAINST EACH OTHER.
I JUST NEED TO BORROW YOUR RIDE FOR A WHILE!
STEP TWO: KILL MY BOOT JETS.
AND OF COURSE, STEP THREE:
CROSS FINGERS AND TOES!
WHEW

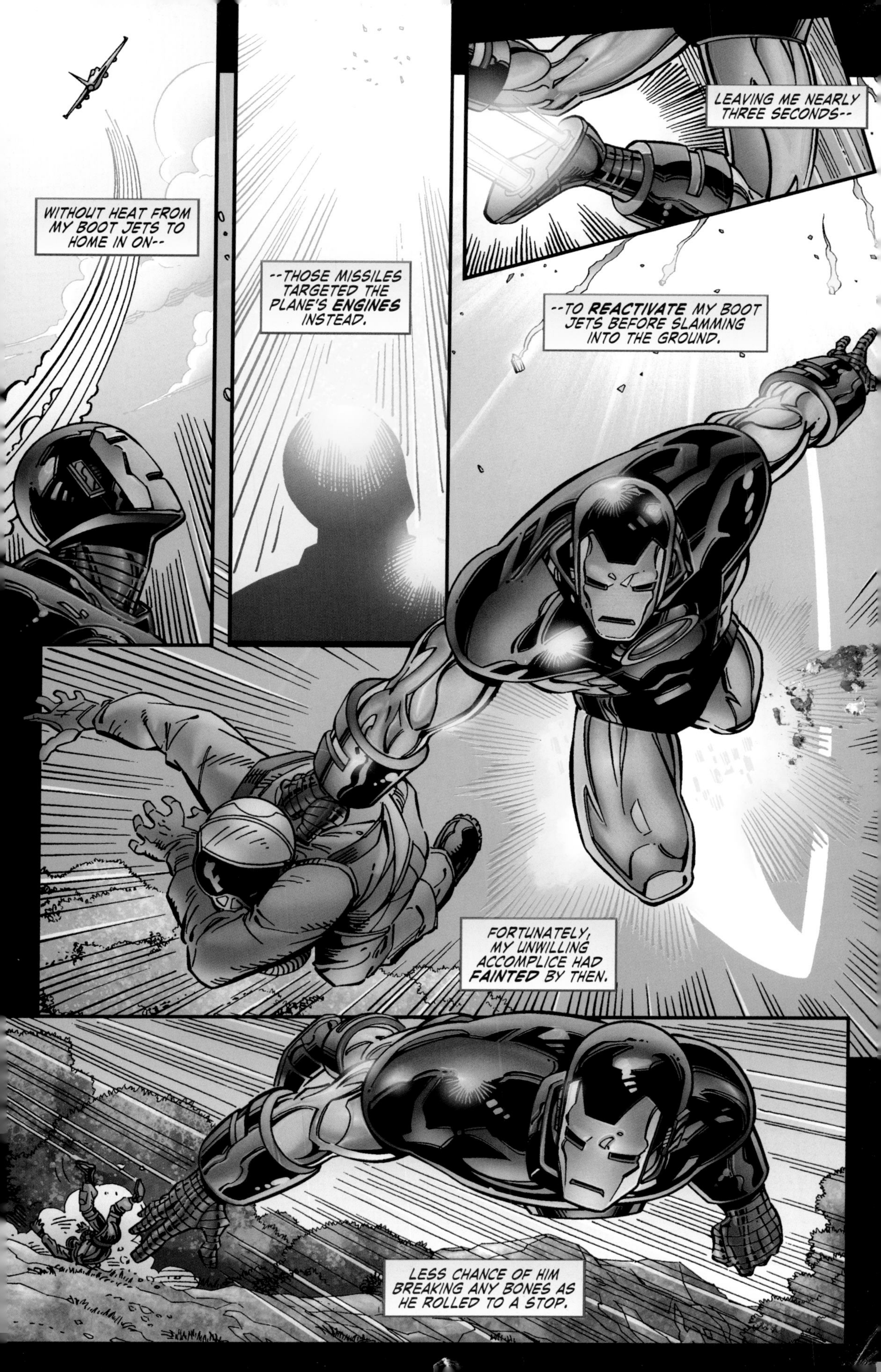

WITHOUT HEAT FROM MY BOOT JETS TO HOME IN ON--
--THOSE MISSILES TARGETED THE PLANE'S **ENGINES** INSTEAD.
LEAVING ME NEARLY THREE SECONDS--
--TO **REACTIVATE** MY BOOT JETS BEFORE SLAMMING INTO THE GROUND.
FORTUNATELY, MY UNWILLING ACCOMPLICE HAD **FAINTED** BY THEN.
LESS CHANCE OF HIM BREAKING ANY BONES AS HE ROLLED TO A STOP.

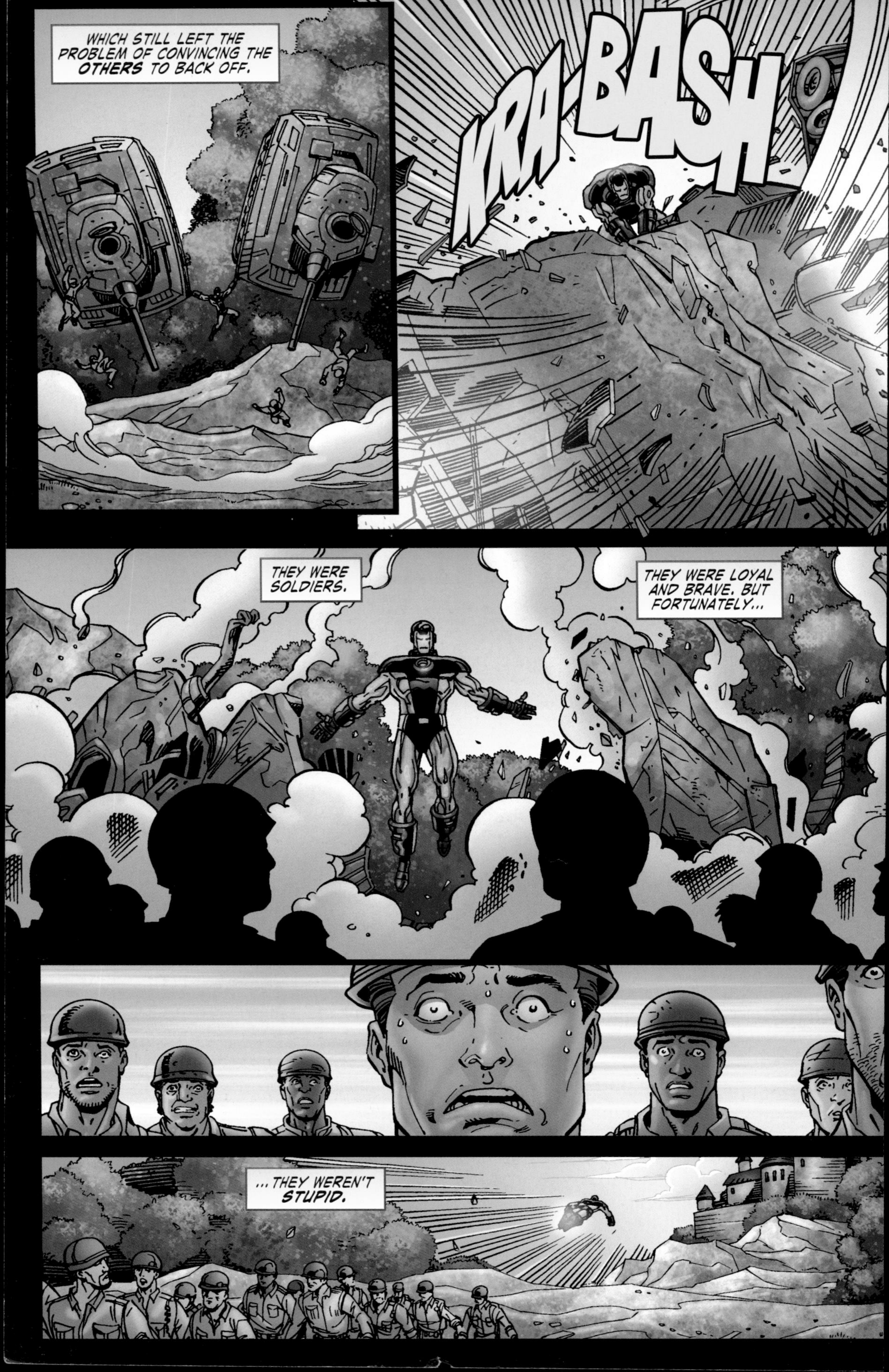
WHICH STILL LEFT THE PROBLEM OF CONVINCING THE OTHERS TO BACK OFF.
KRA-BASH
THEY WERE SOLDIERS.
THEY WERE LOYAL AND BRAVE. BUT FORTUNATELY...
...THEY WEREN'T STUPID.

ARE YOU *QUITE* THROUGH...?

GOOD. IT'S TIME TO GO.

GO? WHERE?

MY CABALISTIC PROBES HAVE DISCOVERED THAT *MEPHISTO* HAS FOUND A WAY TO HASTEN THE END OF DAYS. IN LAYMAN'S TERMS:

THE END OF THE WORLD! I FIND THAT PRESUMPTIVE.

THEREFORE, I'VE MODIFIED MY *TIME CUBE* TO TRAVERSE OTHER DIMENSIONS, TO TAKE US TO MEPHISTO'S REALM.

SEEMS TO ME WE HAD A LITTLE TROUBLE GETTING *BACK* THE LAST TIME.

NO LONGER. REMOTE TRANSMITTERS WILL SIGNAL THE CUBE TO RETRIEVE US.

THIS ONE IS YOURS.

AND I'LL HAVE *YOURS* AS WELL. GIVE.

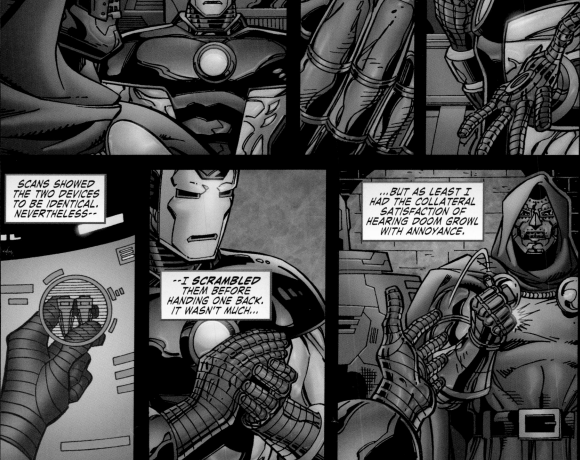

SCANS SHOWED THE TWO DEVICES TO BE IDENTICAL. NEVERTHELESS--

--I *SCRAMBLED* THEM BEFORE HANDING ONE BACK. IT WASN'T MUCH...

...BUT AS LEAST I HAD THE COLLATERAL SATISFACTION OF HEARING DOOM GROWL WITH ANNOYANCE.

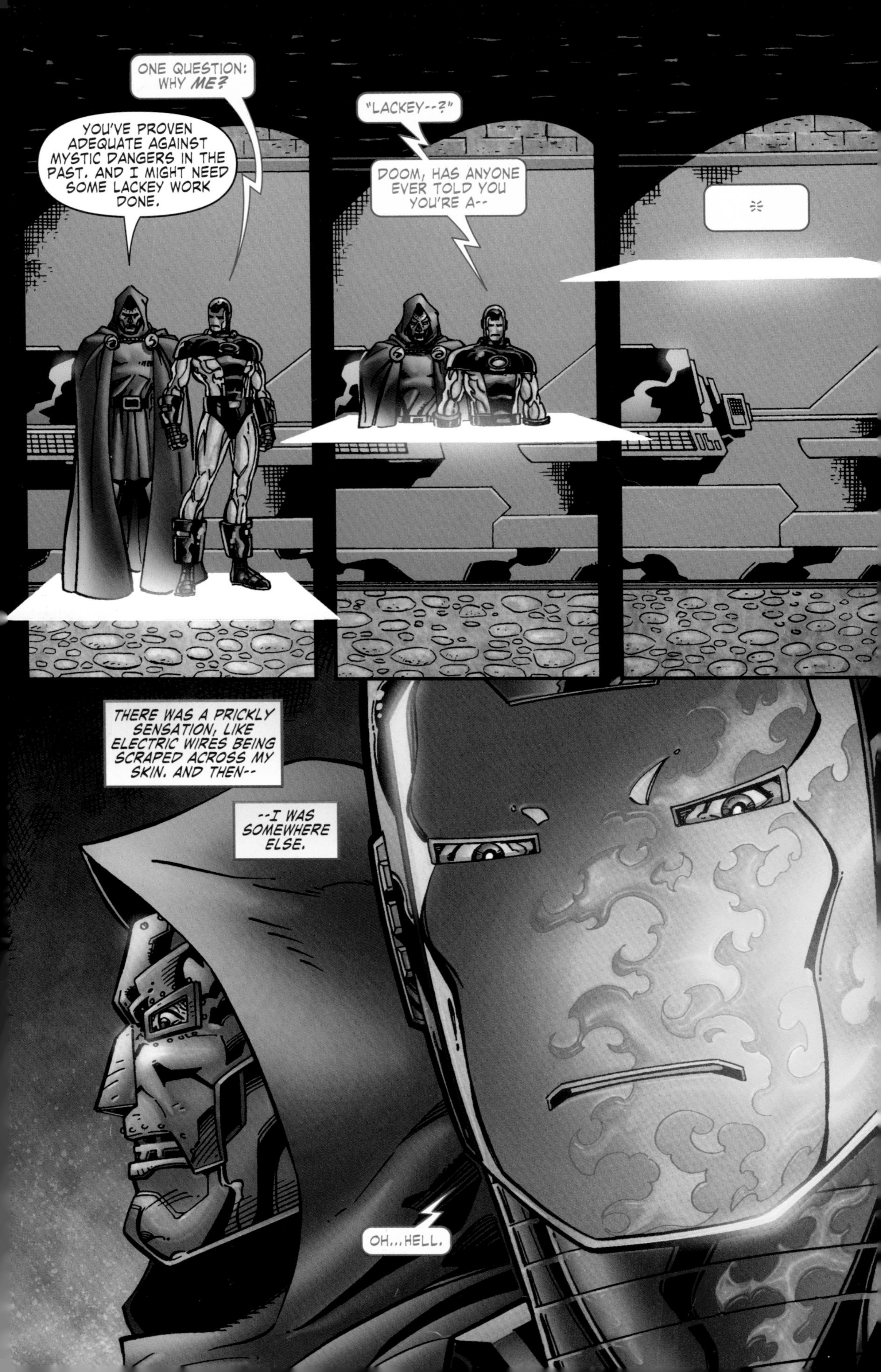
ONE QUESTION: WHY ME?
YOU'VE PROVEN ADEQUATE AGAINST MYSTIC DANGERS IN THE PAST. AND I MIGHT NEED SOME LACKEY WORK DONE.
"LACKEY--?"
DOOM, HAS ANYONE EVER TOLD YOU YOU'RE A--
THERE WAS A PRICKLY SENSATION, LIKE ELECTRIC WIRES BEING SCRAPED ACROSS MY SKIN. AND THEN--
--I WAS SOMEWHERE ELSE.
OH...HELL.

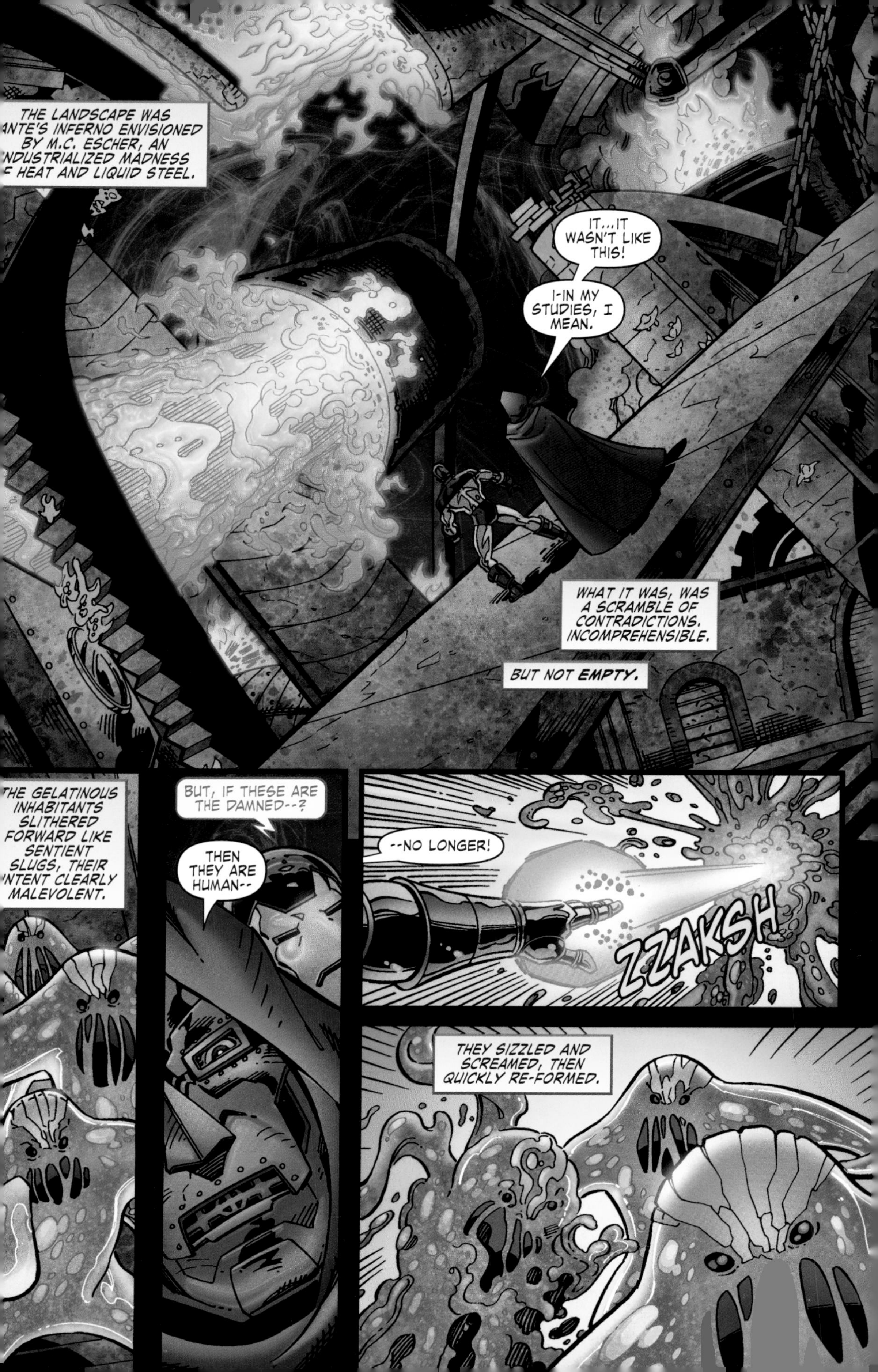

THE LANDSCAPE WAS ANTE'S INFERNO ENVISIONED BY M.C. ESCHER, AN NDUSTRIALIZED MADNESS F HEAT AND LIQUID STEEL.
IT...IT WASN'T LIKE THIS!
I-IN MY STUDIES, I MEAN.
WHAT IT WAS, WAS A SCRAMBLE OF CONTRADICTIONS. INCOMPREHENSIBLE.
BUT NOT EMPTY.
THE GELATINOUS INHABITANTS SLITHERED FORWARD LIKE SENTIENT SLUGS, THEIR NTENT CLEARLY MALEVOLENT.
BUT, IF THESE ARE THE DAMNED--?
THEN THEY ARE HUMAN--
--NO LONGER!
ZZAKSH
THEY SIZZLED AND SCREAMED, THEN QUICKLY RE-FORMED.

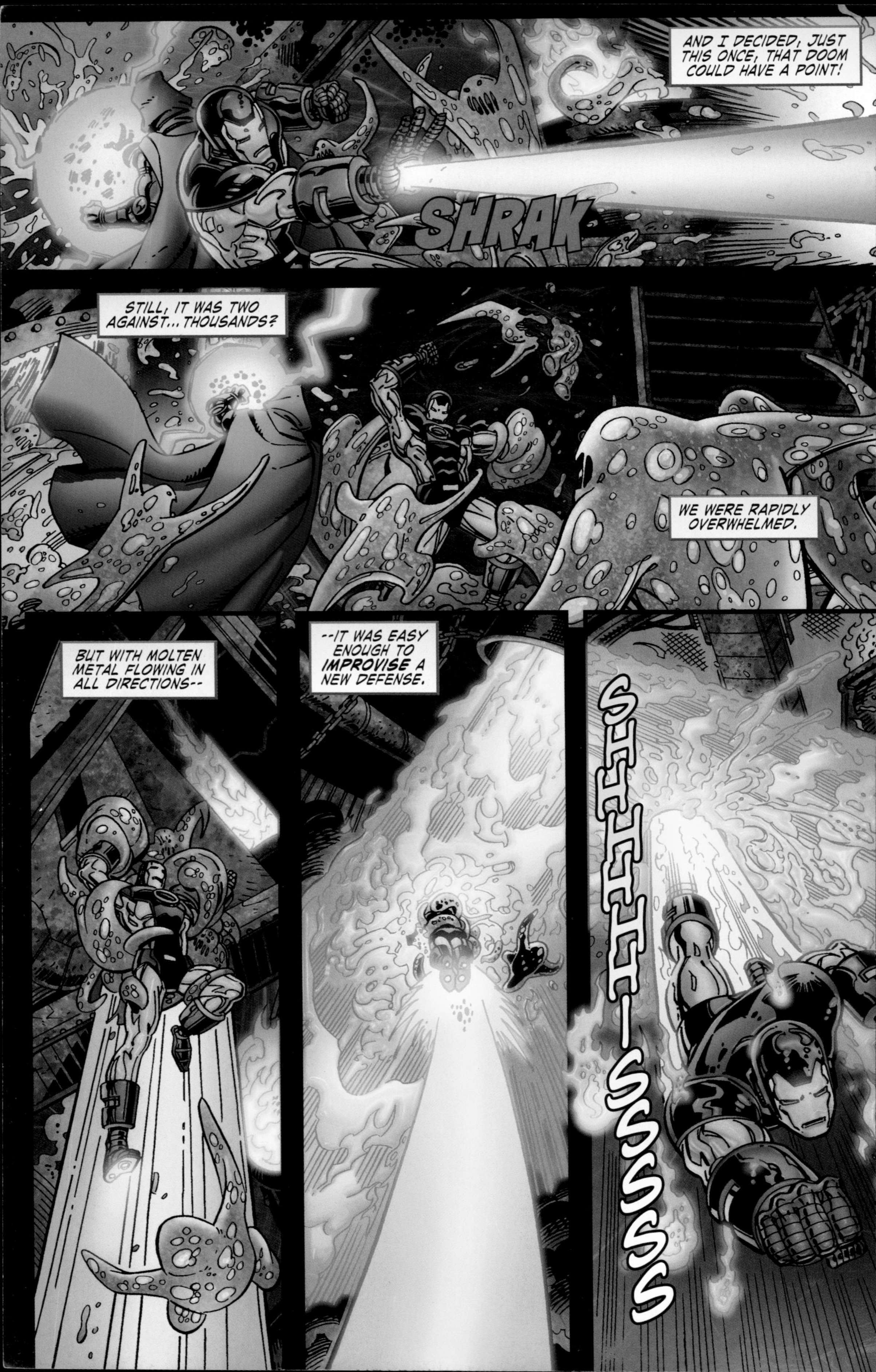
AND I DECIDED, JUST THIS ONCE, THAT DOOM COULD HAVE A POINT!
SHRAK
STILL, IT WAS TWO AGAINST... THOUSANDS?
WE WERE RAPIDLY OVERWHELMED.
BUT WITH MOLTEN METAL FLOWING IN ALL DIRECTIONS--
--IT WAS EASY ENOUGH TO IMPROVISE A NEW DEFENSE.
SHHHHHHISSSSS

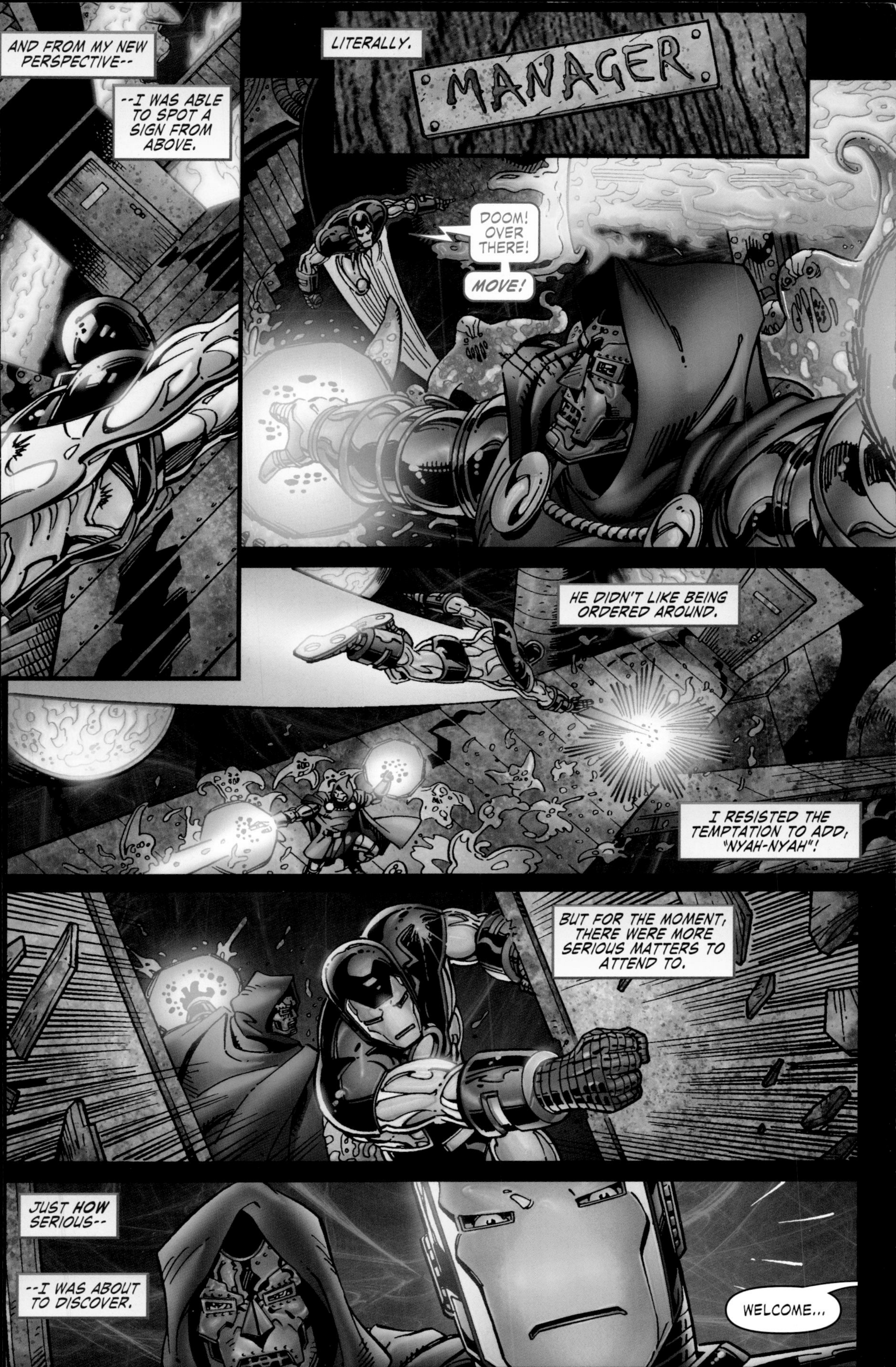
AND FROM MY NEW PERSPECTIVE--
--I WAS ABLE TO SPOT A SIGN FROM ABOVE.
LITERALLY.
MANAGER
DOOM! OVER THERE!
MOVE!
HE DIDN'T LIKE BEING ORDERED AROUND.
I RESISTED THE TEMPTATION TO ADD, "NYAH-NYAH"!
BUT FOR THE MOMENT, THERE WERE MORE SERIOUS MATTERS TO ATTEND TO.
JUST HOW SERIOUS--
--I WAS ABOUT TO DISCOVER.
WELCOME...

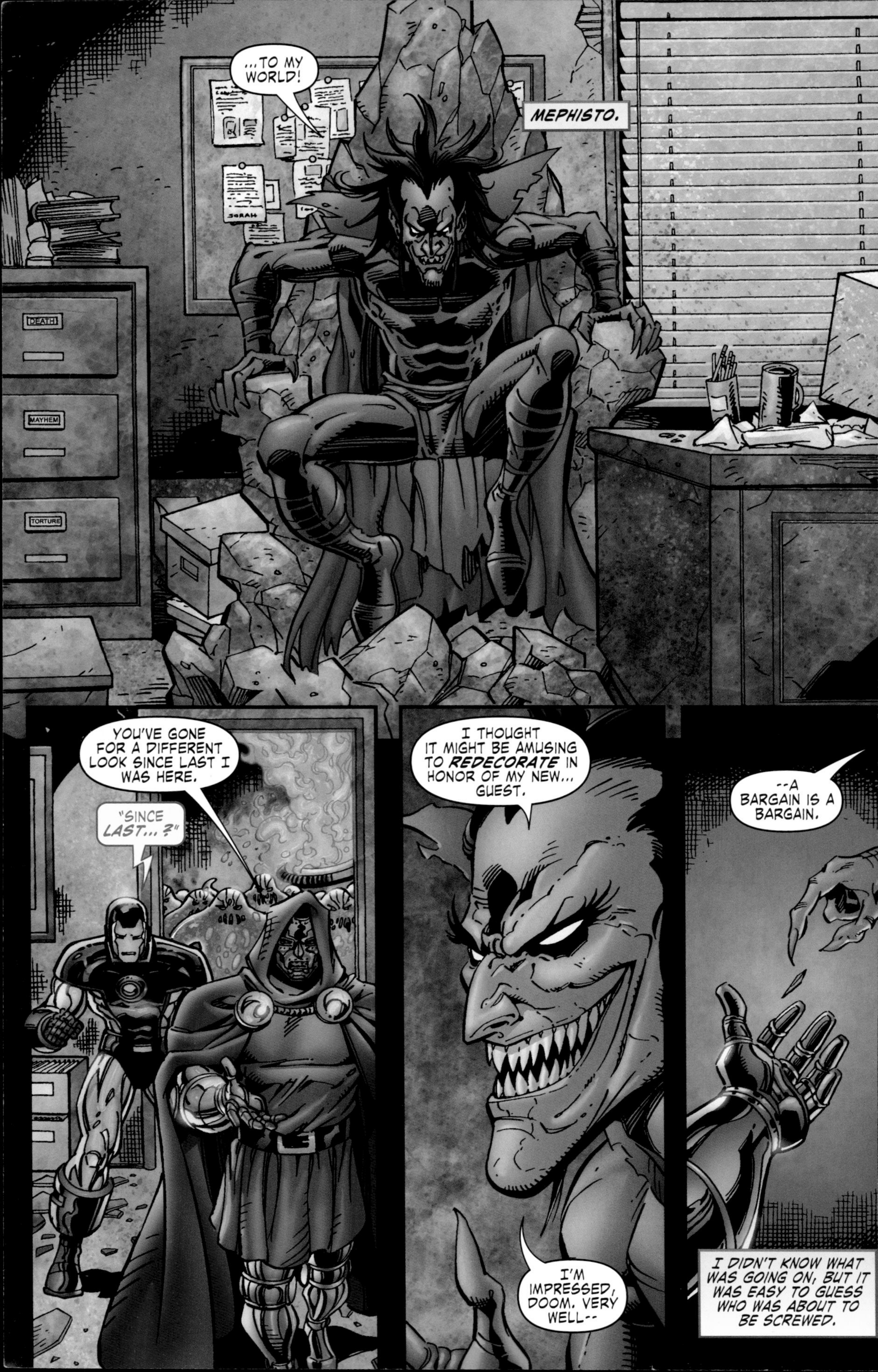
...TO MY WORLD!
MEPHISTO.
DEATH
MAYHEM
TORTURE
YOU'VE GONE FOR A DIFFERENT LOOK SINCE LAST I WAS HERE.
"SINCE LAST... ?"
I THOUGHT IT MIGHT BE AMUSING TO REDECORATE IN HONOR OF MY NEW... GUEST.
I'M IMPRESSED, DOOM. VERY WELL--
--A BARGAIN IS A BARGAIN.
I DIDN'T KNOW WHAT WAS GOING ON, BUT IT WAS EASY TO GUESS WHO WAS ABOUT TO BE SCREWED.

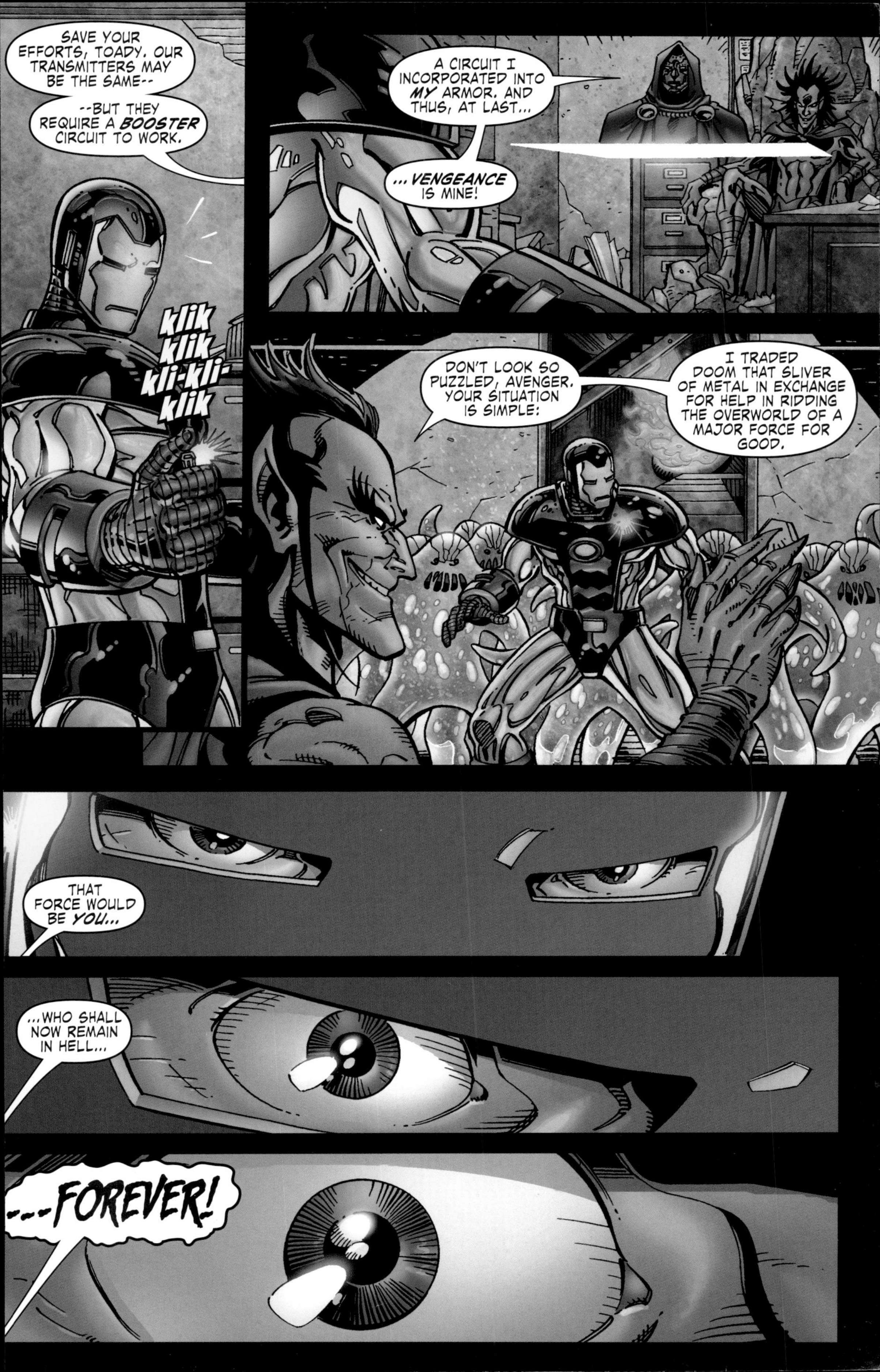
SAVE YOUR EFFORTS, TOADY. OUR TRANSMITTERS MAY BE THE SAME--
--BUT THEY REQUIRE A BOOSTER CIRCUIT TO WORK.
A CIRCUIT I INCORPORATED INTO MY ARMOR. AND THUS, AT LAST...
...VENGEANCE IS MINE!
klik klik kli-kli-klik
DON'T LOOK SO PUZZLED, AVENGER. YOUR SITUATION IS SIMPLE:
I TRADED DOOM THAT SLIVER OF METAL IN EXCHANGE FOR HELP IN RIDDING THE OVERWORLD OF A MAJOR FORCE FOR GOOD.
THAT FORCE WOULD BE YOU...
...WHO SHALL NOW REMAIN IN HELL...
...FOREVER!

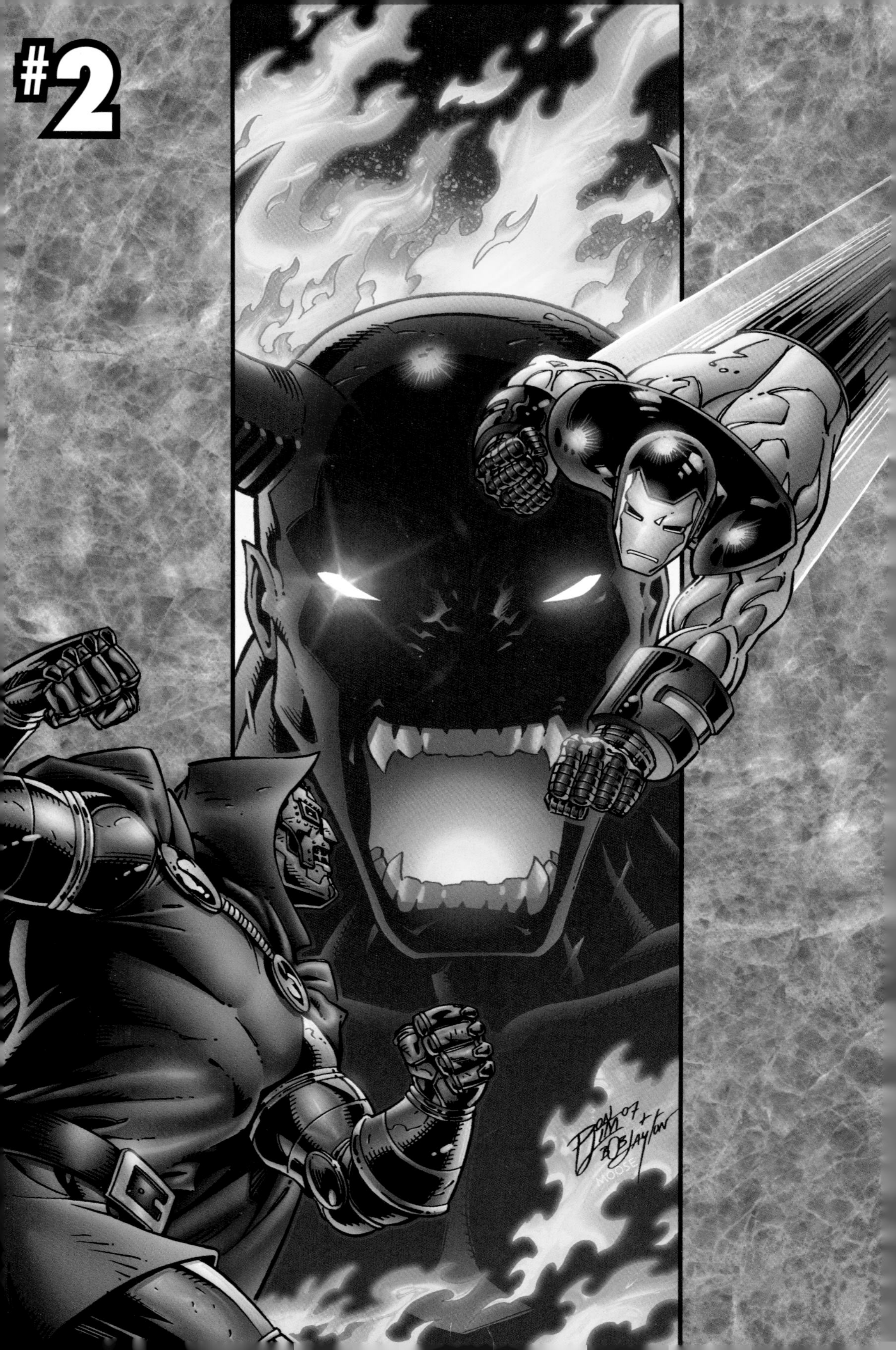
#2

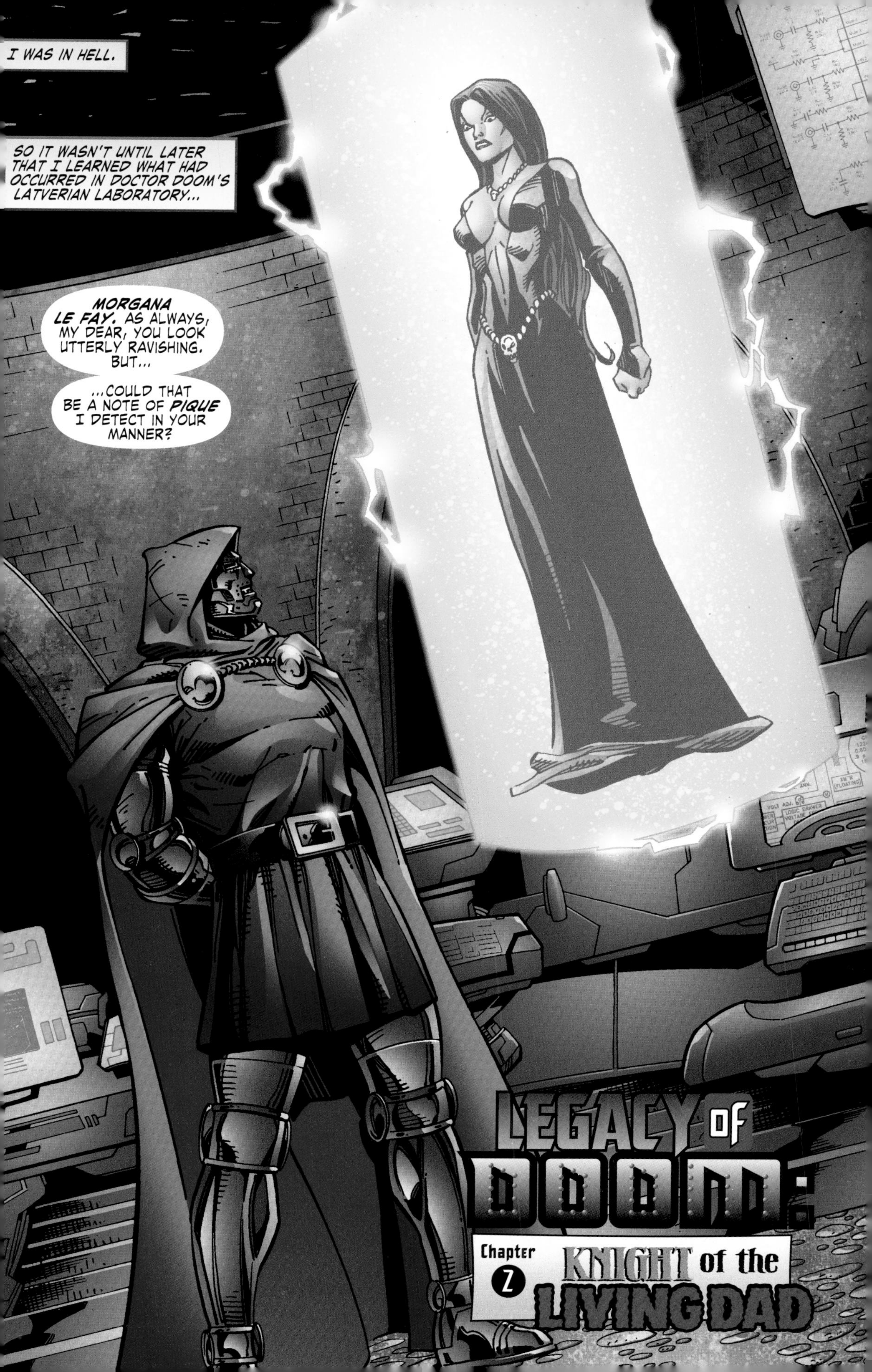

I WAS IN HELL.
SO IT WASN'T UNTIL LATER THAT I LEARNED WHAT HAD OCCURRED IN DOCTOR DOOM'S LATVERIAN LABORATORY...
MORGANA LE FAY. AS ALWAYS, MY DEAR, YOU LOOK UTTERLY RAVISHING. BUT...
...COULD THAT BE A NOTE OF PIQUE I DETECT IN YOUR MANNER?
LEGACY of DOOM:
Chapter 2 KNIGHT of the LIVING DAD

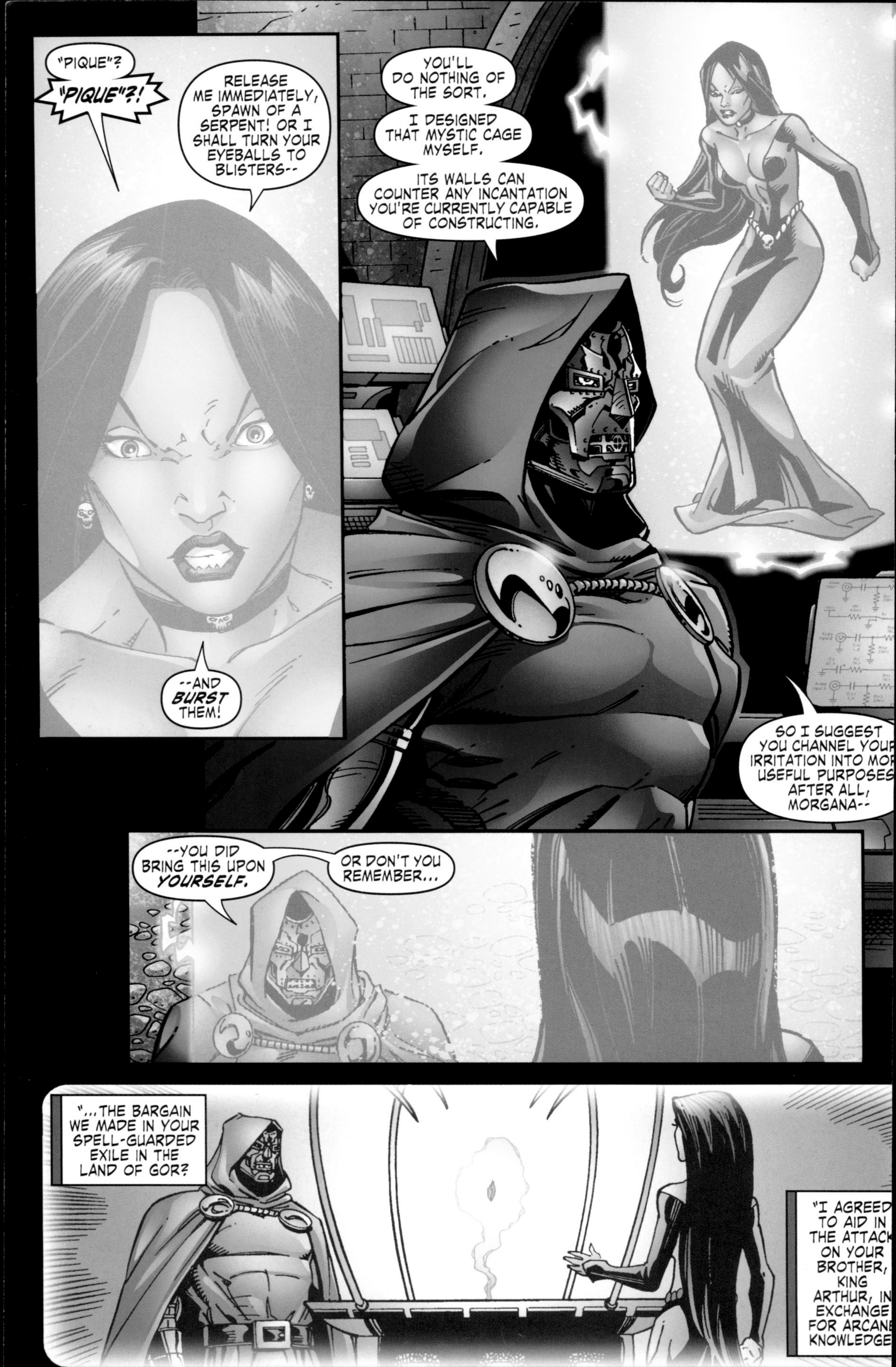

"PIQUE"?
"PIQUE"?!
RELEASE ME IMMEDIATELY, SPAWN OF A SERPENT! OR I SHALL TURN YOUR EYEBALLS TO BLISTERS--
--AND BURST THEM!
YOU'LL DO NOTHING OF THE SORT.
I DESIGNED THAT MYSTIC CAGE MYSELF.
ITS WALLS CAN COUNTER ANY INCANTATION YOU'RE CURRENTLY CAPABLE OF CONSTRUCTING.
SO I SUGGEST YOU CHANNEL YOUR IRRITATION INTO MORE USEFUL PURPOSES. AFTER ALL, MORGANA--
--YOU DID BRING THIS UPON YOURSELF.
OR DON'T YOU REMEMBER...
"...THE BARGAIN WE MADE IN YOUR SPELL-GUARDED EXILE IN THE LAND OF GOR?
"I AGREED TO AID IN THE ATTACK ON YOUR BROTHER, KING ARTHUR, IN EXCHANGE FOR ARCANE KNOWLEDGE

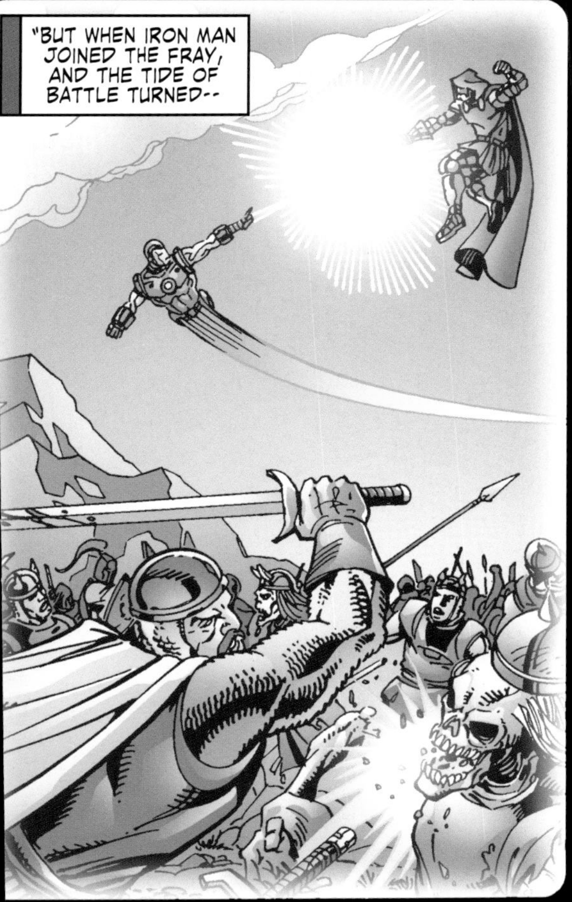
"BUT WHEN IRON MAN JOINED THE FRAY, AND THE TIDE OF BATTLE TURNED--

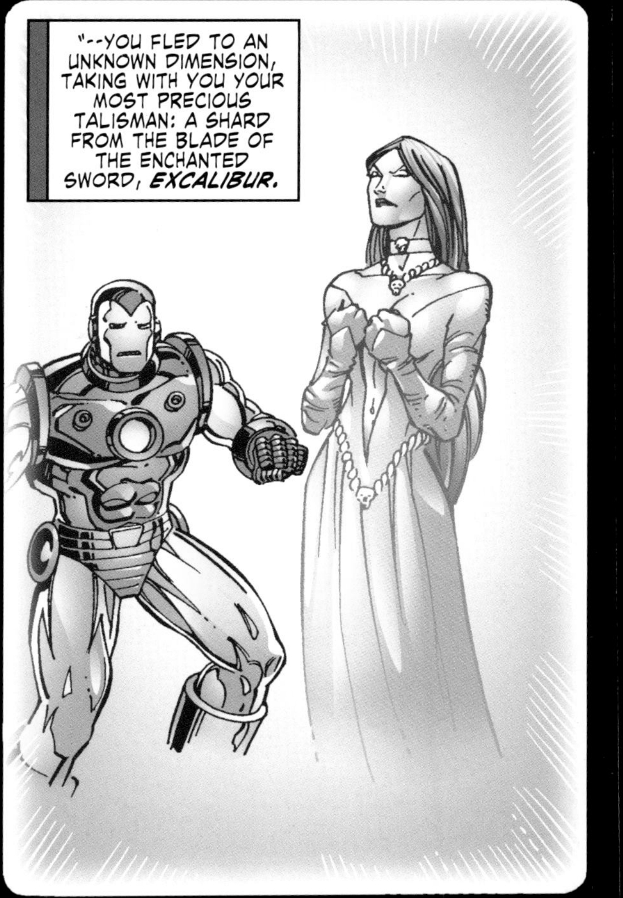
"--YOU FLED TO AN UNKNOWN DIMENSION, TAKING WITH YOU YOUR MOST PRECIOUS TALISMAN: A SHARD FROM THE BLADE OF THE ENCHANTED SWORD, EXCALIBUR.

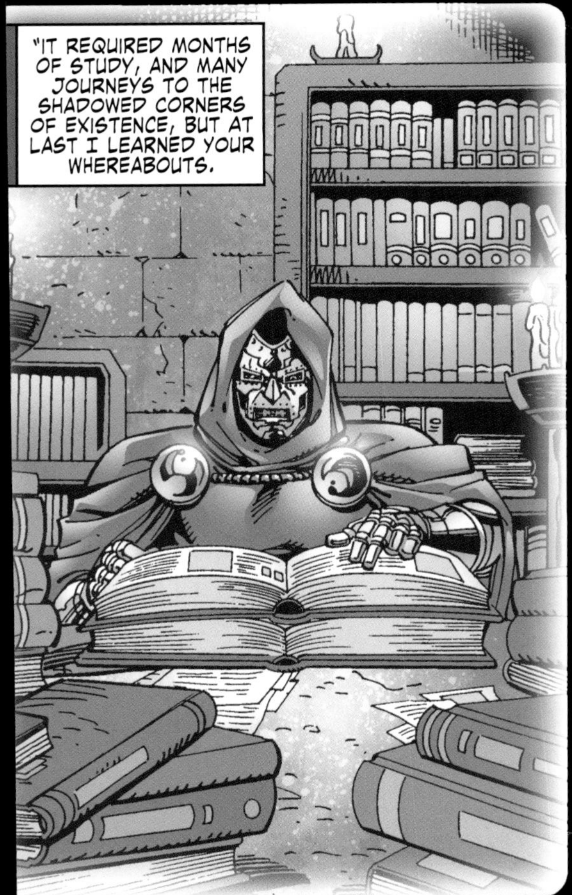
"IT REQUIRED MONTHS OF STUDY, AND MANY JOURNEYS TO THE SHADOWED CORNERS OF EXISTENCE, BUT AT LAST I LEARNED YOUR WHEREABOUTS.

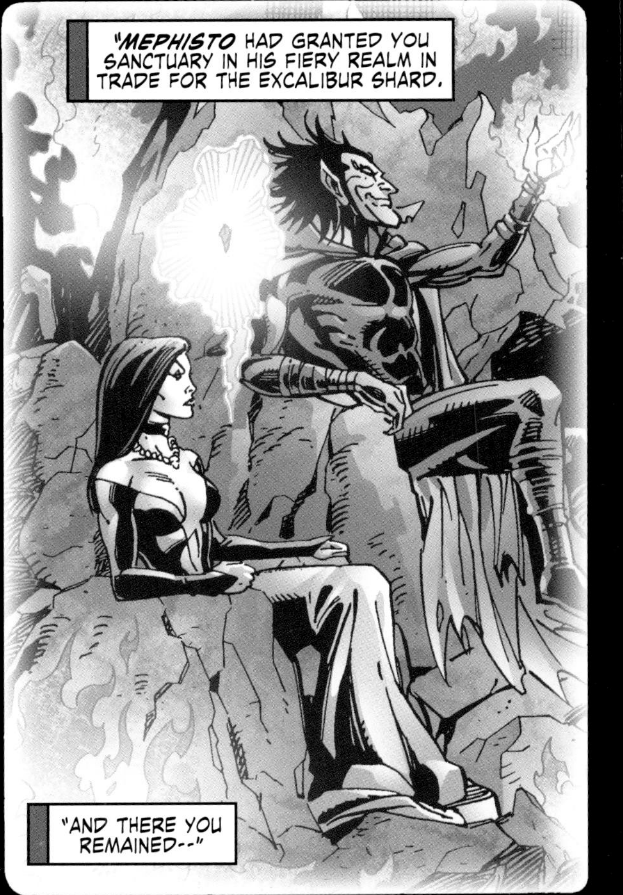
"MEPHISTO HAD GRANTED YOU SANCTUARY IN HIS FIERY REALM IN TRADE FOR THE EXCALIBUR SHARD.
"AND THERE YOU REMAINED--"

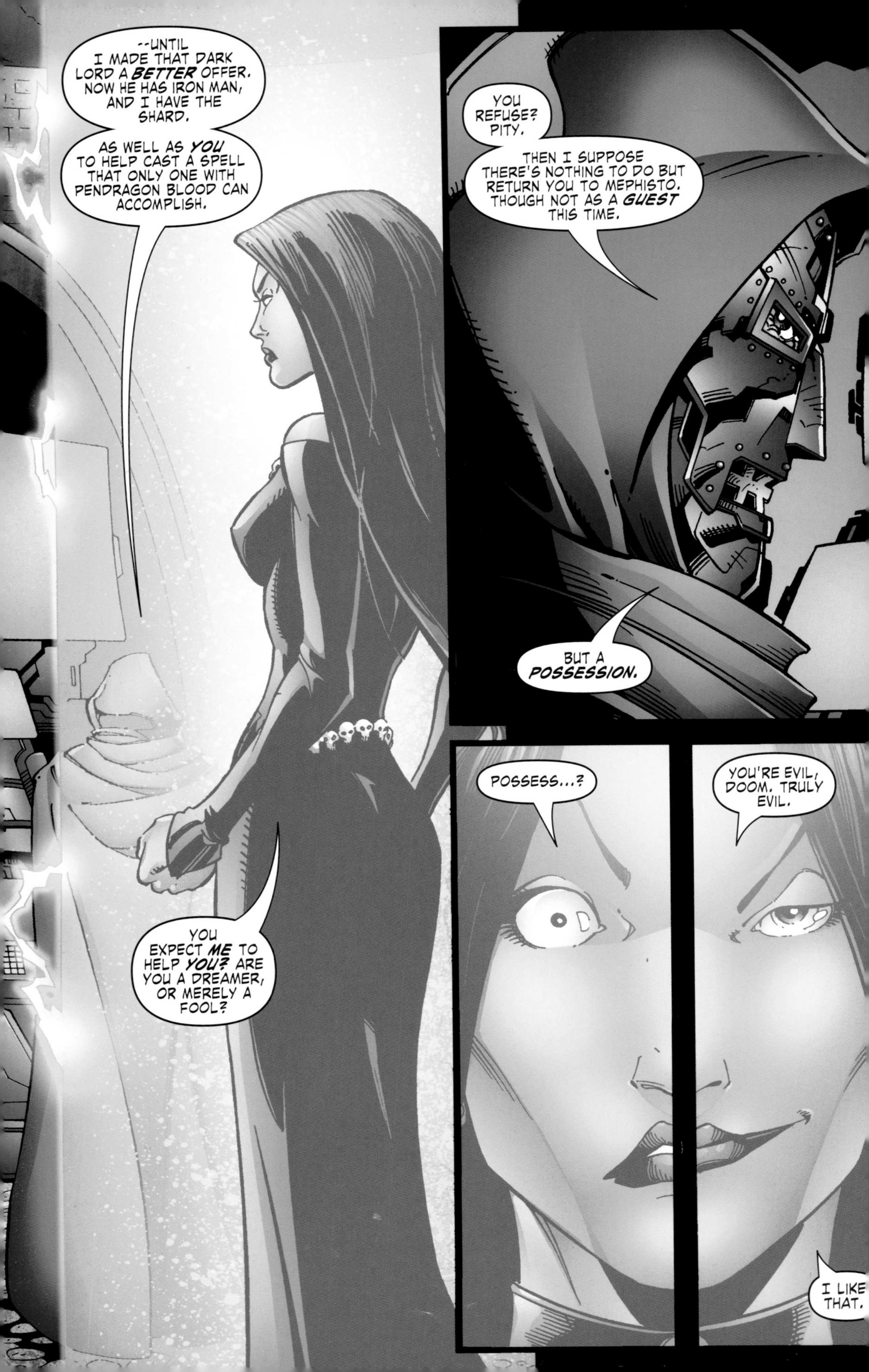
--UNTIL I MADE THAT DARK LORD A BETTER OFFER. NOW HE HAS IRON MAN, AND I HAVE THE SHARD.
AS WELL AS YOU TO HELP CAST A SPELL THAT ONLY ONE WITH PENDRAGON BLOOD CAN ACCOMPLISH.
YOU EXPECT ME TO HELP YOU? ARE YOU A DREAMER, OR MERELY A FOOL?
YOU REFUSE? PITY.
THEN I SUPPOSE THERE'S NOTHING TO DO BUT RETURN YOU TO MEPHISTO. THOUGH NOT AS A GUEST THIS TIME.
BUT A POSSESSION.
POSSESS...?
YOU'RE EVIL, DOOM. TRULY EVIL.
I LIKE THAT.

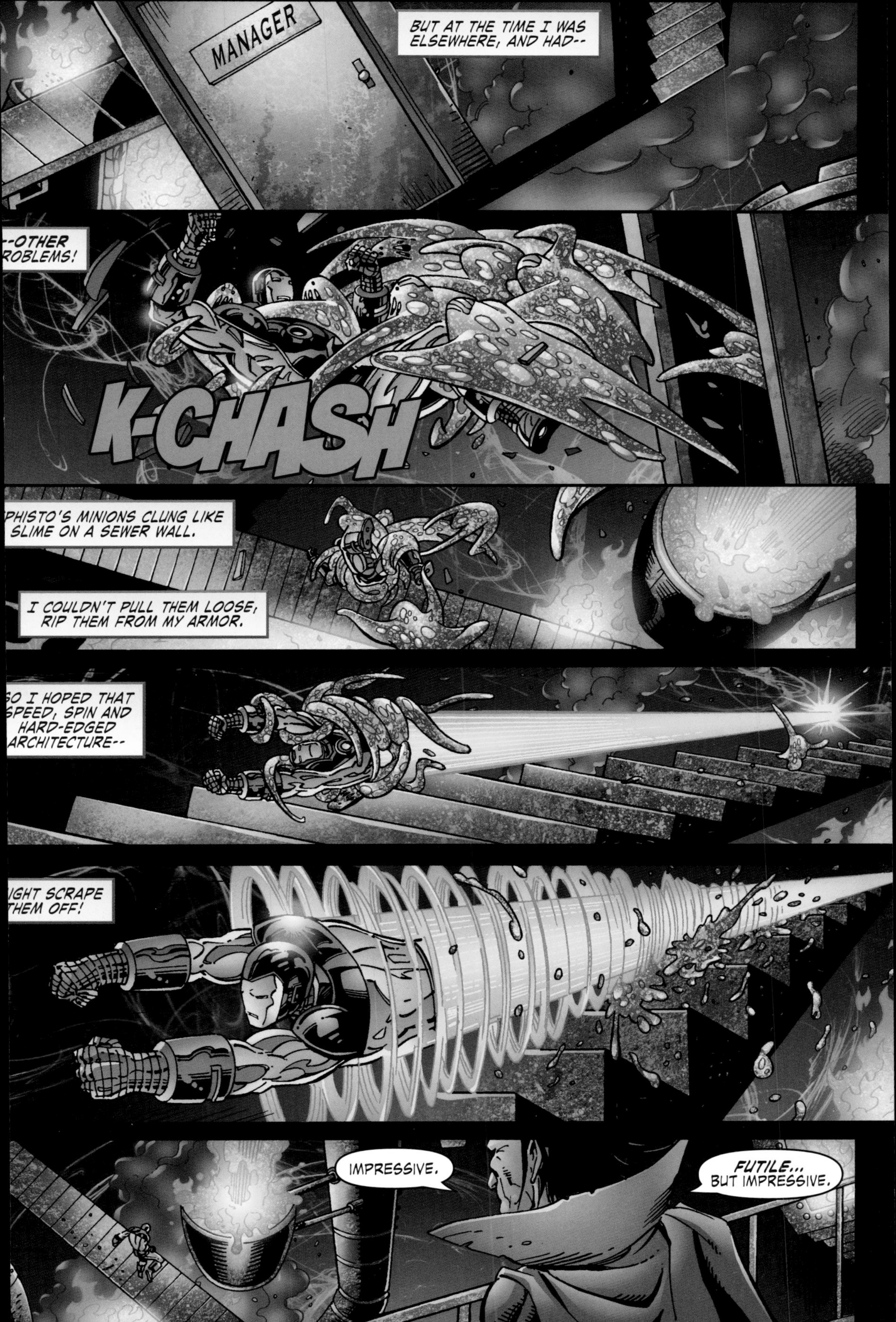

MANAGER
BUT AT THE TIME I WAS ELSEWHERE, AND HAD--
--OTHER ROBLEMS!
K-CHASH
PHISTO'S MINIONS CLUNG LIKE SLIME ON A SEWER WALL.
I COULDN'T PULL THEM LOOSE, RIP THEM FROM MY ARMOR.
SO I HOPED THAT SPEED, SPIN AND HARD-EDGED ARCHITECTURE--
IGHT SCRAPE THEM OFF!
IMPRESSIVE.
FUTILE... BUT IMPRESSIVE.

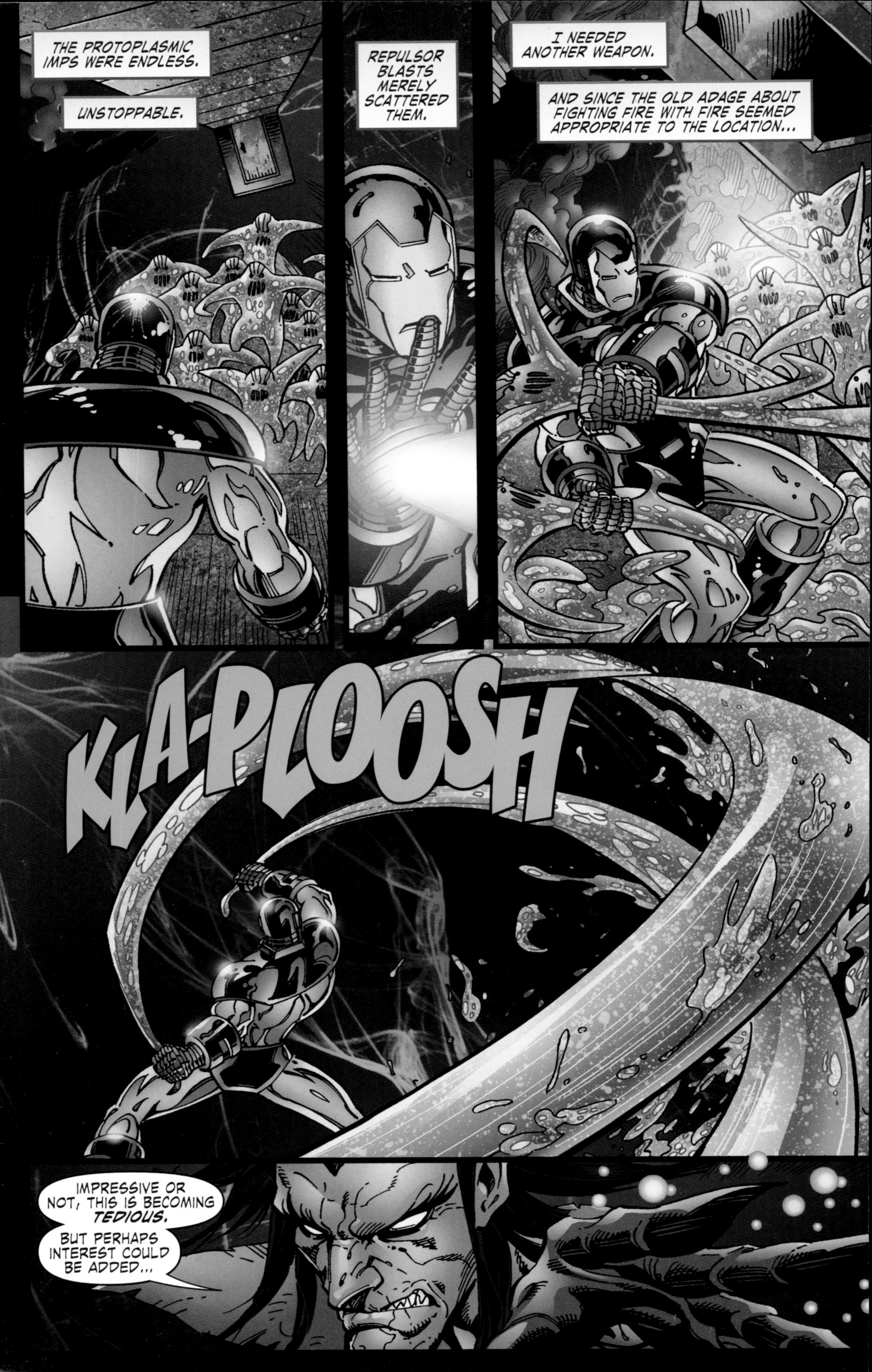
THE PROTOPLASMIC IMPS WERE ENDLESS.
UNSTOPPABLE.
REPULSOR BLASTS MERELY SCATTERED THEM.
I NEEDED ANOTHER WEAPON.
AND SINCE THE OLD ADAGE ABOUT FIGHTING FIRE WITH FIRE SEEMED APPROPRIATE TO THE LOCATION...
KLA-PLOOSH
IMPRESSIVE OR NOT, THIS IS BECOMING *TEDIOUS.*
BUT PERHAPS INTEREST COULD BE ADDED...

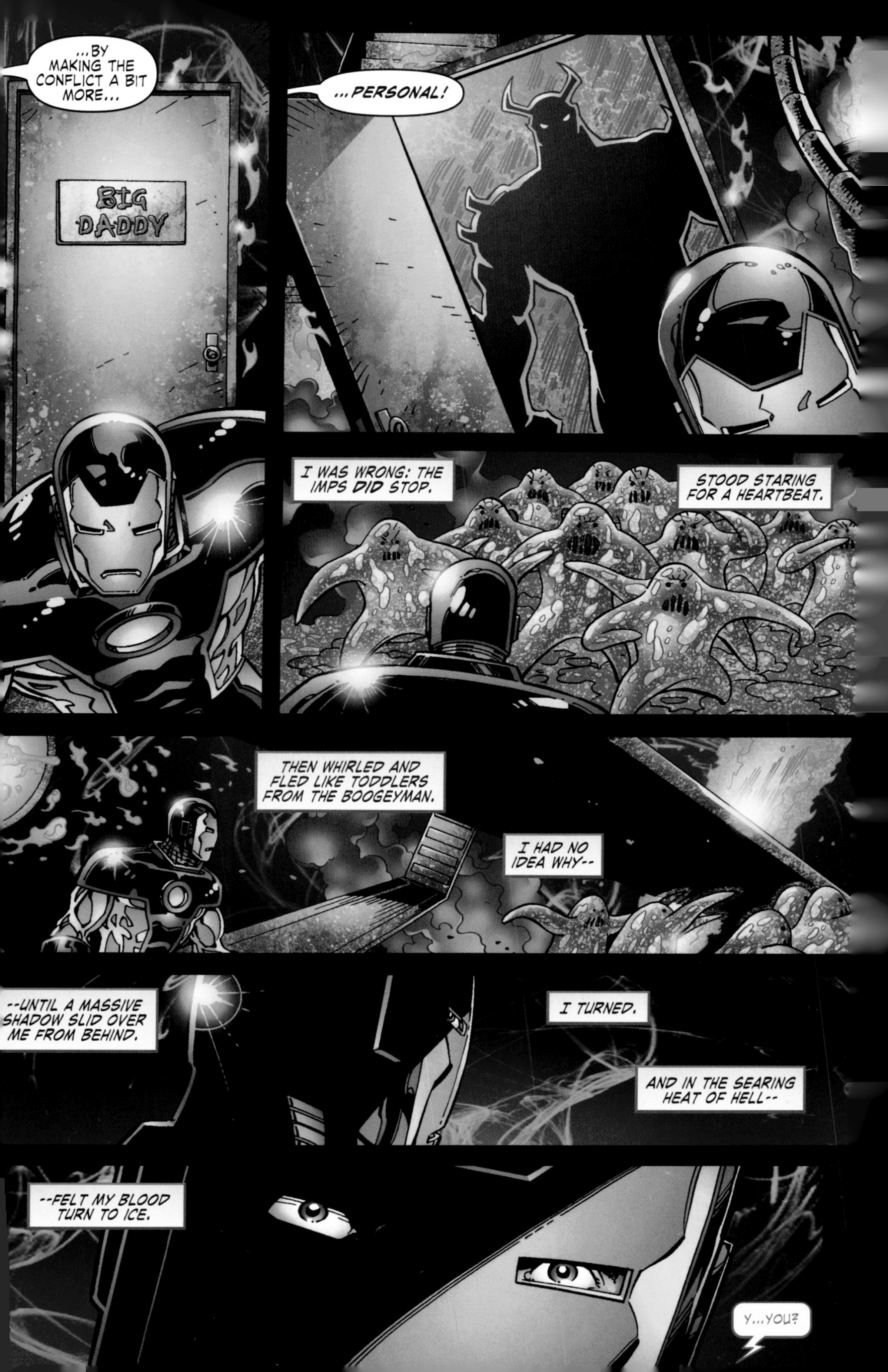
...BY MAKING THE CONFLICT A BIT MORE...
BIG DADDY
...PERSONAL!
I WAS WRONG: THE IMPS DID STOP.
STOOD STARING FOR A HEARTBEAT.
THEN WHIRLED AND FLED LIKE TODDLERS FROM THE BOOGEYMAN.
I HAD NO IDEA WHY--
--UNTIL A MASSIVE SHADOW SLID OVER ME FROM BEHIND.
I TURNED.
AND IN THE SEARING HEAT OF HELL--
--FELT MY BLOOD TURN TO ICE.
Y...YOU?

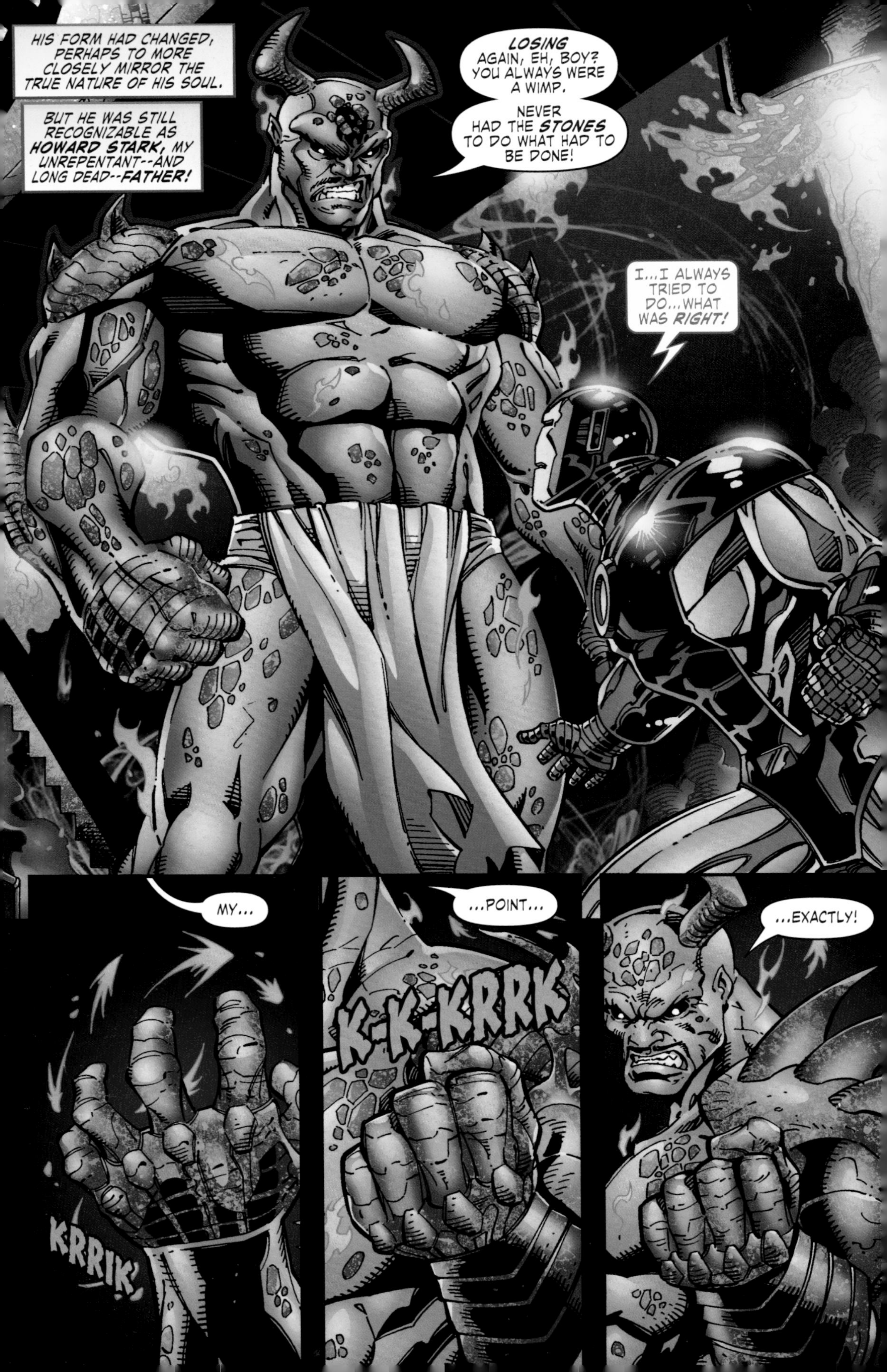
HIS FORM HAD CHANGED, PERHAPS TO MORE CLOSELY MIRROR THE TRUE NATURE OF HIS SOUL.
BUT HE WAS STILL RECOGNIZABLE AS HOWARD STARK, MY UNREPENTANT--AND LONG DEAD--FATHER!
LOSING AGAIN, EH, BOY? YOU ALWAYS WERE A WIMP.
NEVER HAD THE STONES TO DO WHAT HAD TO BE DONE!
I...I ALWAYS TRIED TO DO...WHAT WAS RIGHT!
MY...
KRRIK
...POINT...
K-K-KRRK
...EXACTLY!

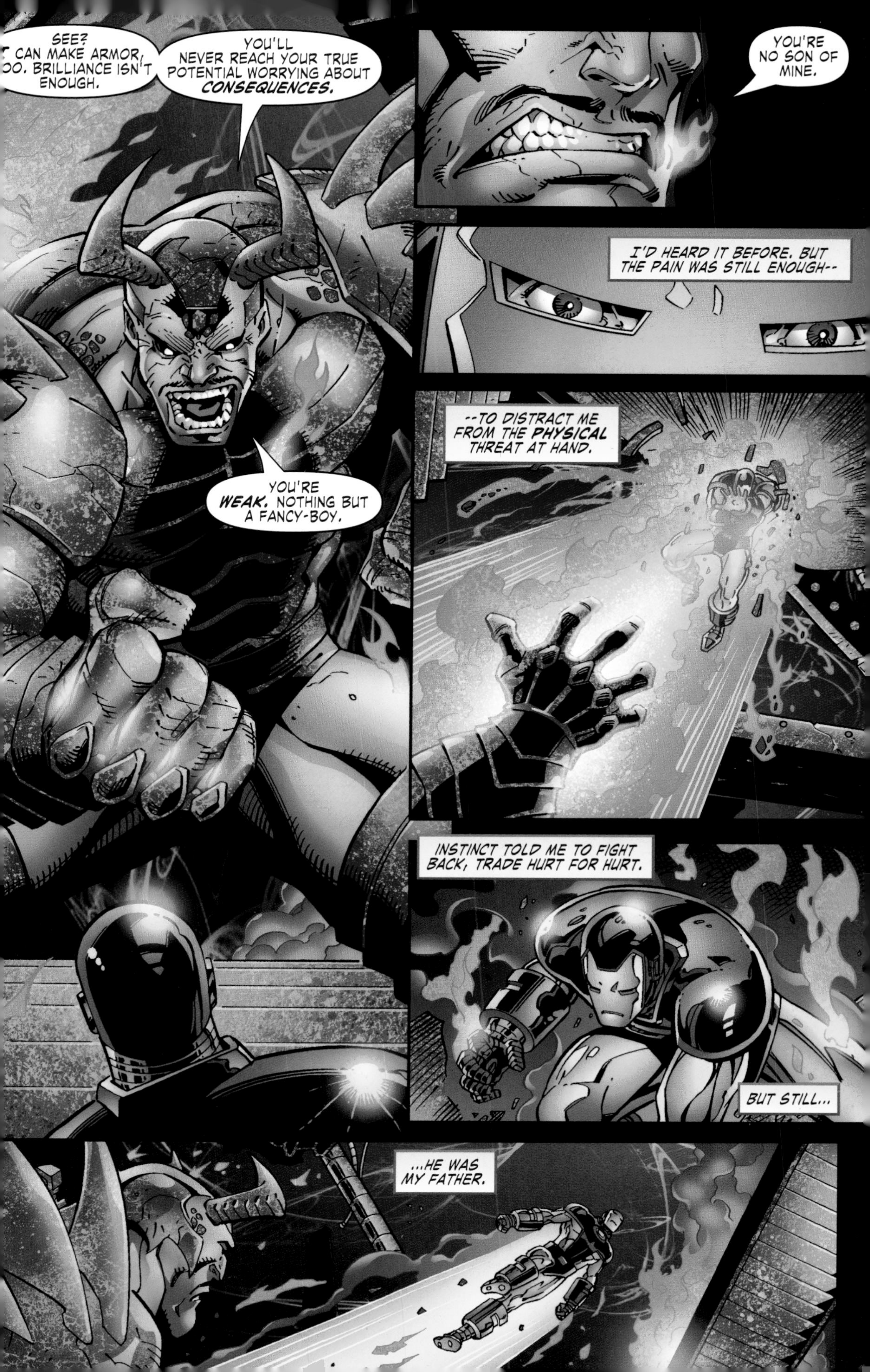
SEE? T CAN MAKE ARMOR, OO. BRILLIANCE ISN'T ENOUGH.
YOU'LL NEVER REACH YOUR TRUE POTENTIAL WORRYING ABOUT CONSEQUENCES.
YOU'RE WEAK. NOTHING BUT A FANCY-BOY.
YOU'RE NO SON OF MINE.
I'D HEARD IT BEFORE. BUT THE PAIN WAS STILL ENOUGH--
--TO DISTRACT ME FROM THE PHYSICAL THREAT AT HAND.
INSTINCT TOLD ME TO FIGHT BACK, TRADE HURT FOR HURT.
BUT STILL...
...HE WAS MY FATHER.

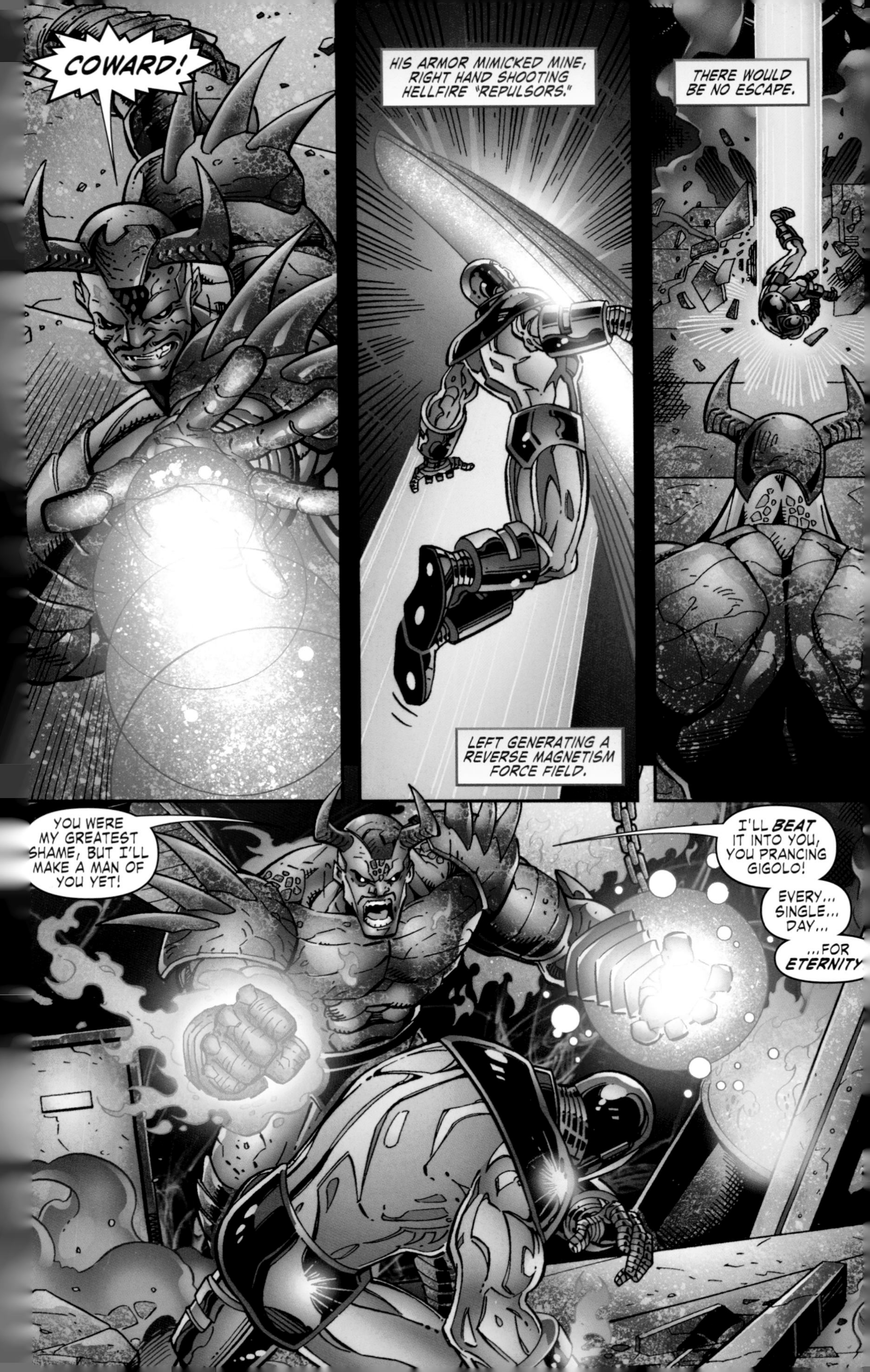
COWARD!
HIS ARMOR MIMICKED MINE, RIGHT HAND SHOOTING HELLFIRE "REPULSORS."
LEFT GENERATING A REVERSE MAGNETISM FORCE FIELD.
THERE WOULD BE NO ESCAPE.
YOU WERE MY GREATEST SHAME, BUT I'LL MAKE A MAN OF YOU YET!
I'LL BEAT IT INTO YOU, YOU PRANCING GIGOLO!
EVERY... SINGLE... DAY...
...FOR ETERNITY

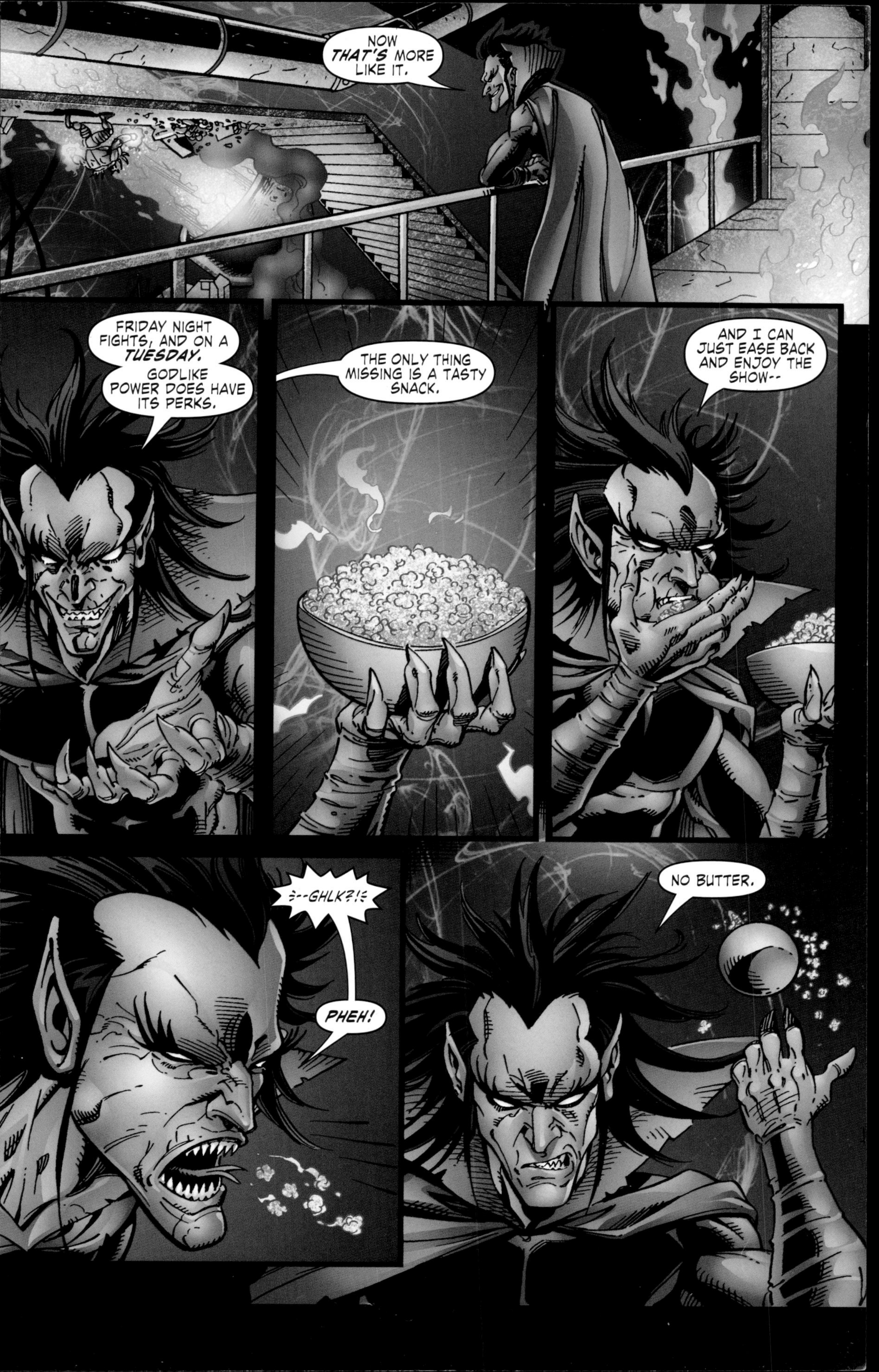
NOW THAT'S MORE LIKE IT.
FRIDAY NIGHT FIGHTS, AND ON A TUESDAY.
GODLIKE POWER DOES HAVE ITS PERKS.
THE ONLY THING MISSING IS A TASTY SNACK.
AND I CAN JUST EASE BACK AND ENJOY THE SHOW--
--GHLK?!
PHEH!
NO BUTTER.

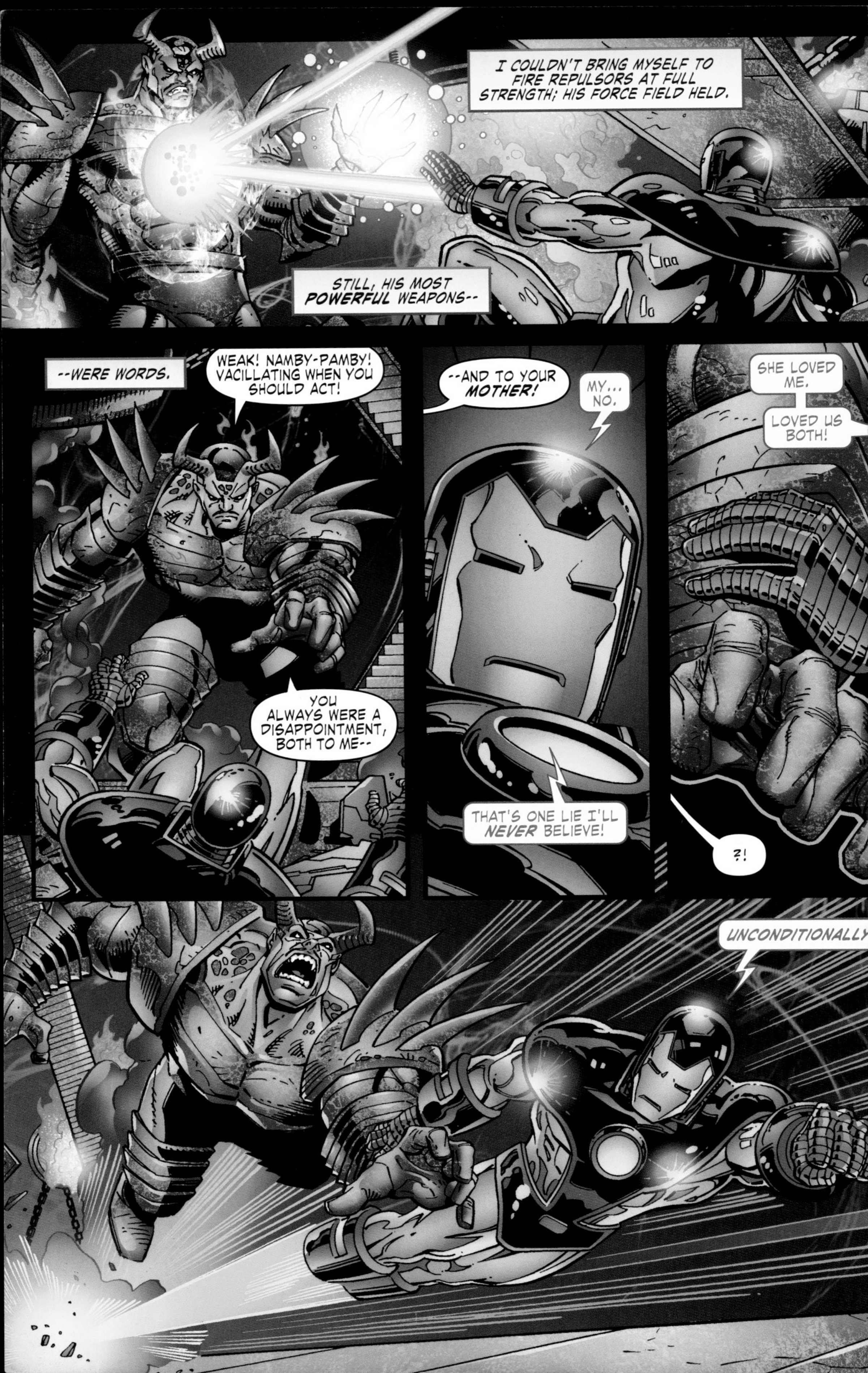

I COULDN'T BRING MYSELF TO FIRE REPULSORS AT FULL STRENGTH; HIS FORCE FIELD HELD.
STILL, HIS MOST POWERFUL WEAPONS--
--WERE WORDS.
WEAK! NAMBY-PAMBY! VACILLATING WHEN YOU SHOULD ACT!
YOU ALWAYS WERE A DISAPPOINTMENT, BOTH TO ME--
--AND TO YOUR MOTHER!
MY... NO.
THAT'S ONE LIE I'LL NEVER BELIEVE!
SHE LOVED ME.
LOVED US BOTH!
?!
UNCONDITIONALLY

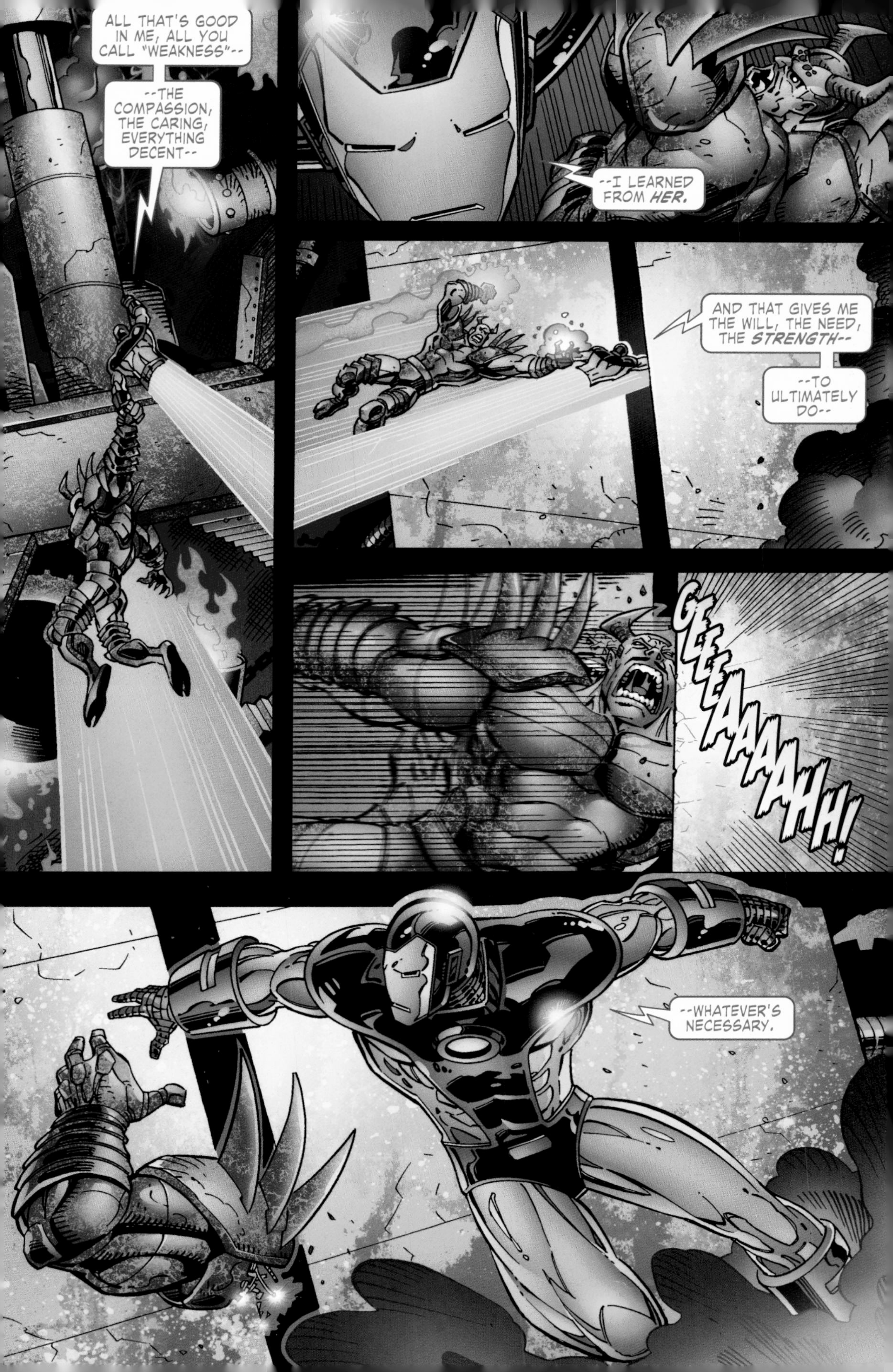
ALL THAT'S GOOD IN ME, ALL YOU CALL "WEAKNESS"--
--THE COMPASSION, THE CARING, EVERYTHING DECENT--
--I LEARNED FROM HER.
AND THAT GIVES ME THE WILL, THE NEED, THE STRENGTH--
--TO ULTIMATELY DO--
GEEEAAAAAHH!
--WHATEVER'S NECESSARY.

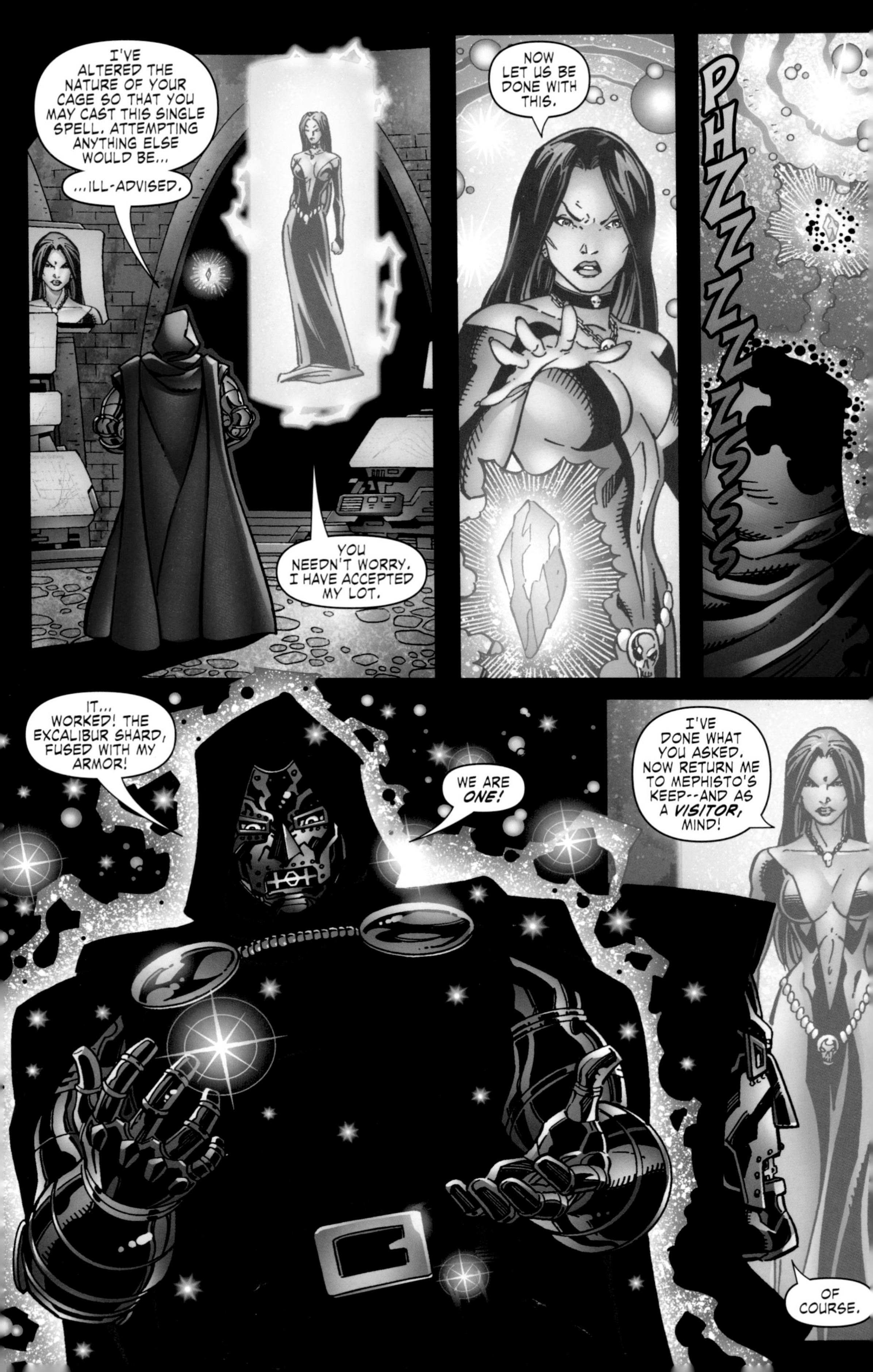
I'VE ALTERED THE NATURE OF YOUR CAGE SO THAT YOU MAY CAST THIS SINGLE SPELL. ATTEMPTING ANYTHING ELSE WOULD BE...
...ILL-ADVISED.
YOU NEEDN'T WORRY. I HAVE ACCEPTED MY LOT.
NOW LET US BE DONE WITH THIS.
PHZZZZZSSSS
IT... WORKED! THE EXCALIBUR SHARD, FUSED WITH MY ARMOR!
WE ARE ONE!
I'VE DONE WHAT YOU ASKED. NOW RETURN ME TO MEPHISTO'S KEEP--AND AS A VISITOR, MIND!
OF COURSE.

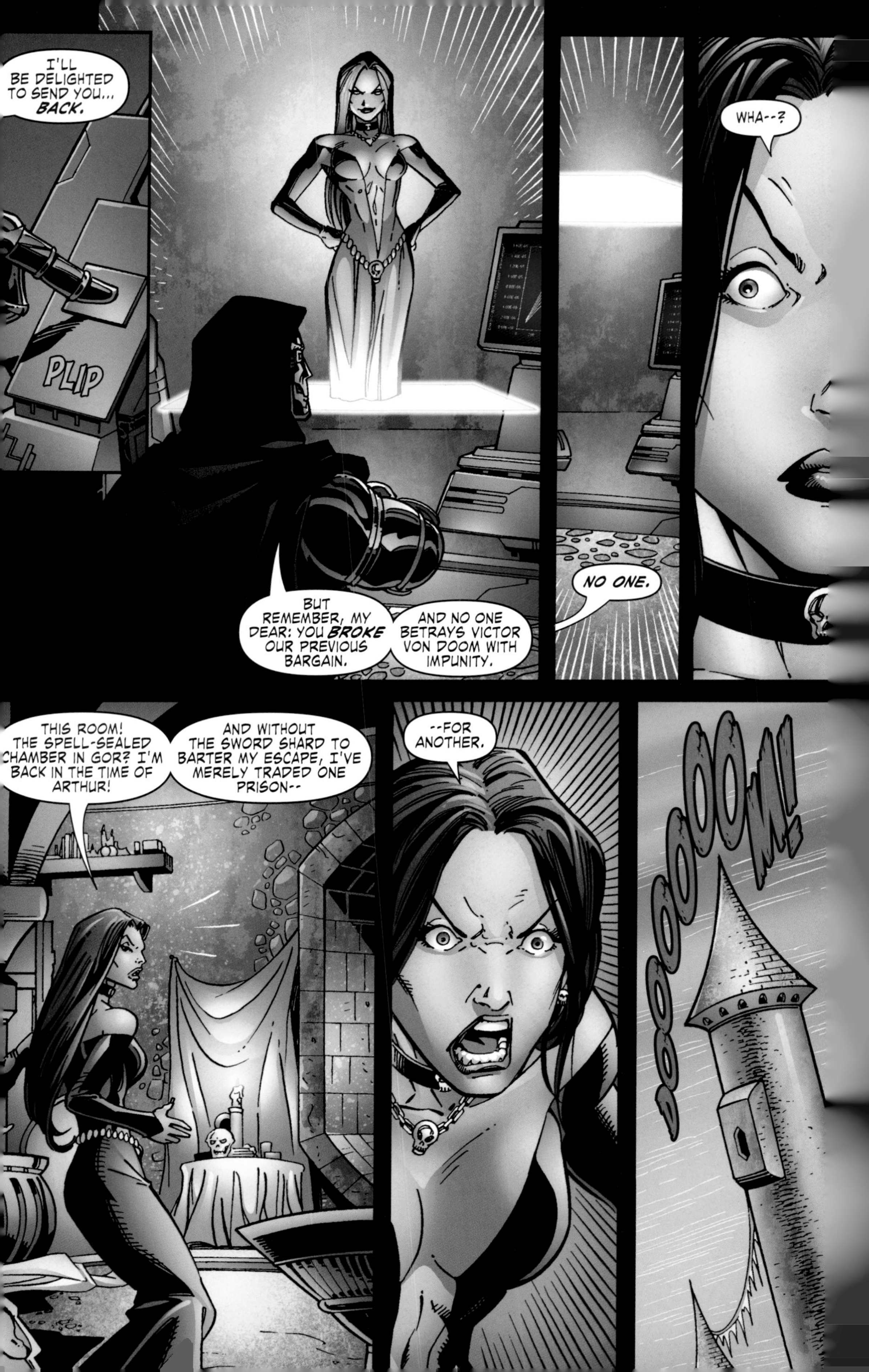
I'LL BE DELIGHTED TO SEND YOU... BACK.
PLIP
BUT REMEMBER, MY DEAR: YOU BROKE OUR PREVIOUS BARGAIN.
AND NO ONE BETRAYS VICTOR VON DOOM WITH IMPUNITY.
NO ONE.
WHA--?
THIS ROOM! THE SPELL-SEALED CHAMBER IN GOR? I'M BACK IN THE TIME OF ARTHUR!
AND WITHOUT THE SWORD SHARD TO BARTER MY ESCAPE, I'VE MERELY TRADED ONE PRISON--
--FOR ANOTHER.
DOOOOOOOM!

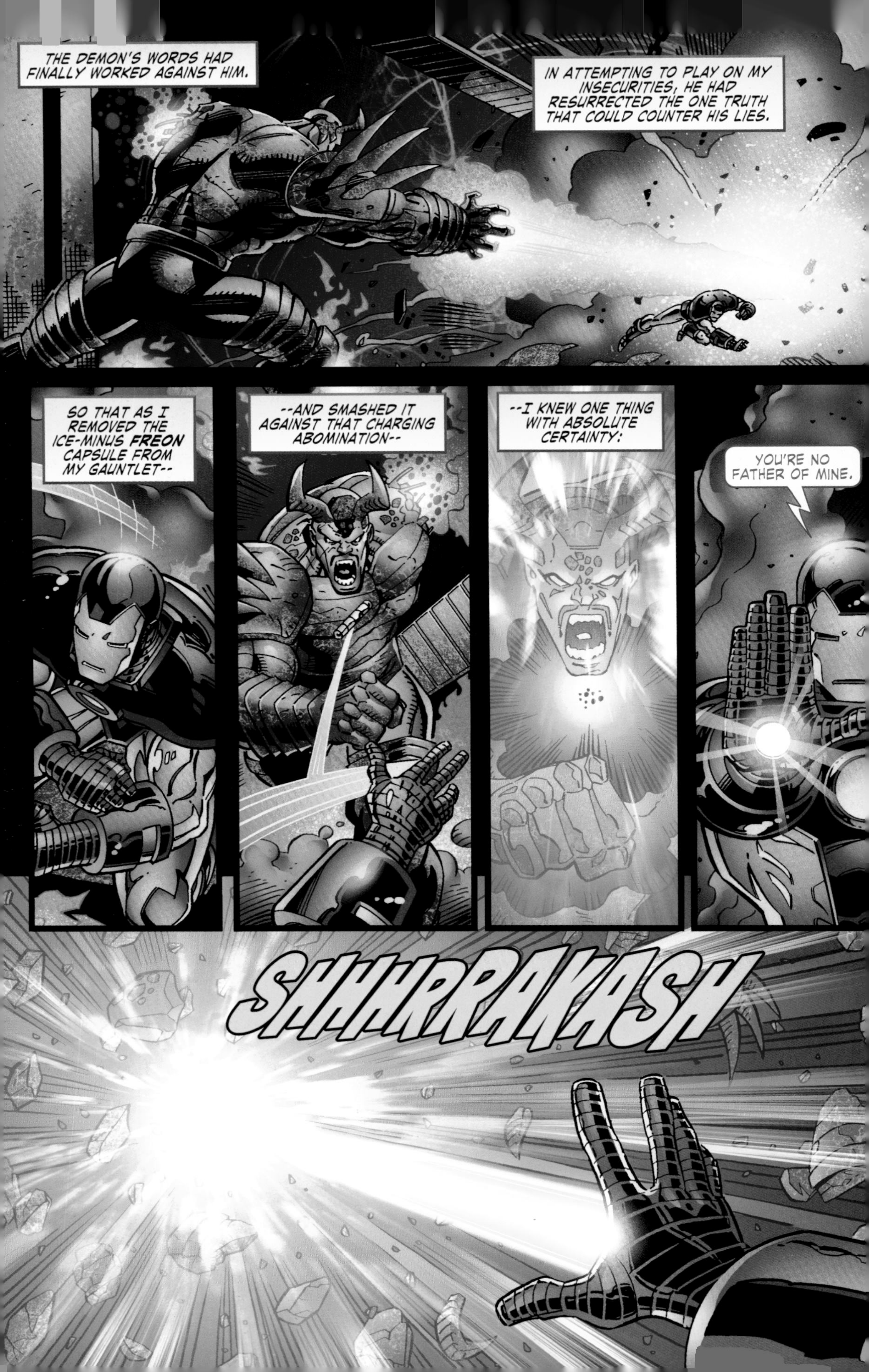
THE DEMON'S WORDS HAD FINALLY WORKED AGAINST HIM.
IN ATTEMPTING TO PLAY ON MY INSECURITIES, HE HAD RESURRECTED THE ONE TRUTH THAT COULD COUNTER HIS LIES.
SO THAT AS I REMOVED THE ICE-MINUS FREON CAPSULE FROM MY GAUNTLET--
--AND SMASHED IT AGAINST THAT CHARGING ABOMINATION--
--I KNEW ONE THING WITH ABSOLUTE CERTAINTY:
YOU'RE NO FATHER OF MINE.
SHHHRRAKASH

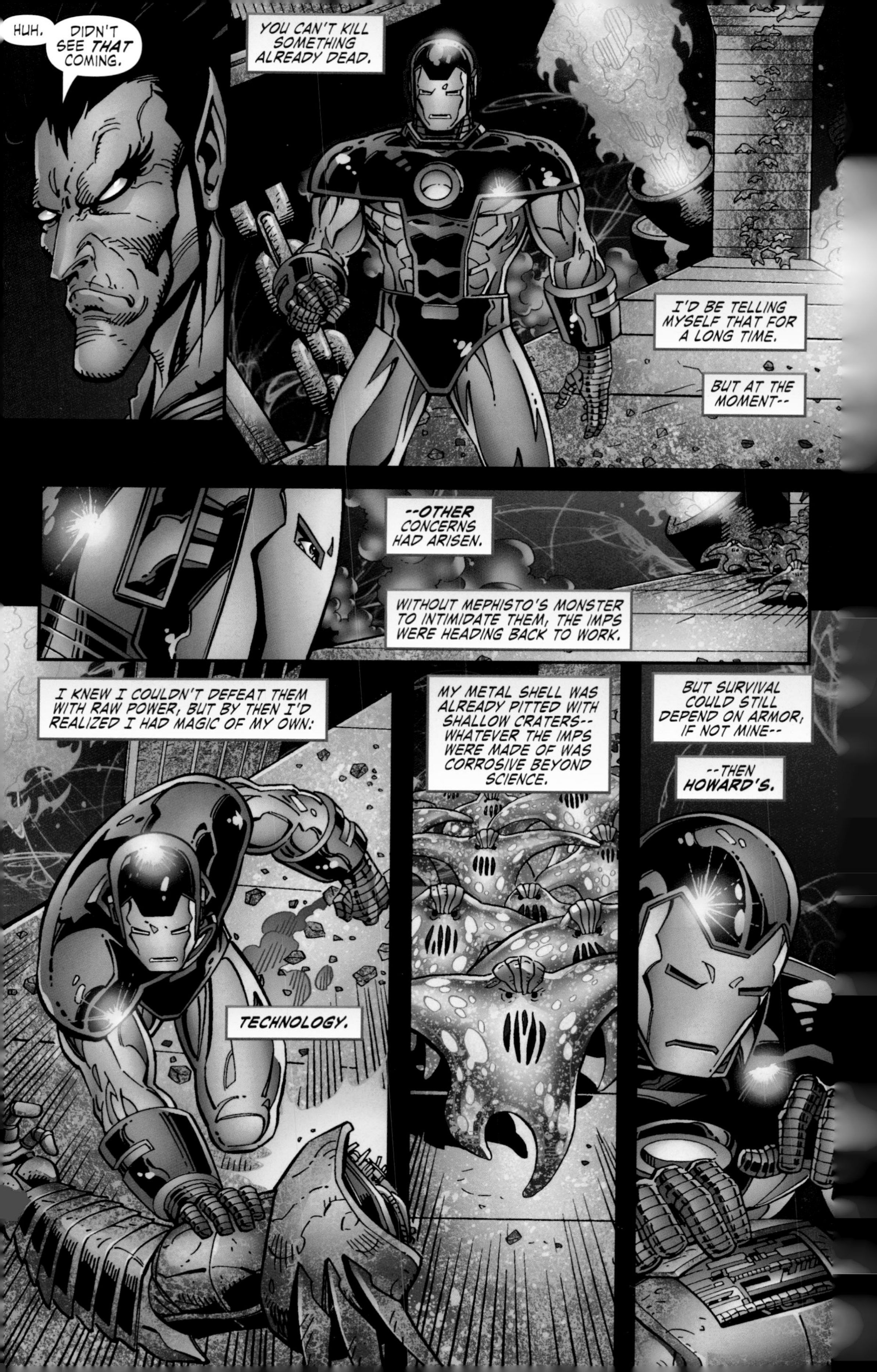
HUH.
DIDN'T SEE THAT COMING.
YOU CAN'T KILL SOMETHING ALREADY DEAD.
I'D BE TELLING MYSELF THAT FOR A LONG TIME.
BUT AT THE MOMENT--
--OTHER CONCERNS HAD ARISEN.
WITHOUT MEPHISTO'S MONSTER TO INTIMIDATE THEM, THE IMPS WERE HEADING BACK TO WORK.
I KNEW I COULDN'T DEFEAT THEM WITH RAW POWER, BUT BY THEN I'D REALIZED I HAD MAGIC OF MY OWN:
TECHNOLOGY.
MY METAL SHELL WAS ALREADY PITTED WITH SHALLOW CRATERS-- WHATEVER THE IMPS WERE MADE OF WAS CORROSIVE BEYOND SCIENCE.
BUT SURVIVAL COULD STILL DEPEND ON ARMOR, IF NOT MINE--
--THEN HOWARD'S.

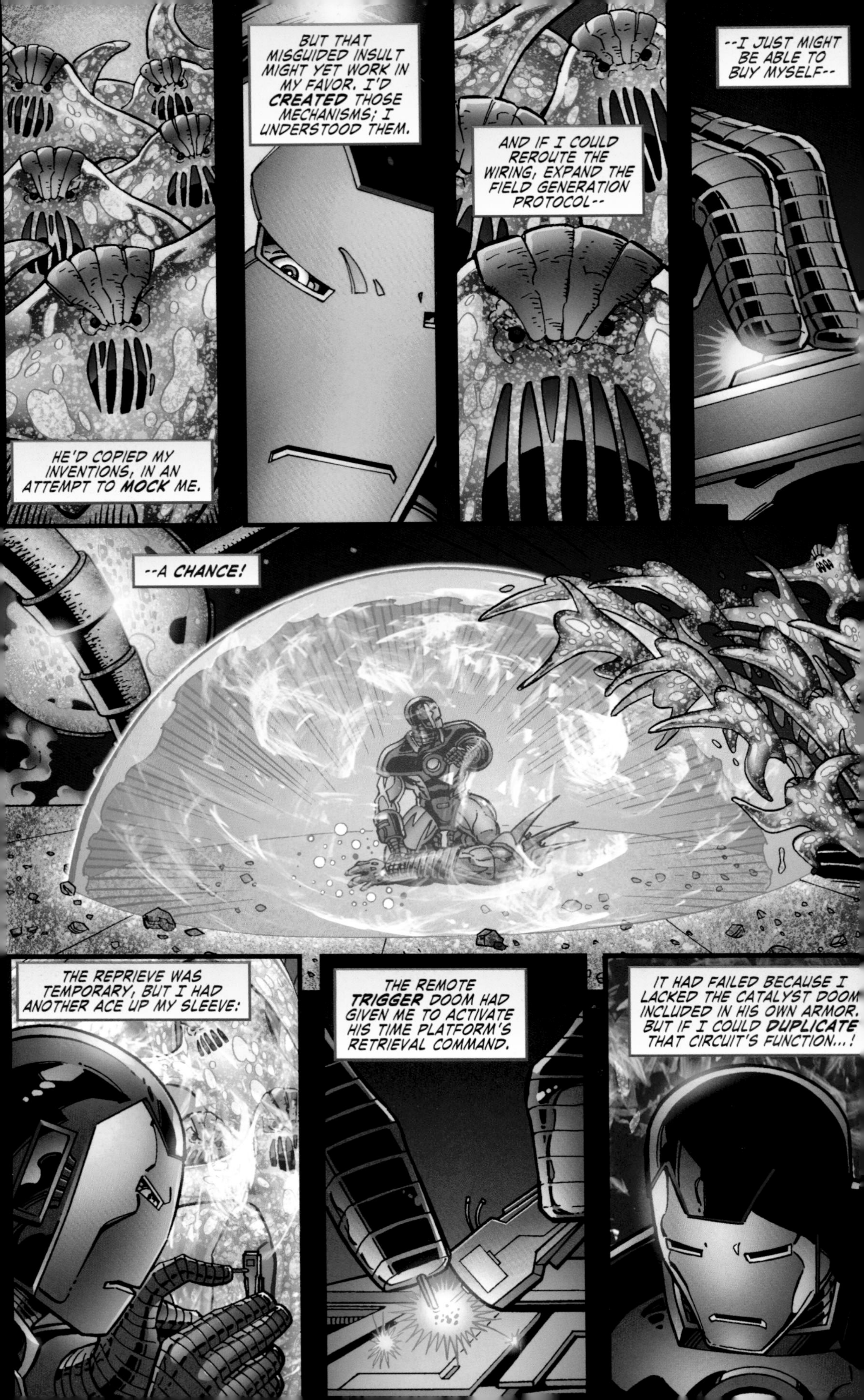

HE'D COPIED MY INVENTIONS, IN AN ATTEMPT TO MOCK ME.
BUT THAT MISGUIDED INSULT MIGHT YET WORK IN MY FAVOR. I'D CREATED THOSE MECHANISMS; I UNDERSTOOD THEM.
AND IF I COULD REROUTE THE WIRING, EXPAND THE FIELD GENERATION PROTOCOL--
--I JUST MIGHT BE ABLE TO BUY MYSELF--
--A CHANCE!
THE REPRIEVE WAS TEMPORARY, BUT I HAD ANOTHER ACE UP MY SLEEVE:
THE REMOTE TRIGGER DOOM HAD GIVEN ME TO ACTIVATE HIS TIME PLATFORM'S RETRIEVAL COMMAND.
IT HAD FAILED BECAUSE I LACKED THE CATALYST DOOM INCLUDED IN HIS OWN ARMOR. BUT IF I COULD DUPLICATE THAT CIRCUIT'S FUNCTION...!

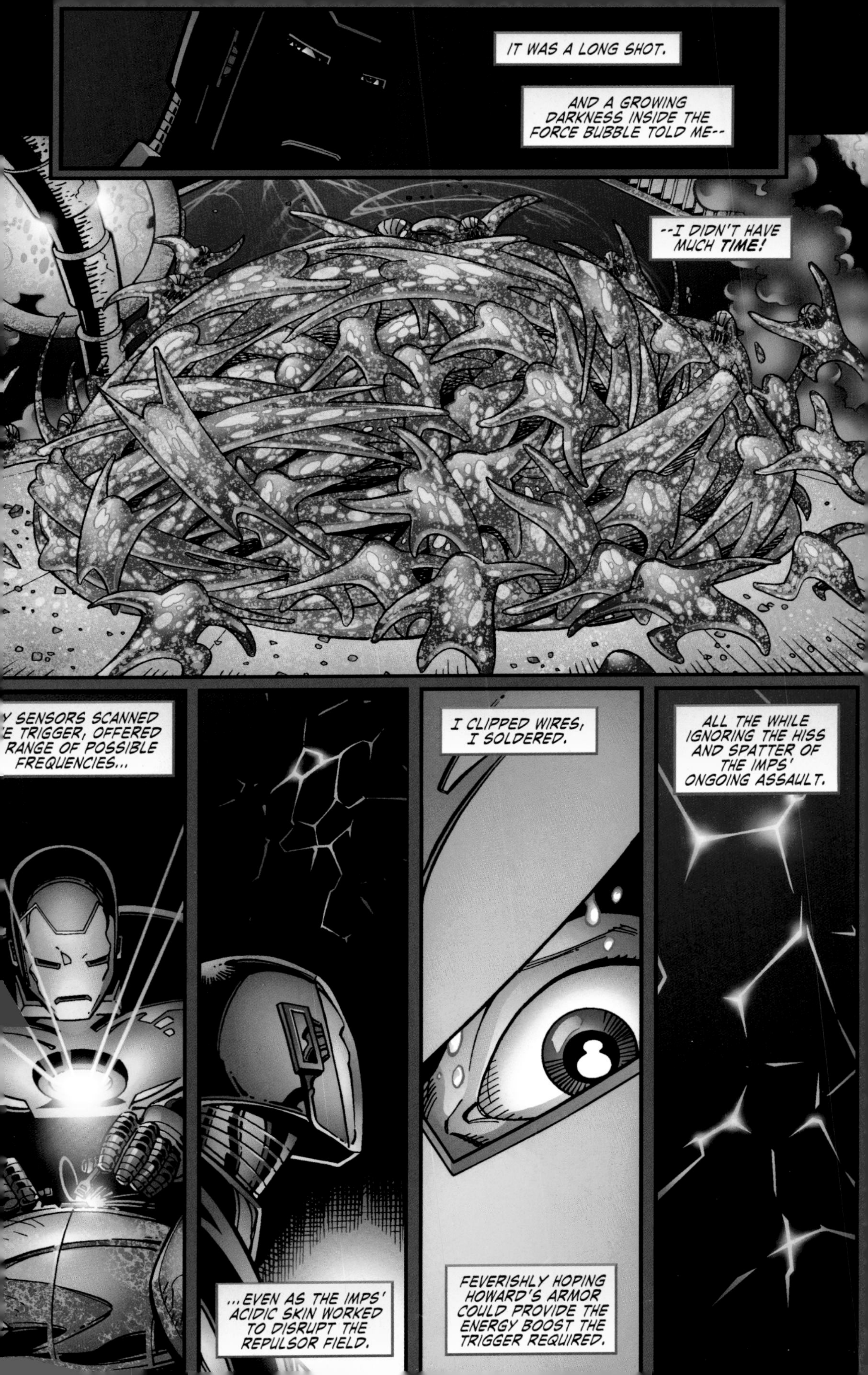
IT WAS A LONG SHOT.
AND A GROWING DARKNESS INSIDE THE FORCE BUBBLE TOLD ME--
--I DIDN'T HAVE MUCH TIME!
Y SENSORS SCANNED E TRIGGER, OFFERED RANGE OF POSSIBLE FREQUENCIES...
...EVEN AS THE IMPS' ACIDIC SKIN WORKED TO DISRUPT THE REPULSOR FIELD.
I CLIPPED WIRES, I SOLDERED.
FEVERISHLY HOPING HOWARD'S ARMOR COULD PROVIDE THE ENERGY BOOST THE TRIGGER REQUIRED.
ALL THE WHILE IGNORING THE HISS AND SPATTER OF THE IMPS' ONGOING ASSAULT.

--THE SIMPLE PUSH OF A BUTTON.

PEEP

KPLASH

AND THEN... THEY WERE THROUGH! THERE WAS NO TIME TO TEST THE FREQUENCY I'D CHOSEN.

THERE WAS ONLY TIME FOR--

I HA WHEN T HAPPE

REAL

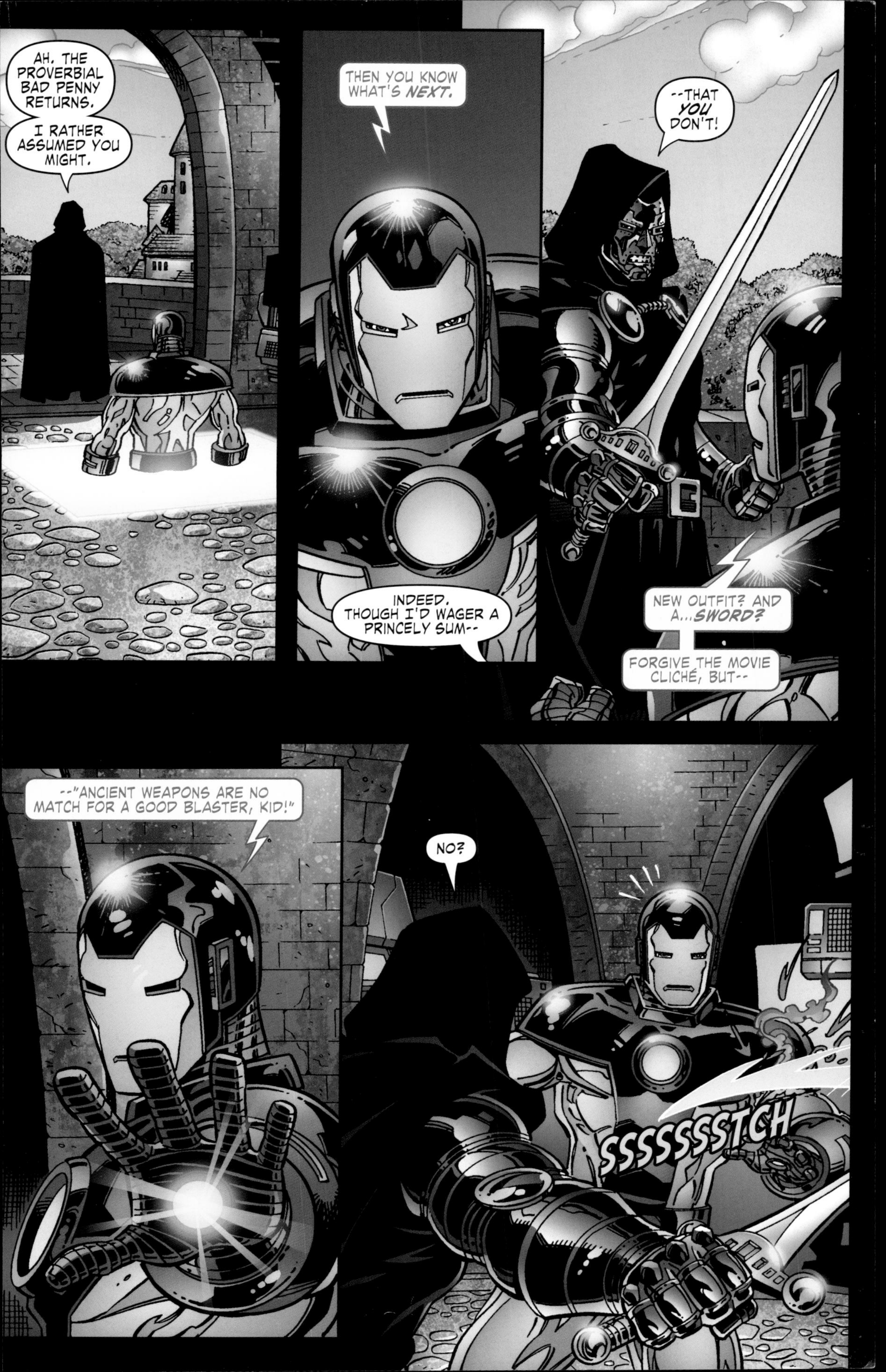

AH. THE PROVERBIAL BAD PENNY RETURNS.
I RATHER ASSUMED YOU MIGHT.
THEN YOU KNOW WHAT'S NEXT.
INDEED. THOUGH I'D WAGER A PRINCELY SUM--
--THAT YOU DON'T!
NEW OUTFIT? AND A...SWORD?
FORGIVE THE MOVIE CLICHÉ, BUT--
--"ANCIENT WEAPONS ARE NO MATCH FOR A GOOD BLASTER, KID!"
NO?
SSSSSSSTCH

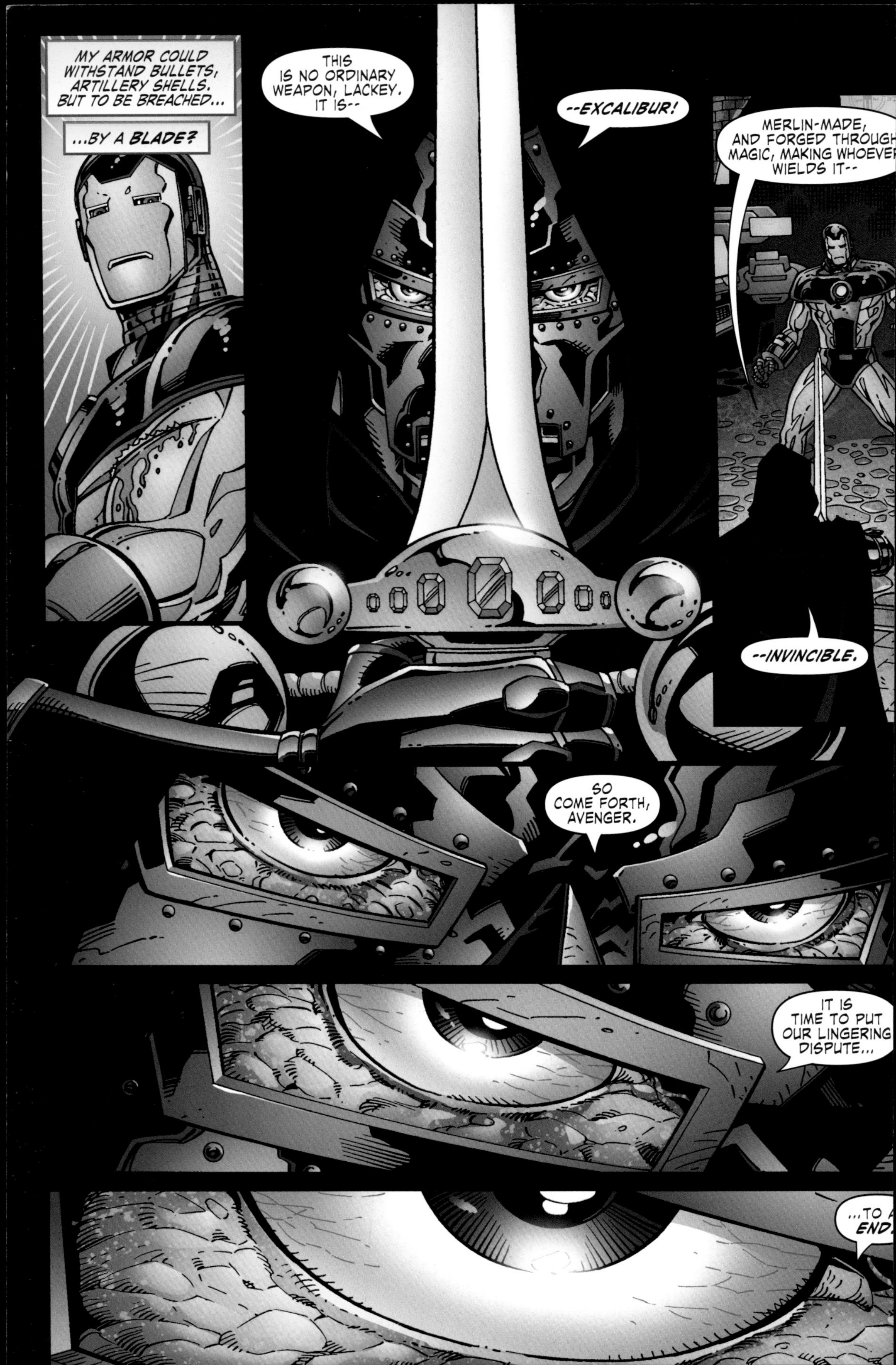
MY ARMOR COULD WITHSTAND BULLETS, ARTILLERY SHELLS. BUT TO BE BREACHED...
...BY A BLADE?
THIS IS NO ORDINARY WEAPON, LACKEY. IT IS--
--EXCALIBUR!
MERLIN-MADE, AND FORGED THROUGH MAGIC, MAKING WHOEVER WIELDS IT--
--INVINCIBLE.
SO COME FORTH, AVENGER.
IT IS TIME TO PUT OUR LINGERING DISPUTE...
...TO A END!

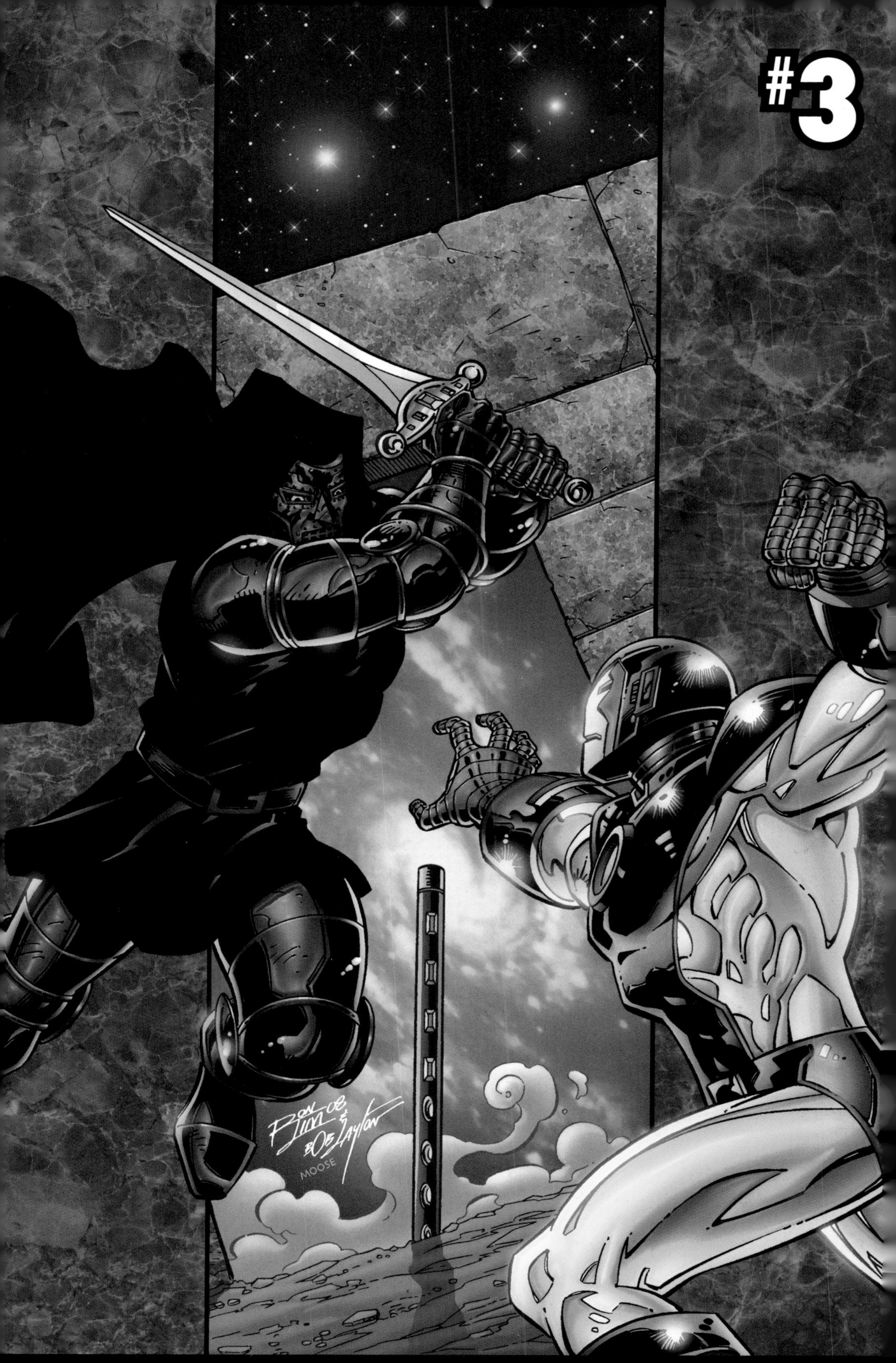
#3
MOOSE

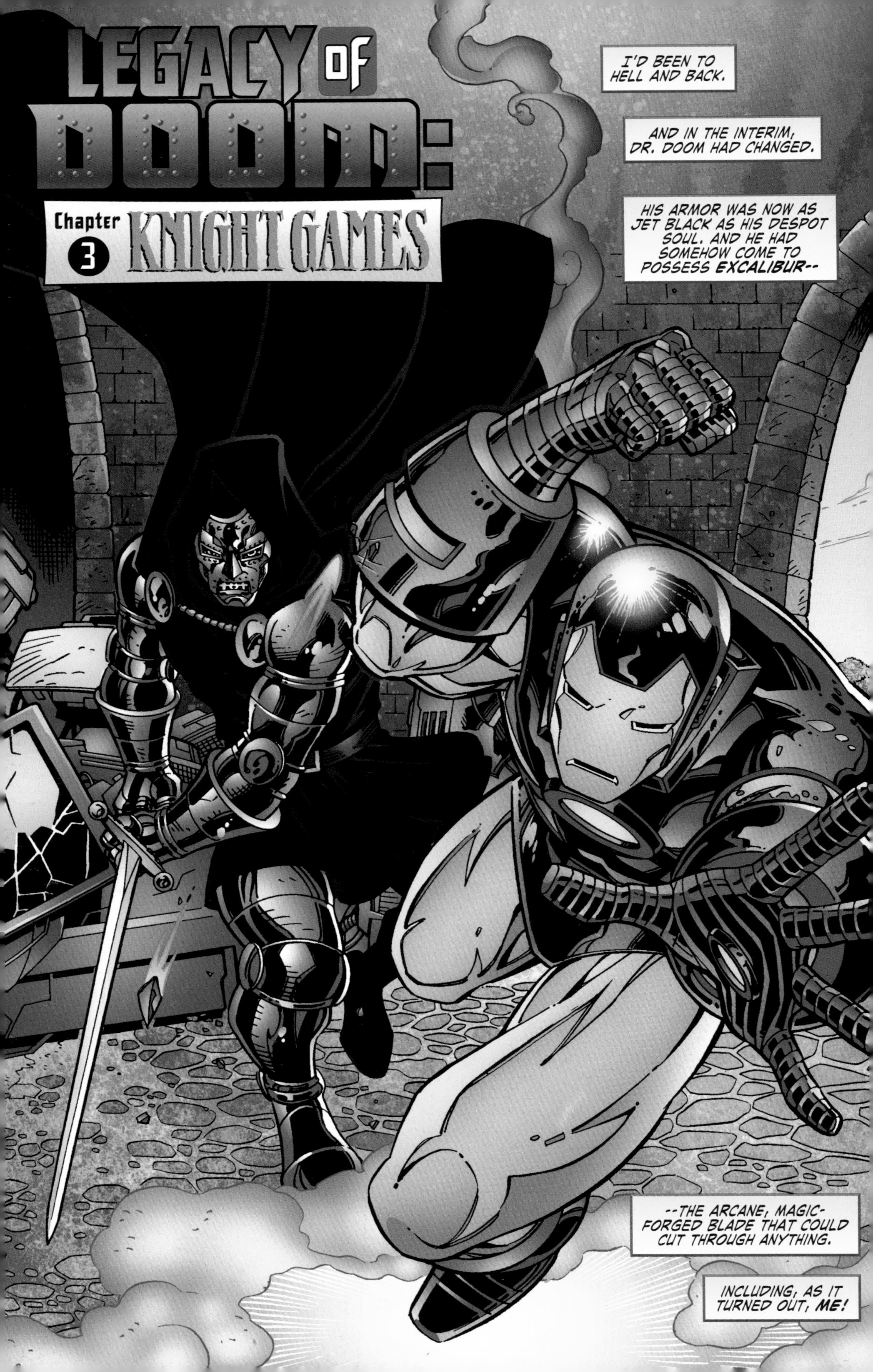
LEGACY OF DOOM:
Chapter 3 KNIGHT GAMES
I'D BEEN TO HELL AND BACK.
AND IN THE INTERIM, DR. DOOM HAD CHANGED.
HIS ARMOR WAS NOW AS JET BLACK AS HIS DESPOT SOUL. AND HE HAD SOMEHOW COME TO POSSESS EXCALIBUR--
--THE ARCANE, MAGIC-FORGED BLADE THAT COULD CUT THROUGH ANYTHING.
INCLUDING, AS IT TURNED OUT, ME!

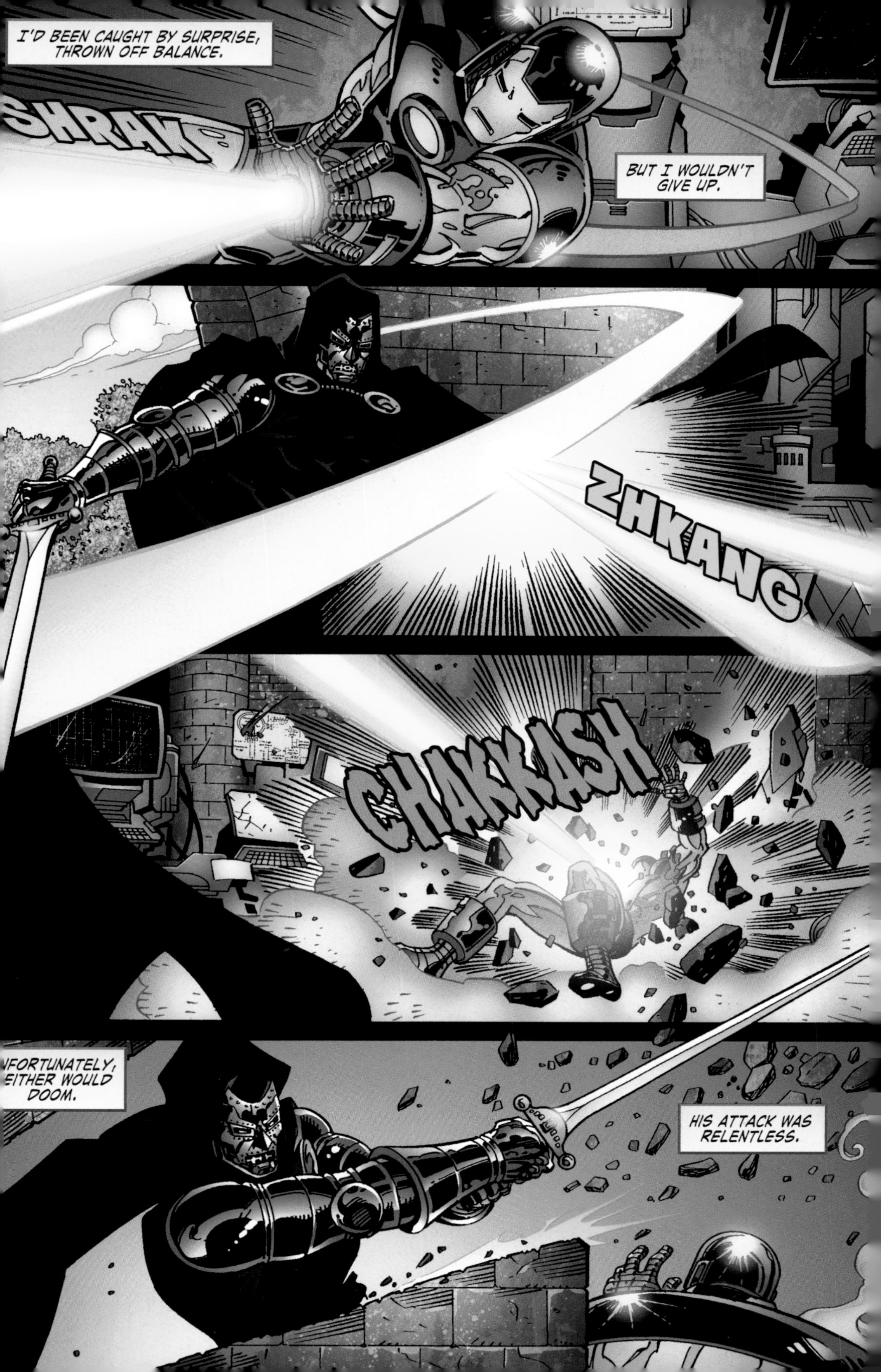
I'D BEEN CAUGHT BY SURPRISE, THROWN OFF BALANCE.
SHRAK
BUT I WOULDN'T GIVE UP.
ZHKANG
CHAKKASH
NFORTUNATELY, EITHER WOULD DOOM.
HIS ATTACK WAS RELENTLESS.

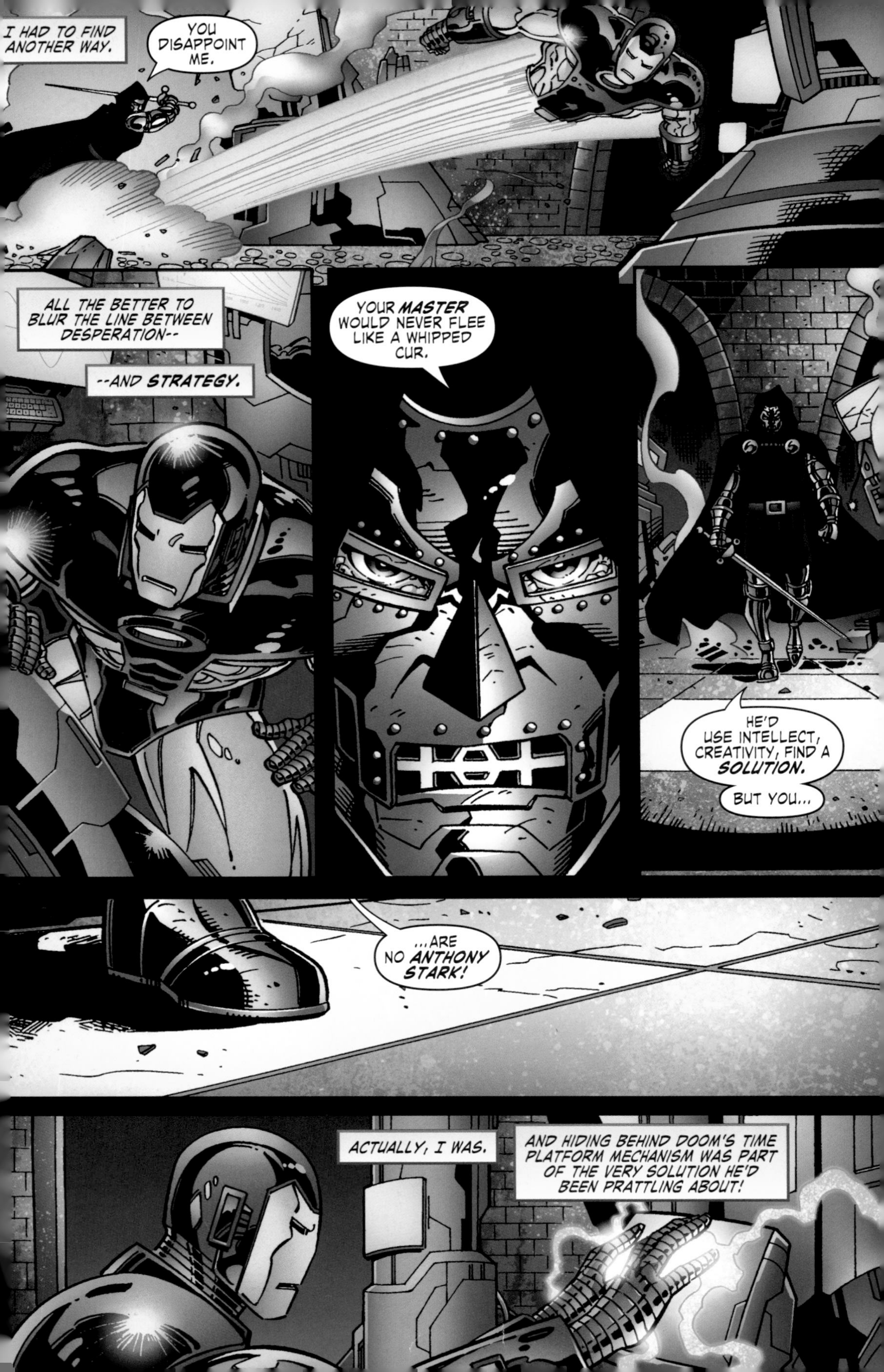
I HAD TO FIND ANOTHER WAY.
YOU DISAPPOINT ME.
ALL THE BETTER TO BLUR THE LINE BETWEEN DESPERATION--
--AND STRATEGY.
YOUR MASTER WOULD NEVER FLEE LIKE A WHIPPED CUR.
HE'D USE INTELLECT, CREATIVITY, FIND A SOLUTION.
BUT YOU...
...ARE NO ANTHONY STARK!
ACTUALLY, I WAS.
AND HIDING BEHIND DOOM'S TIME PLATFORM MECHANISM WAS PART OF THE VERY SOLUTION HE'D BEEN PRATTLING ABOUT!

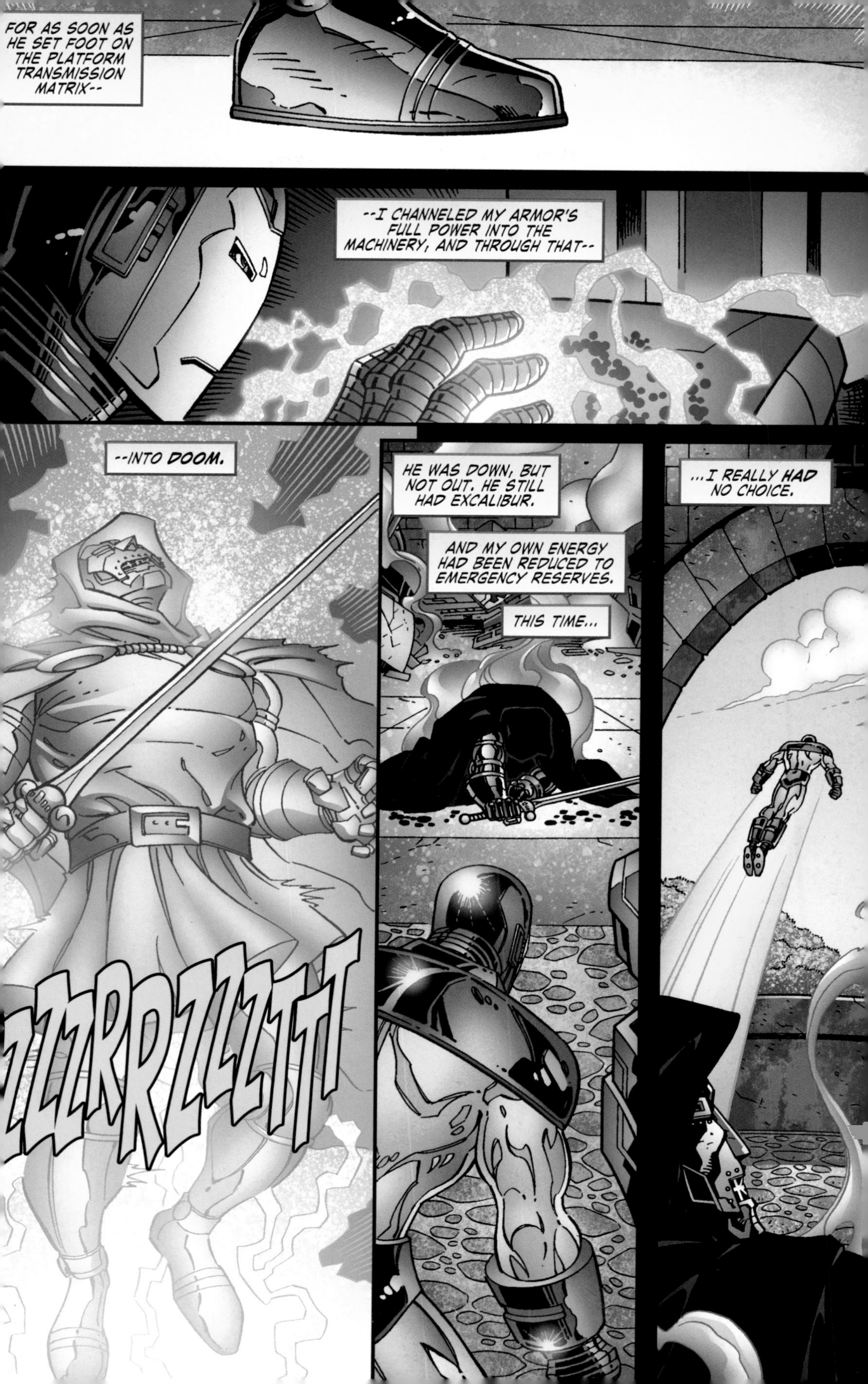
FOR AS SOON AS HE SET FOOT ON THE PLATFORM TRANSMISSION MATRIX--
--I CHANNELED MY ARMOR'S FULL POWER INTO THE MACHINERY, AND THROUGH THAT--
--INTO DOOM.
ZZZRZZZTTT
HE WAS DOWN, BUT NOT OUT. HE STILL HAD EXCALIBUR.
AND MY OWN ENERGY HAD BEEN REDUCED TO EMERGENCY RESERVES.
THIS TIME...
...I REALLY HAD NO CHOICE.

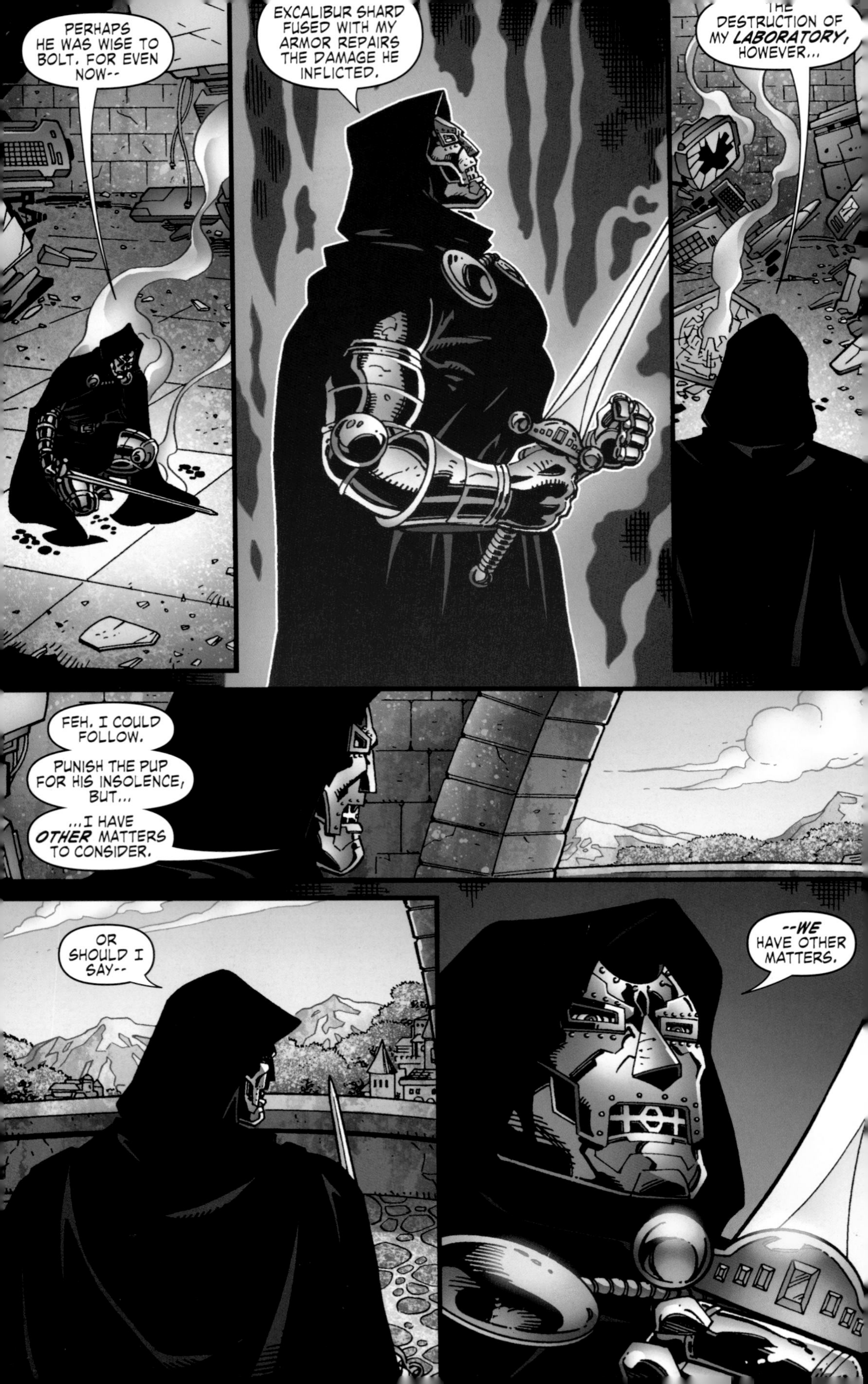
PERHAPS HE WAS WISE TO BOLT. FOR EVEN NOW--
EXCALIBUR SHARD FUSED WITH MY ARMOR REPAIRS THE DAMAGE HE INFLICTED.
THE DESTRUCTION OF MY LABORATORY, HOWEVER...
FEH. I COULD FOLLOW.
PUNISH THE PUP FOR HIS INSOLENCE, BUT...
...I HAVE OTHER MATTERS TO CONSIDER.
OR SHOULD I SAY--
--WE HAVE OTHER MATTERS.

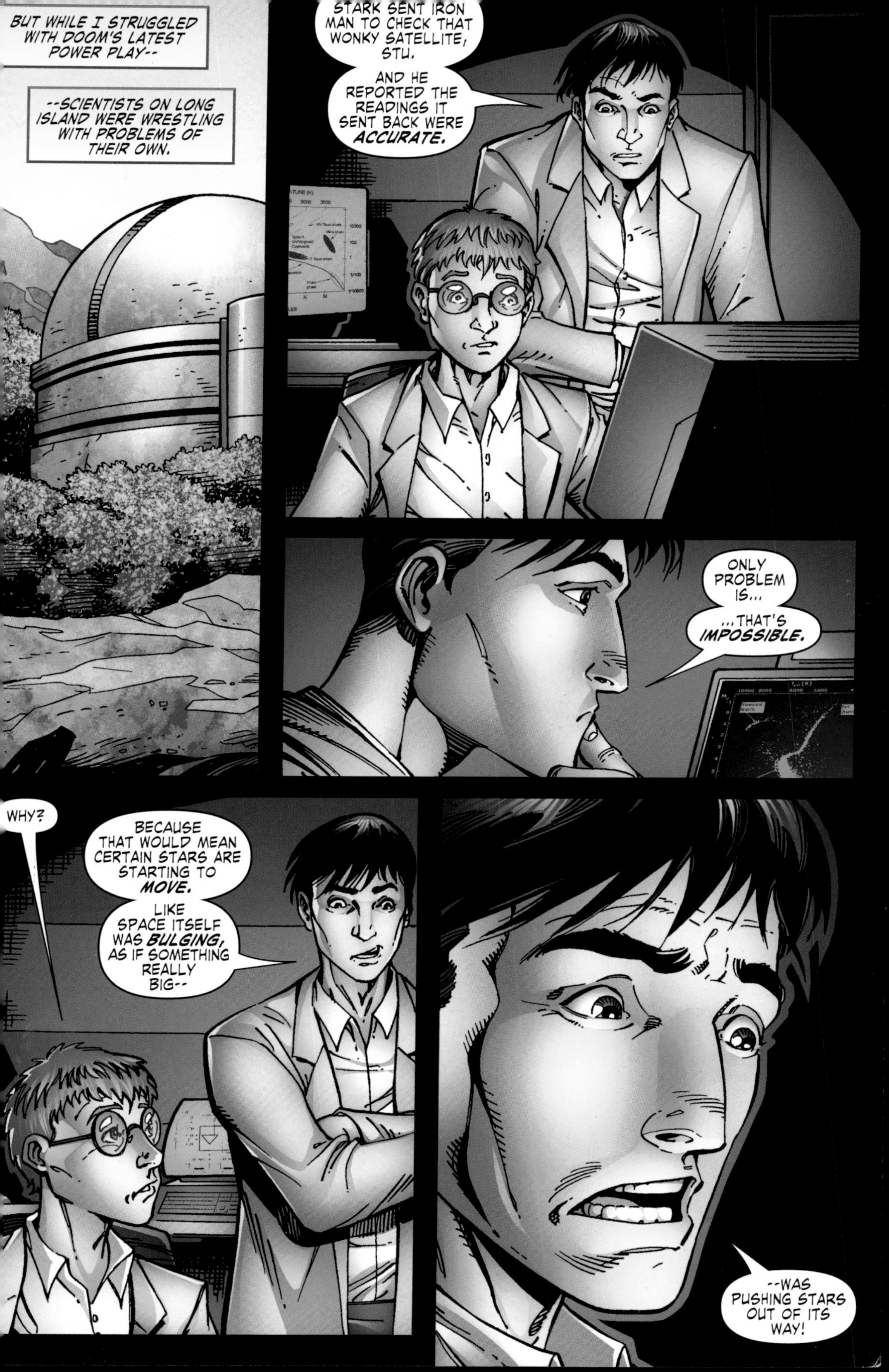
BUT WHILE I STRUGGLED WITH DOOM'S LATEST POWER PLAY--
--SCIENTISTS ON LONG ISLAND WERE WRESTLING WITH PROBLEMS OF THEIR OWN.
STARK SENT IRON MAN TO CHECK THAT WONKY SATELLITE, STU.
AND HE REPORTED THE READINGS IT SENT BACK WERE ACCURATE.
ONLY PROBLEM IS...
...THAT'S IMPOSSIBLE.
WHY?
BECAUSE THAT WOULD MEAN CERTAIN STARS ARE STARTING TO MOVE.
LIKE SPACE ITSELF WAS BULGING, AS IF SOMETHING REALLY BIG--
--WAS PUSHING STARS OUT OF ITS WAY!

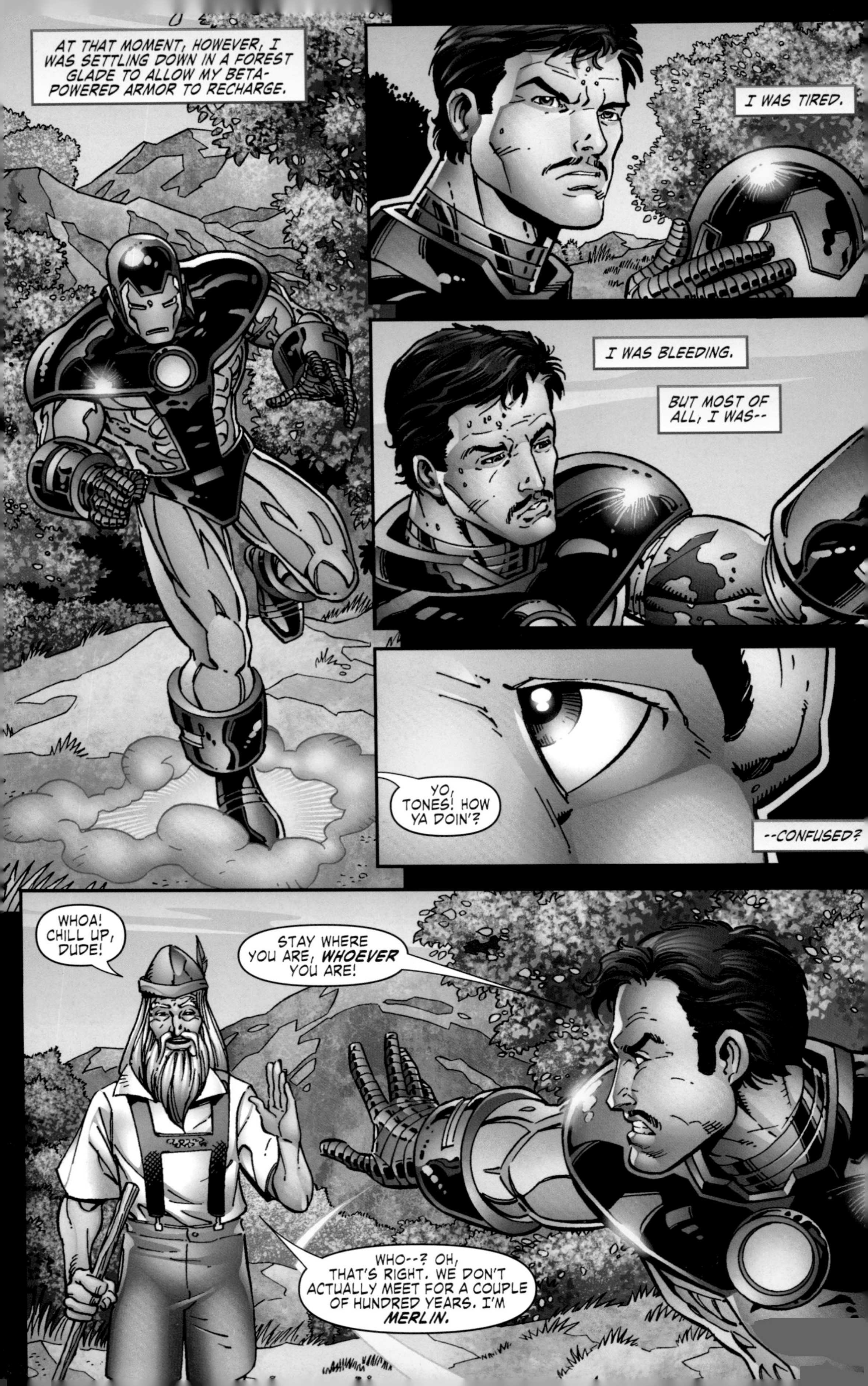
AT THAT MOMENT, HOWEVER, I WAS SETTLING DOWN IN A FOREST GLADE TO ALLOW MY BETA-POWERED ARMOR TO RECHARGE.
I WAS TIRED.
I WAS BLEEDING.
BUT MOST OF ALL, I WAS--
YO, TONES! HOW YA DOIN'?
--CONFUSED?
WHOA! CHILL UP, DUDE!
STAY WHERE YOU ARE, WHOEVER YOU ARE!
WHO--? OH, THAT'S RIGHT. WE DON'T ACTUALLY MEET FOR A COUPLE OF HUNDRED YEARS. I'M MERLIN.

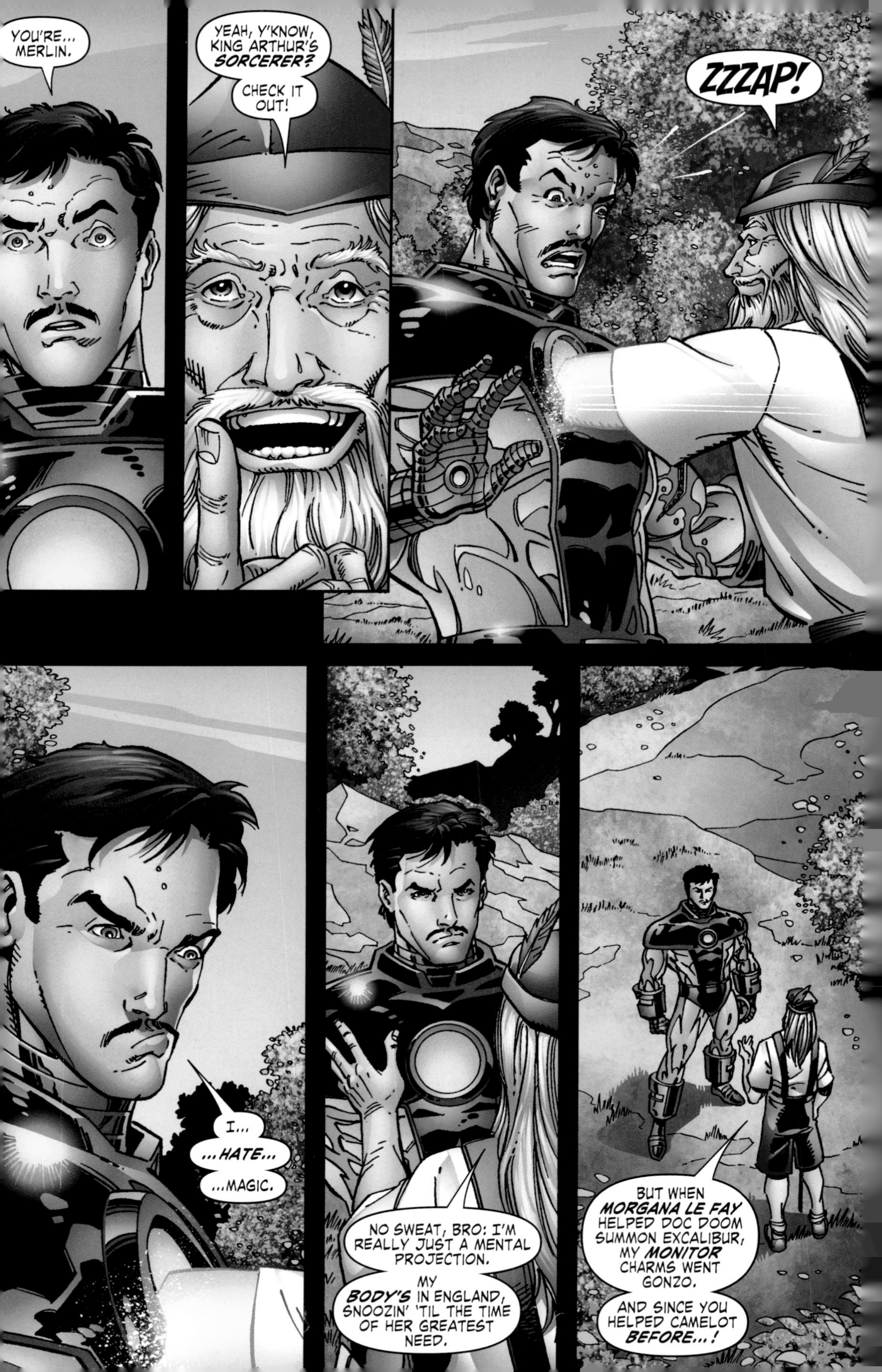
YOU'RE... MERLIN.
YEAH, Y'KNOW, KING ARTHUR'S SORCERER?
CHECK IT OUT!
ZZZAP!
I...
...HATE...
...MAGIC.
NO SWEAT, BRO: I'M REALLY JUST A MENTAL PROJECTION.
MY BODY'S IN ENGLAND, SNOOZIN' 'TIL THE TIME OF HER GREATEST NEED.
BUT WHEN MORGANA LE FAY HELPED DOC DOOM SUMMON EXCALIBUR, MY MONITOR CHARMS WENT GONZO.
AND SINCE YOU HELPED CAMELOT BEFORE...!

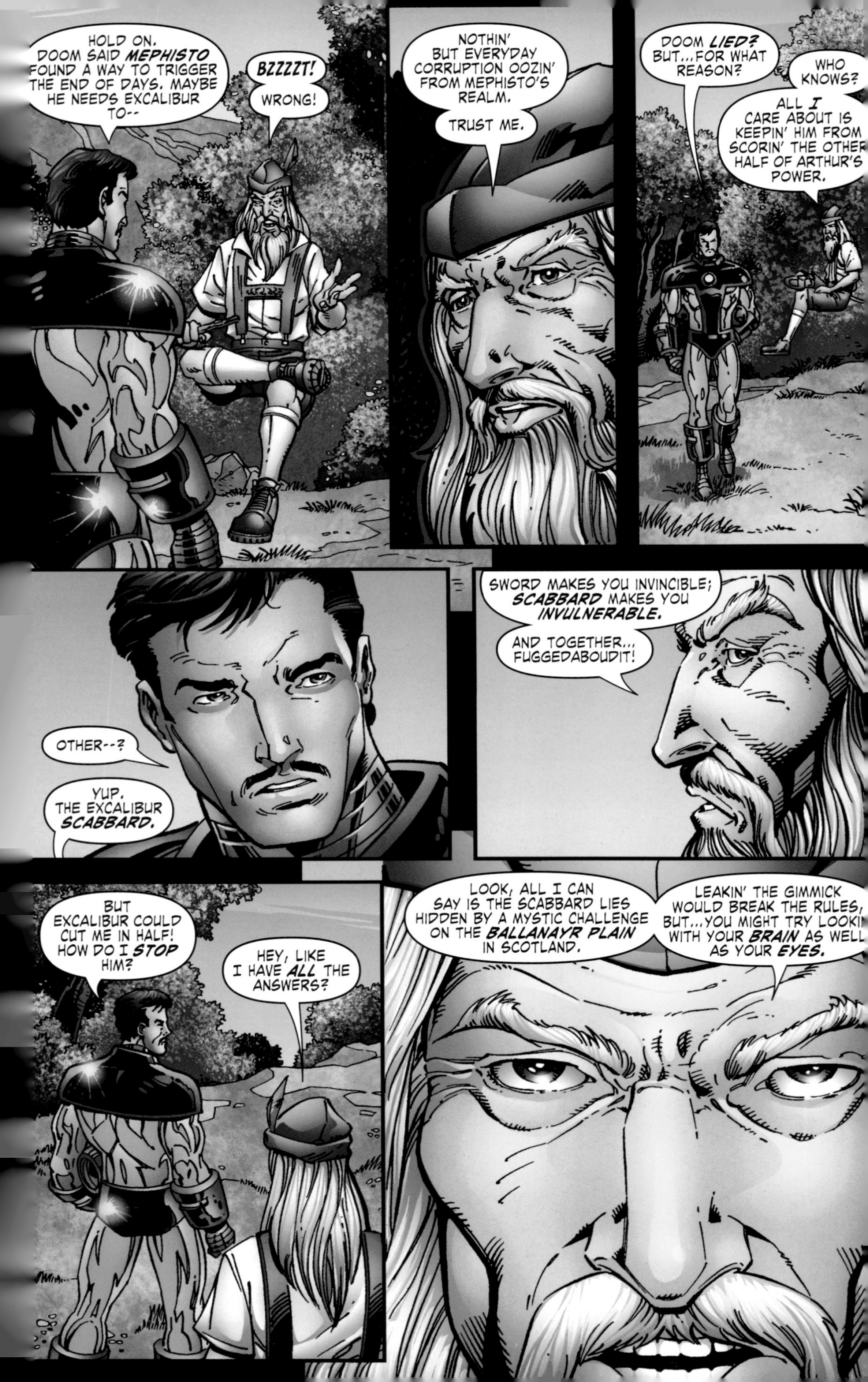
HOLD ON. DOOM SAID *MEPHISTO* FOUND A WAY TO TRIGGER THE END OF DAYS. MAYBE HE NEEDS EXCALIBUR TO--
BZZZZT!
WRONG!
NOTHIN' BUT EVERYDAY CORRUPTION OOZIN' FROM MEPHISTO'S REALM.
TRUST ME.
DOOM *LIED?* BUT...FOR WHAT REASON?
WHO KNOWS?
ALL *I* CARE ABOUT IS KEEPIN' HIM FROM SCORIN' THE OTHER HALF OF ARTHUR'S POWER.
OTHER--?
YUP. THE EXCALIBUR *SCABBARD.*
SWORD MAKES YOU INVINCIBLE; *SCABBARD* MAKES YOU *INVULNERABLE.*
AND TOGETHER... FUGGEDABOUDIT!
BUT EXCALIBUR COULD CUT ME IN HALF! HOW DO I *STOP* HIM?
HEY, LIKE I HAVE *ALL* THE ANSWERS?
LOOK, ALL I CAN SAY IS THE SCABBARD LIES HIDDEN BY A MYSTIC CHALLENGE ON THE *BALLANAYR PLAIN* IN SCOTLAND.
LEAKIN' THE GIMMICK WOULD BREAK THE RULES, BUT...YOU MIGHT TRY LOOKI WITH YOUR *BRAIN* AS WELL AS YOUR *EYES.*

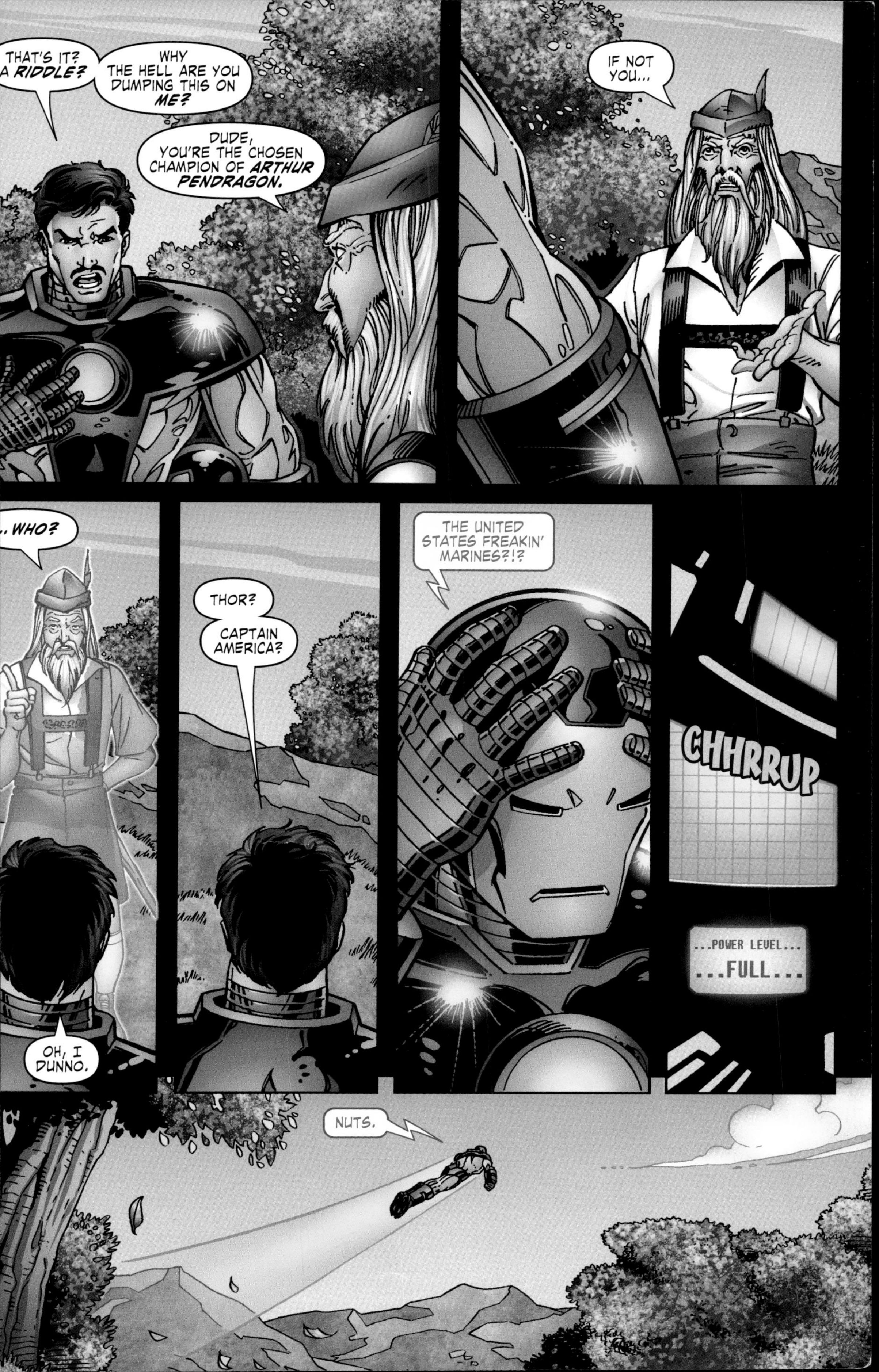
THAT'S IT? A RIDDLE?
WHY THE HELL ARE YOU DUMPING THIS ON ME?
DUDE, YOU'RE THE CHOSEN CHAMPION OF ARTHUR PENDRAGON.
IF NOT YOU...
...WHO?
OH, I DUNNO.
THOR?
CAPTAIN AMERICA?
THE UNITED STATES FREAKIN' MARINES?!?
CHHRRUP
...POWER LEVEL...
...FULL...
NUTS.

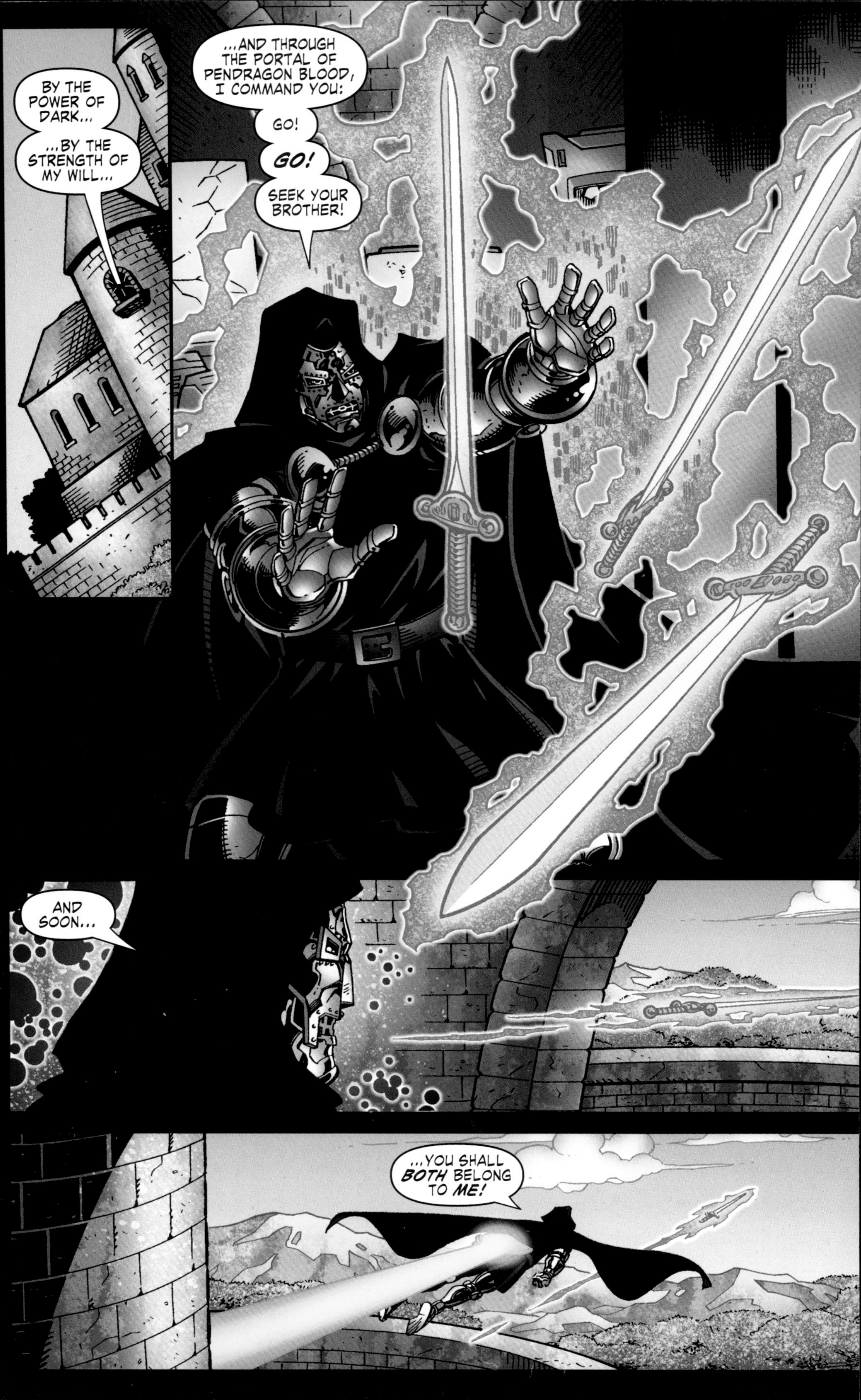
BY THE POWER OF DARK...
...BY THE STRENGTH OF MY WILL...
...AND THROUGH THE PORTAL OF PENDRAGON BLOOD, I COMMAND YOU:
GO!
GO!
SEEK YOUR BROTHER!
AND SOON...
...YOU SHALL BOTH BELONG TO ME!

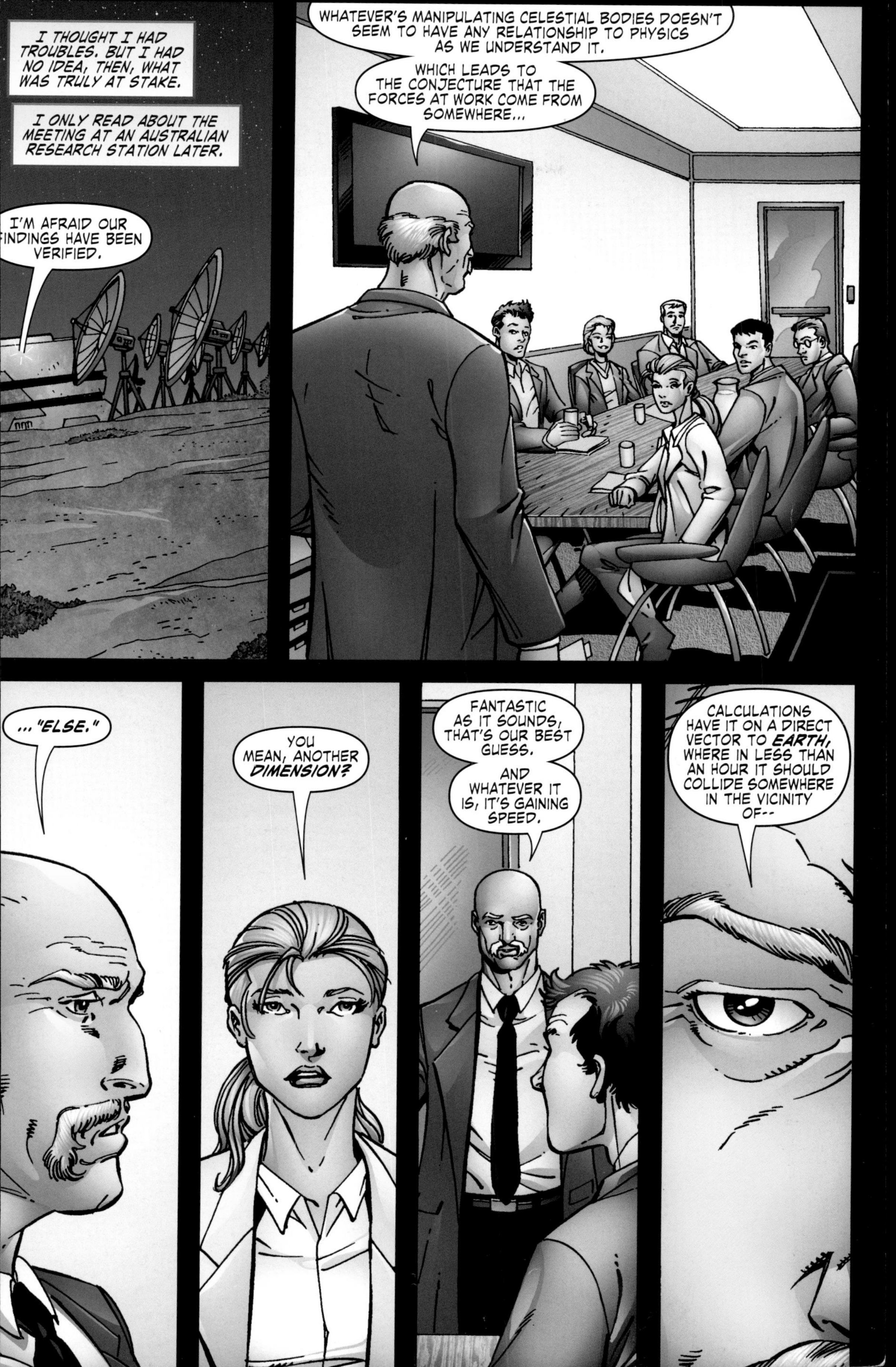

I THOUGHT I HAD TROUBLES. BUT I HAD NO IDEA, THEN, WHAT WAS TRULY AT STAKE.
I ONLY READ ABOUT THE MEETING AT AN AUSTRALIAN RESEARCH STATION LATER.
I'M AFRAID OUR FINDINGS HAVE BEEN VERIFIED.
WHATEVER'S MANIPULATING CELESTIAL BODIES DOESN'T SEEM TO HAVE ANY RELATIONSHIP TO PHYSICS AS WE UNDERSTAND IT.
WHICH LEADS TO THE CONJECTURE THAT THE FORCES AT WORK COME FROM SOMEWHERE...
..."ELSE."
YOU MEAN, ANOTHER DIMENSION?
FANTASTIC AS IT SOUNDS, THAT'S OUR BEST GUESS.
AND WHATEVER IT IS, IT'S GAINING SPEED.
CALCULATIONS HAVE IT ON A DIRECT VECTOR TO EARTH, WHERE IN LESS THAN AN HOUR IT SHOULD COLLIDE SOMEWHERE IN THE VICINITY OF--

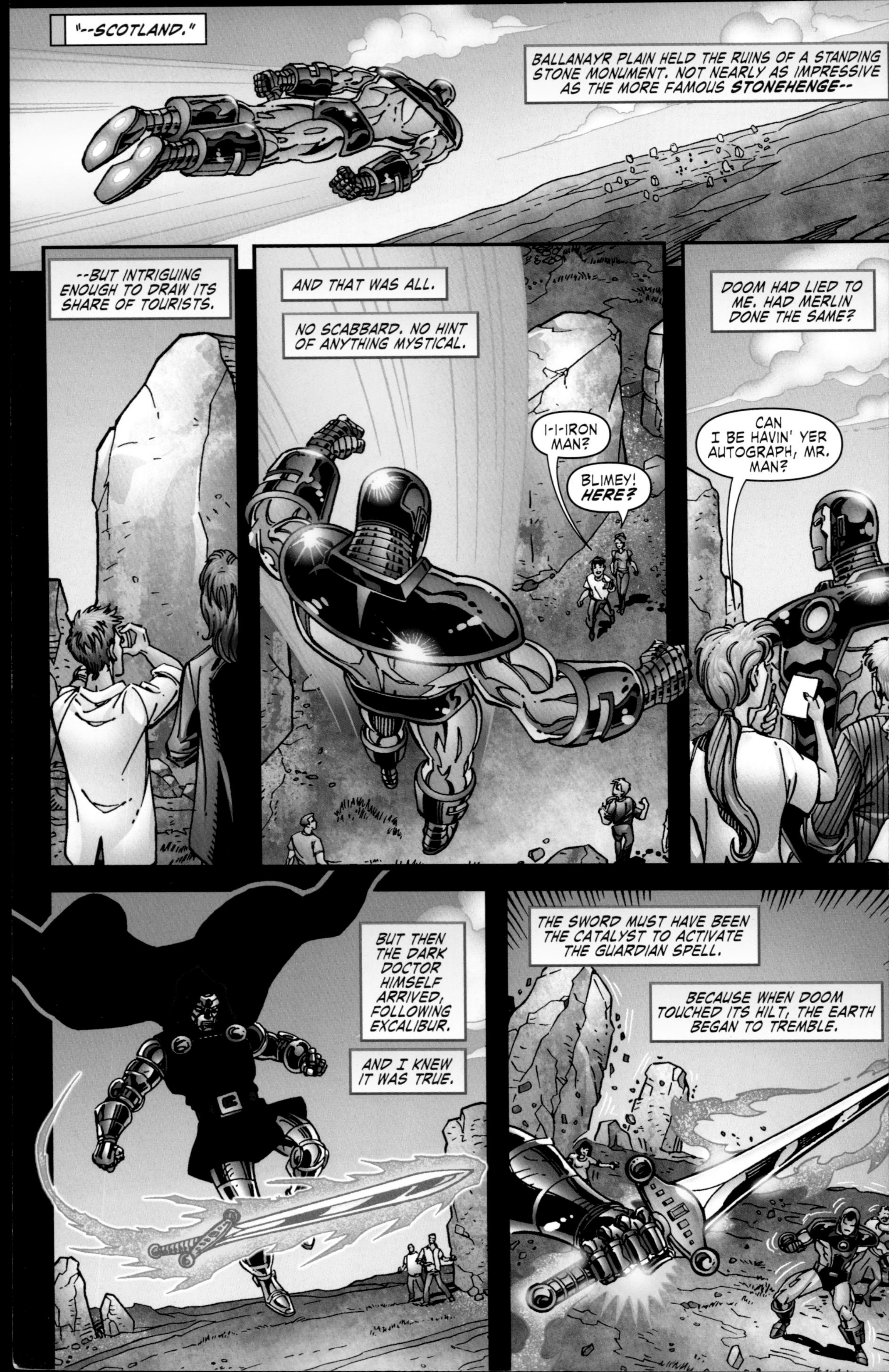
"--SCOTLAND."
BALLANAYR PLAIN HELD THE RUINS OF A STANDING STONE MONUMENT. NOT NEARLY AS IMPRESSIVE AS THE MORE FAMOUS STONEHENGE--
--BUT INTRIGUING ENOUGH TO DRAW ITS SHARE OF TOURISTS.
AND THAT WAS ALL.
NO SCABBARD. NO HINT OF ANYTHING MYSTICAL.
I-I-IRON MAN?
BLIMEY! HERE?
DOOM HAD LIED TO ME. HAD MERLIN DONE THE SAME?
CAN I BE HAVIN' YER AUTOGRAPH, MR. MAN?
BUT THEN THE DARK DOCTOR HIMSELF ARRIVED, FOLLOWING EXCALIBUR.
AND I KNEW IT WAS TRUE.
THE SWORD MUST HAVE BEEN THE CATALYST TO ACTIVATE THE GUARDIAN SPELL.
BECAUSE WHEN DOOM TOUCHED ITS HILT, THE EARTH BEGAN TO TREMBLE.

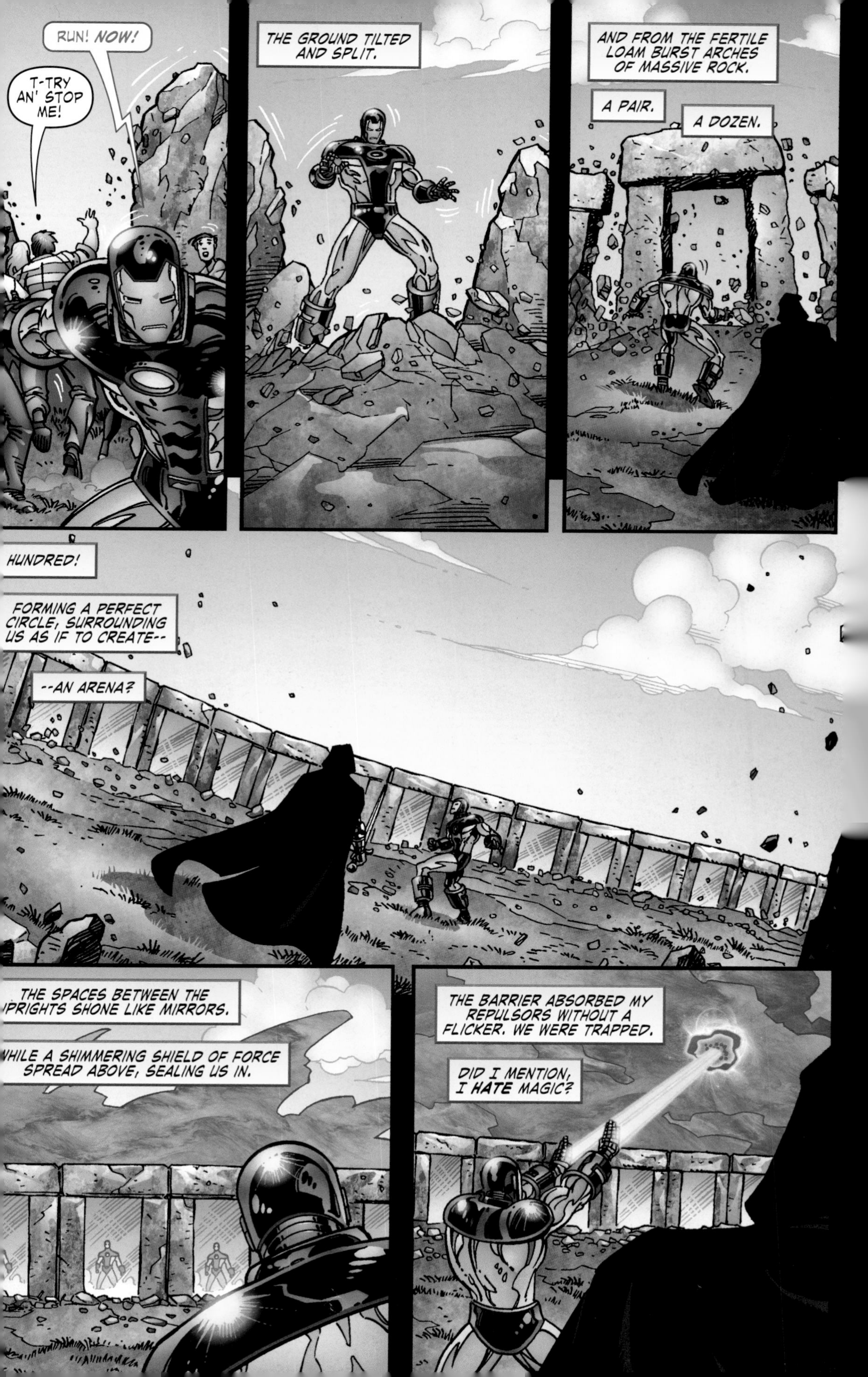

RUN! NOW!
T-TRY AN' STOP ME!
THE GROUND TILTED AND SPLIT.
AND FROM THE FERTILE LOAM BURST ARCHES OF MASSIVE ROCK.
A PAIR.
A DOZEN.
HUNDRED!
FORMING A PERFECT CIRCLE, SURROUNDING US AS IF TO CREATE--
--AN ARENA?
THE SPACES BETWEEN THE UPRIGHTS SHONE LIKE MIRRORS.
WHILE A SHIMMERING SHIELD OF FORCE SPREAD ABOVE, SEALING US IN.
THE BARRIER ABSORBED MY REPULSORS WITHOUT A FLICKER. WE WERE TRAPPED.
DID I MENTION, I HATE MAGIC?

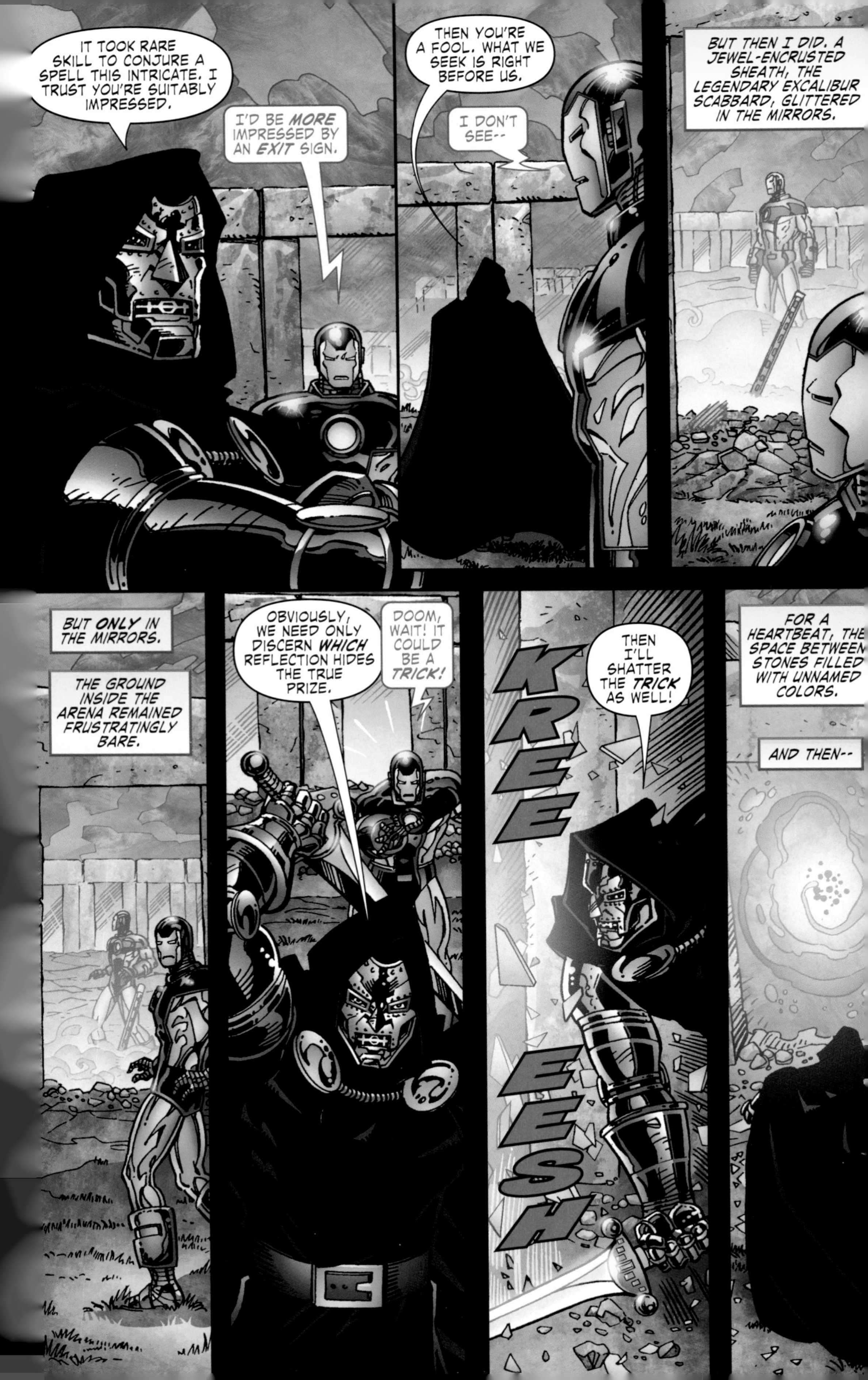
IT TOOK RARE SKILL TO CONJURE A SPELL THIS INTRICATE. I TRUST YOU'RE SUITABLY IMPRESSED.
I'D BE MORE IMPRESSED BY AN EXIT SIGN.
THEN YOU'RE A FOOL. WHAT WE SEEK IS RIGHT BEFORE US.
I DON'T SEE--
BUT THEN I DID. A JEWEL-ENCRUSTED SHEATH, THE LEGENDARY EXCALIBUR SCABBARD, GLITTERED IN THE MIRRORS.
BUT ONLY IN THE MIRRORS.
THE GROUND INSIDE THE ARENA REMAINED FRUSTRATINGLY BARE.
OBVIOUSLY, WE NEED ONLY DISCERN WHICH REFLECTION HIDES THE TRUE PRIZE.
DOOM, WAIT! IT COULD BE A TRICK!
KREEEEESH
THEN I'LL SHATTER THE TRICK AS WELL!
FOR A HEARTBEAT, THE SPACE BETWEEN STONES FILLED WITH UNNAMED COLORS.
AND THEN--

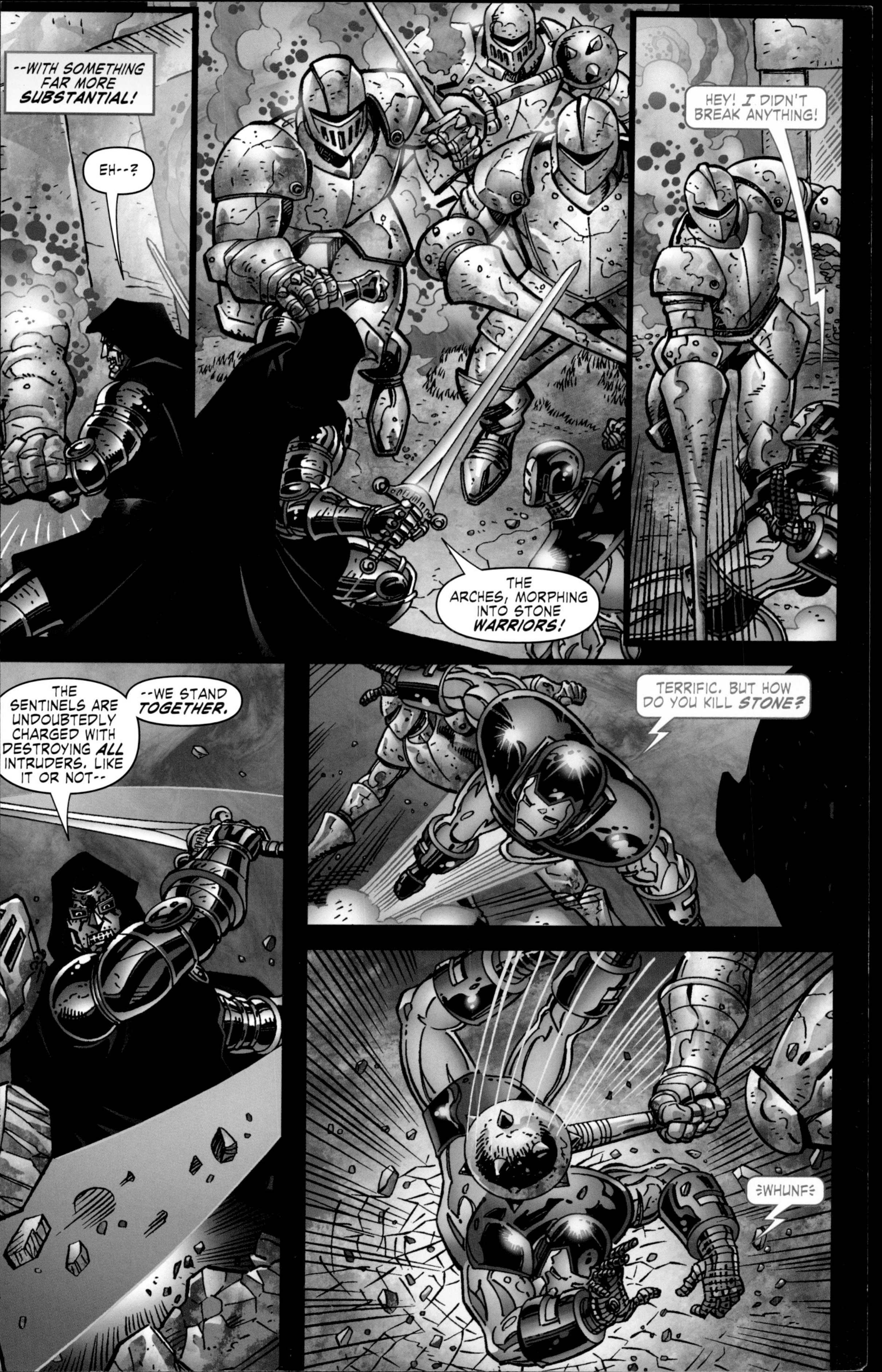
--WITH SOMETHING FAR MORE SUBSTANTIAL!
EH--?
THE ARCHES, MORPHING INTO STONE WARRIORS!
HEY! I DIDN'T BREAK ANYTHING!
THE SENTINELS ARE UNDOUBTEDLY CHARGED WITH DESTROYING ALL INTRUDERS. LIKE IT OR NOT--
--WE STAND TOGETHER.
TERRIFIC. BUT HOW DO YOU KILL STONE?
WHUNF

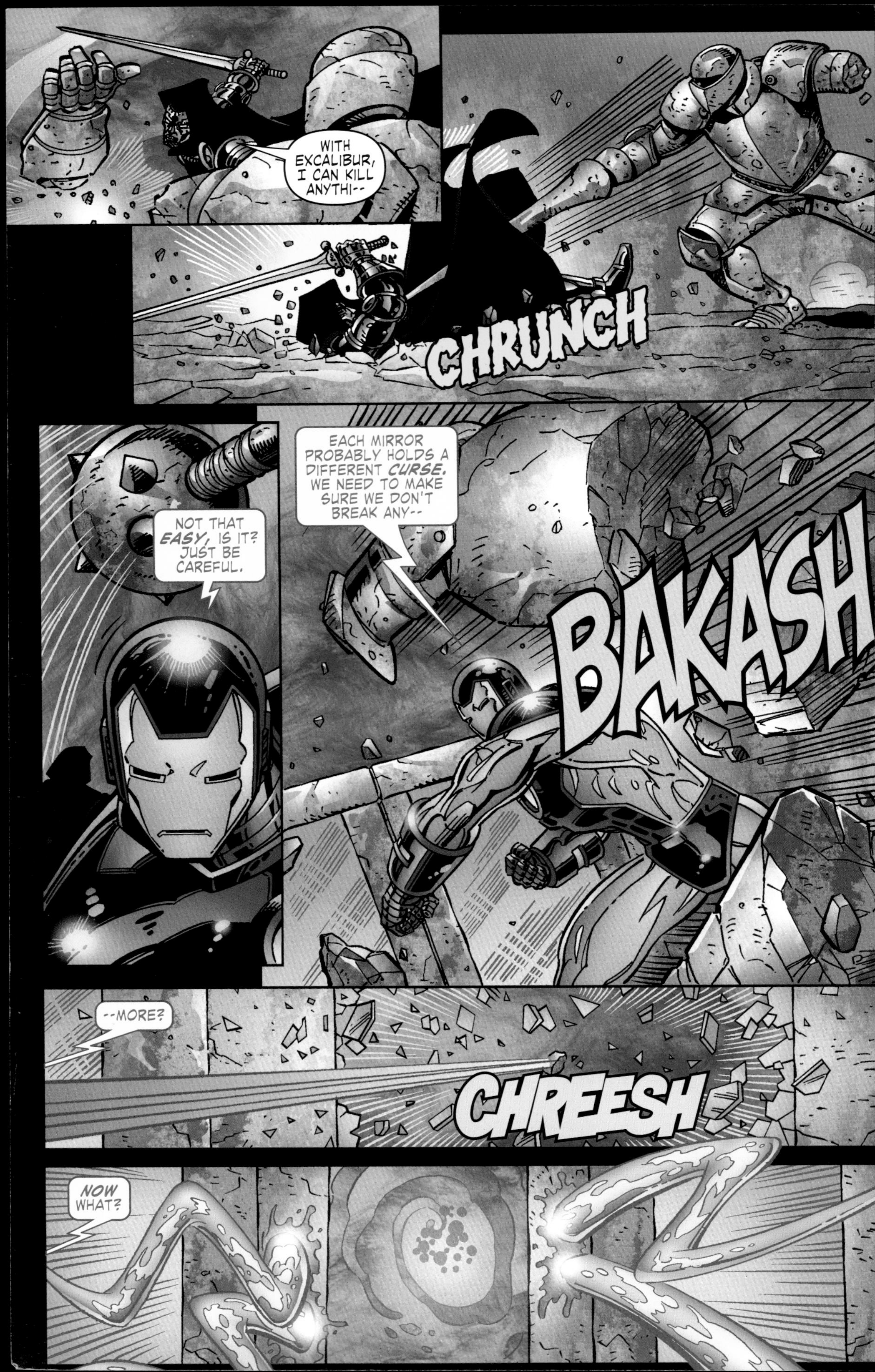
WITH EXCALIBUR, I CAN KILL ANYTHI--
CHRUNCH
NOT THAT EASY, IS IT? JUST BE CAREFUL.
EACH MIRROR PROBABLY HOLDS A DIFFERENT CURSE. WE NEED TO MAKE SURE WE DON'T BREAK ANY--
BAKASH
--MORE?
CHREESH
NOW WHAT?

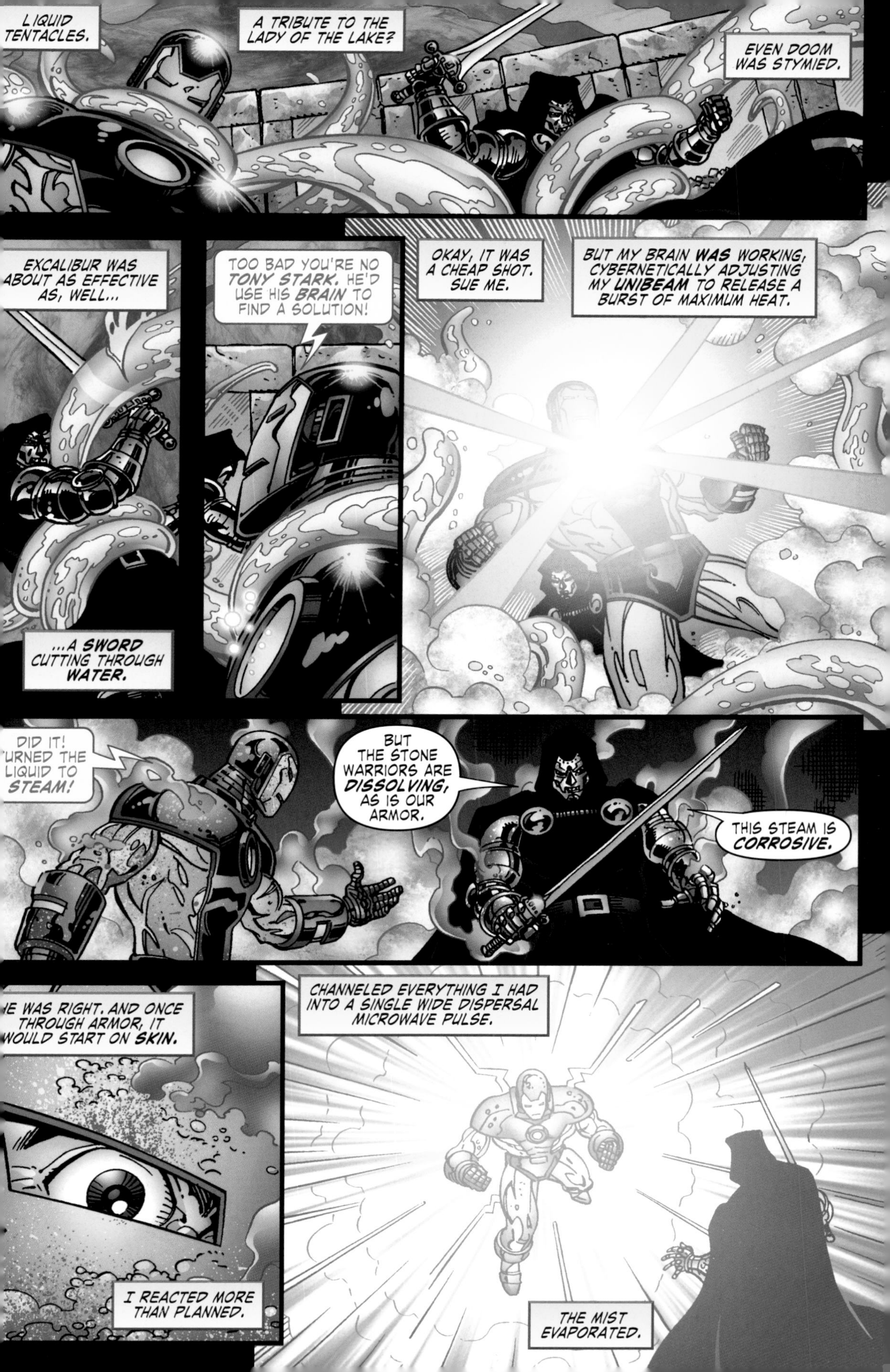

LIQUID TENTACLES.
A TRIBUTE TO THE LADY OF THE LAKE?
EVEN DOOM WAS STYMIED.
EXCALIBUR WAS ABOUT AS EFFECTIVE AS, WELL...
...A SWORD CUTTING THROUGH WATER.
TOO BAD YOU'RE NO TONY STARK. HE'D USE HIS BRAIN TO FIND A SOLUTION!
OKAY, IT WAS A CHEAP SHOT. SUE ME.
BUT MY BRAIN WAS WORKING, CYBERNETICALLY ADJUSTING MY UNIBEAM TO RELEASE A BURST OF MAXIMUM HEAT.
DID IT! URNED THE LIQUID TO STEAM!
BUT THE STONE WARRIORS ARE DISSOLVING, AS IS OUR ARMOR.
THIS STEAM IS CORROSIVE.
E WAS RIGHT. AND ONCE THROUGH ARMOR, IT WOULD START ON SKIN.
I REACTED MORE THAN PLANNED.
CHANNELED EVERYTHING I HAD INTO A SINGLE WIDE DISPERSAL MICROWAVE PULSE.
THE MIST EVAPORATED.

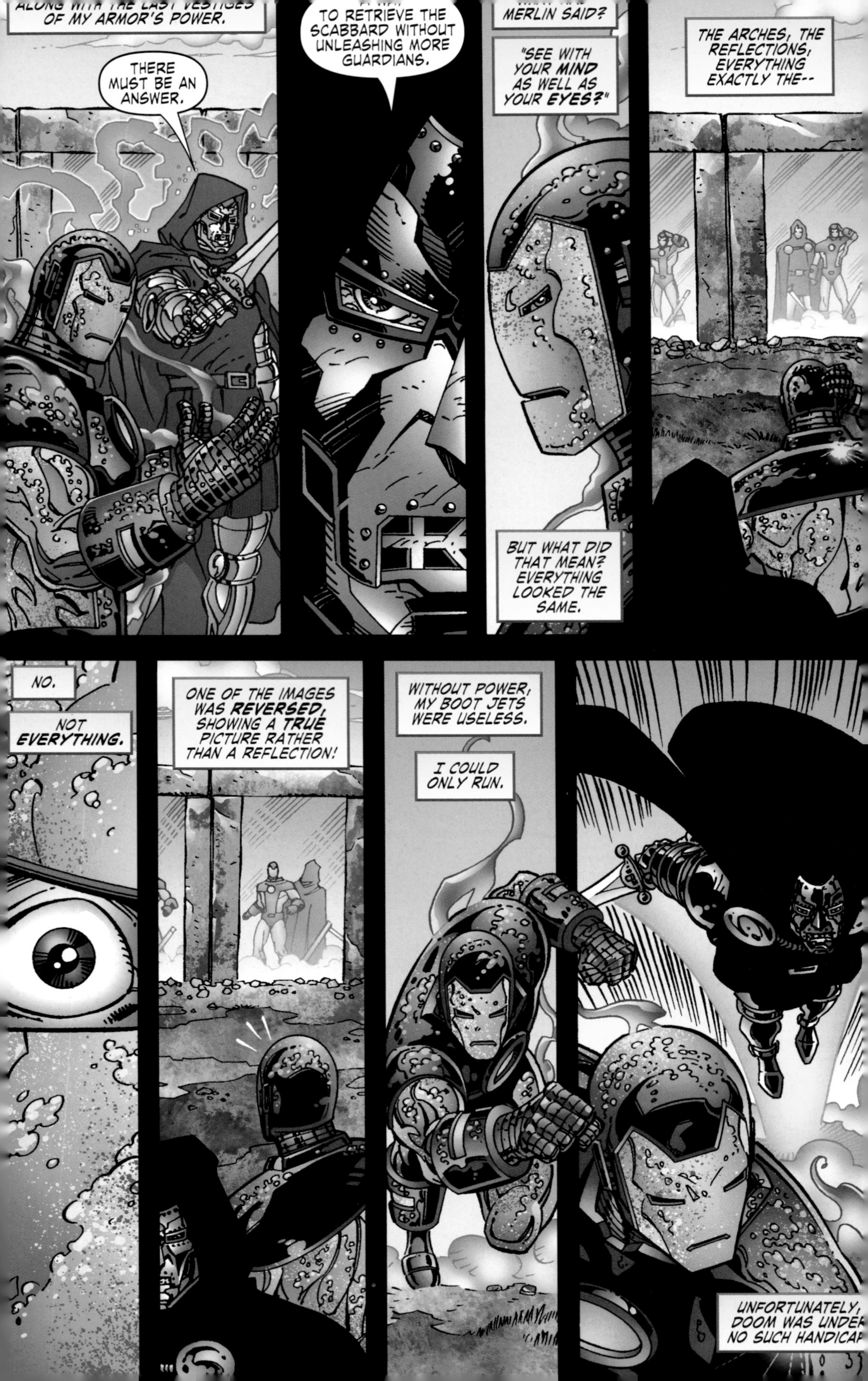
OF MY ARMOR'S POWER.
THERE MUST BE AN ANSWER.
TO RETRIEVE THE SCABBARD WITHOUT UNLEASHING MORE GUARDIANS.
MERLIN SAID?
"SEE WITH YOUR MIND AS WELL AS YOUR EYES?"
BUT WHAT DID THAT MEAN? EVERYTHING LOOKED THE SAME.
THE ARCHES, THE REFLECTIONS, EVERYTHING EXACTLY THE--
NO.
NOT EVERYTHING.
ONE OF THE IMAGES WAS REVERSED, SHOWING A TRUE PICTURE RATHER THAN A REFLECTION!
WITHOUT POWER, MY BOOT JETS WERE USELESS.
I COULD ONLY RUN.
UNFORTUNATELY, DOOM WAS UNDER NO SUCH HANDICAP

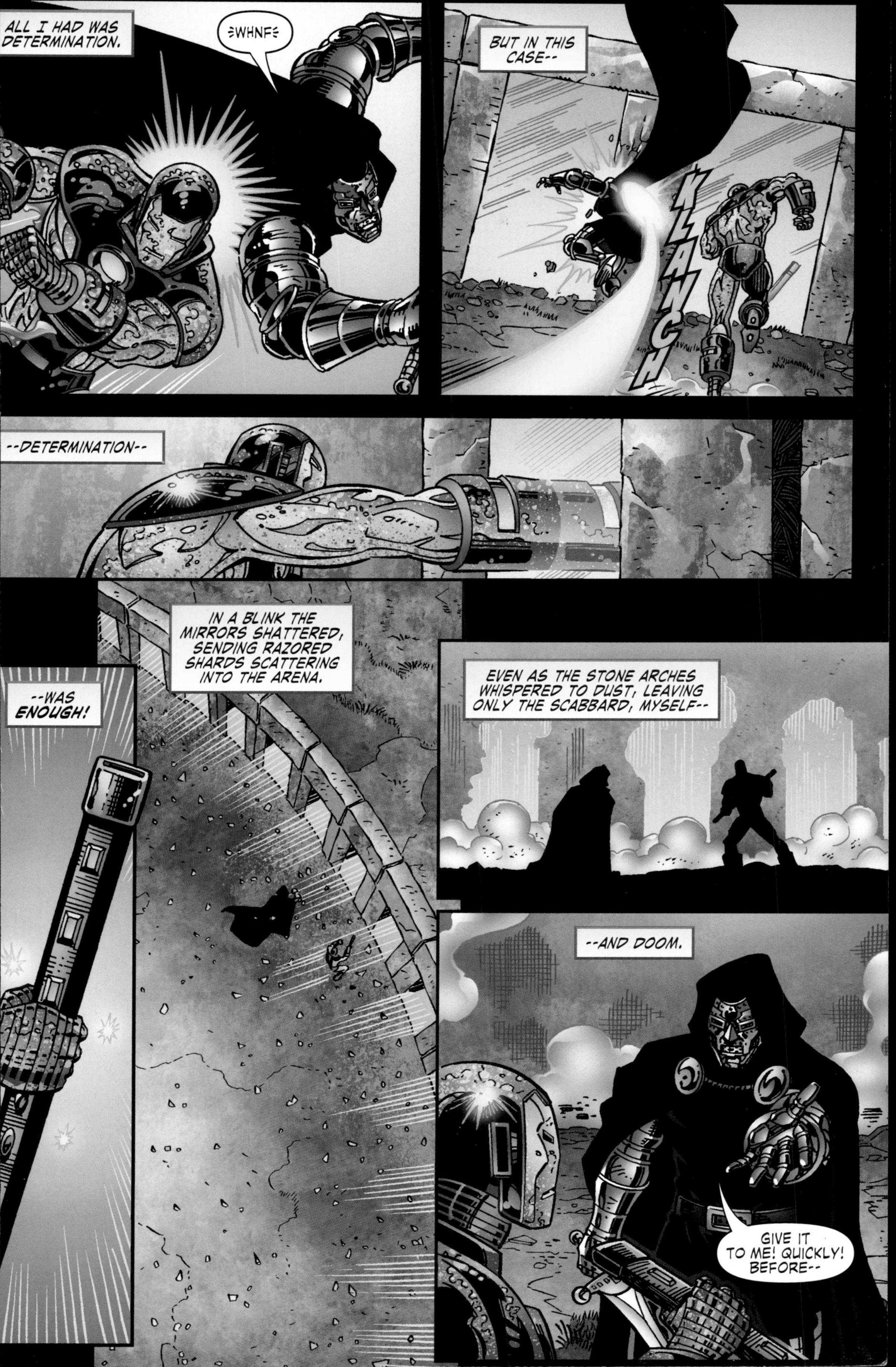

ALL I HAD WAS DETERMINATION.
WHNF
BUT IN THIS CASE--
KLANCH
--DETERMINATION--
IN A BLINK THE MIRRORS SHATTERED, SENDING RAZORED SHARDS SCATTERING INTO THE ARENA.
--WAS ENOUGH!
EVEN AS THE STONE ARCHES WHISPERED TO DUST, LEAVING ONLY THE SCABBARD, MYSELF--
--AND DOOM.
GIVE IT TO ME! QUICKLY! BEFORE--

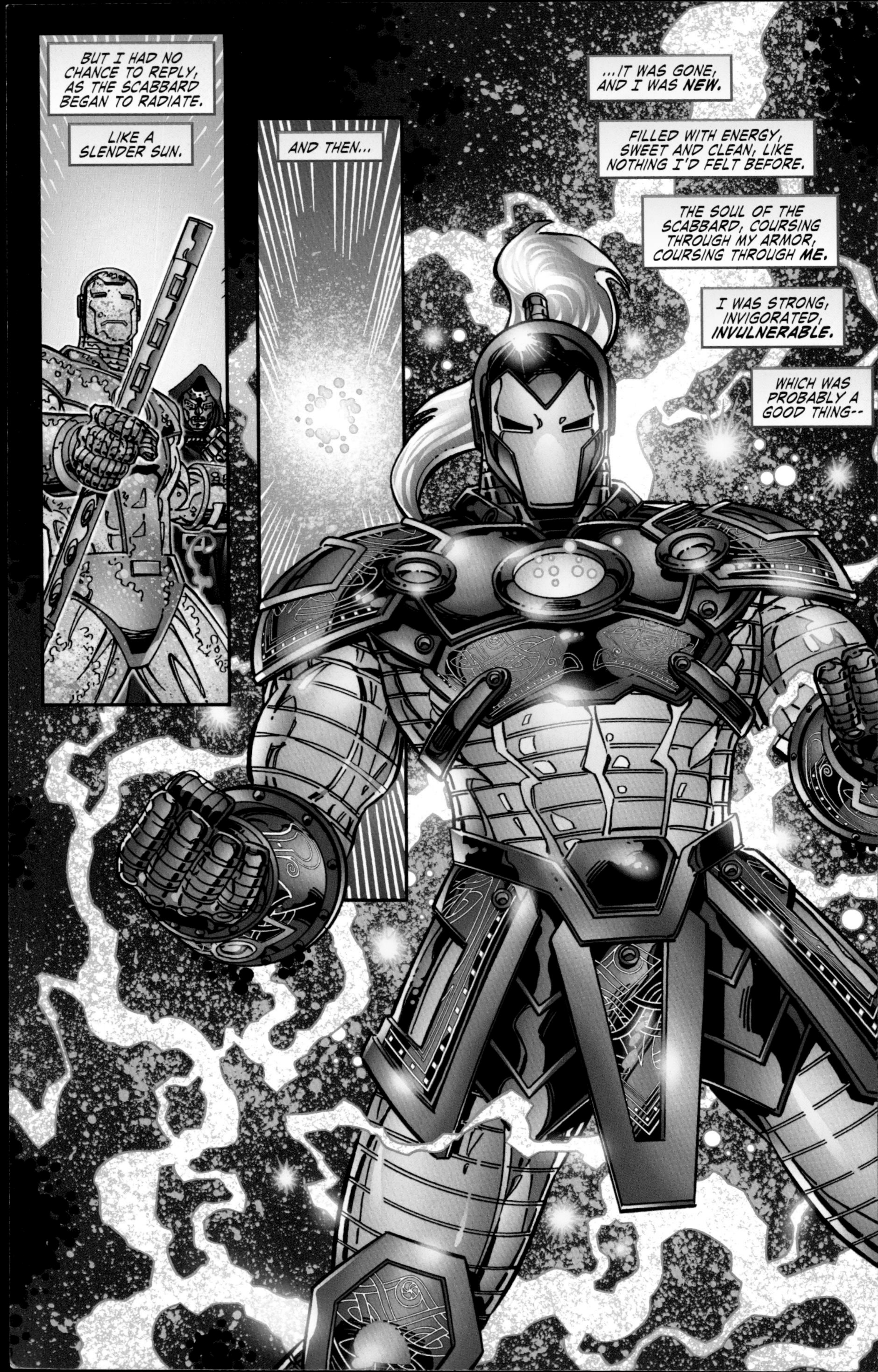
BUT I HAD NO CHANCE TO REPLY, AS THE SCABBARD BEGAN TO RADIATE.
LIKE A SLENDER SUN.
AND THEN...
...IT WAS GONE, AND I WAS NEW.
FILLED WITH ENERGY, SWEET AND CLEAN, LIKE NOTHING I'D FELT BEFORE.
THE SOUL OF THE SCABBARD, COURSING THROUGH MY ARMOR, COURSING THROUGH ME.
I WAS STRONG, INVIGORATED, INVULNERABLE.
WHICH WAS PROBABLY A GOOD THING--

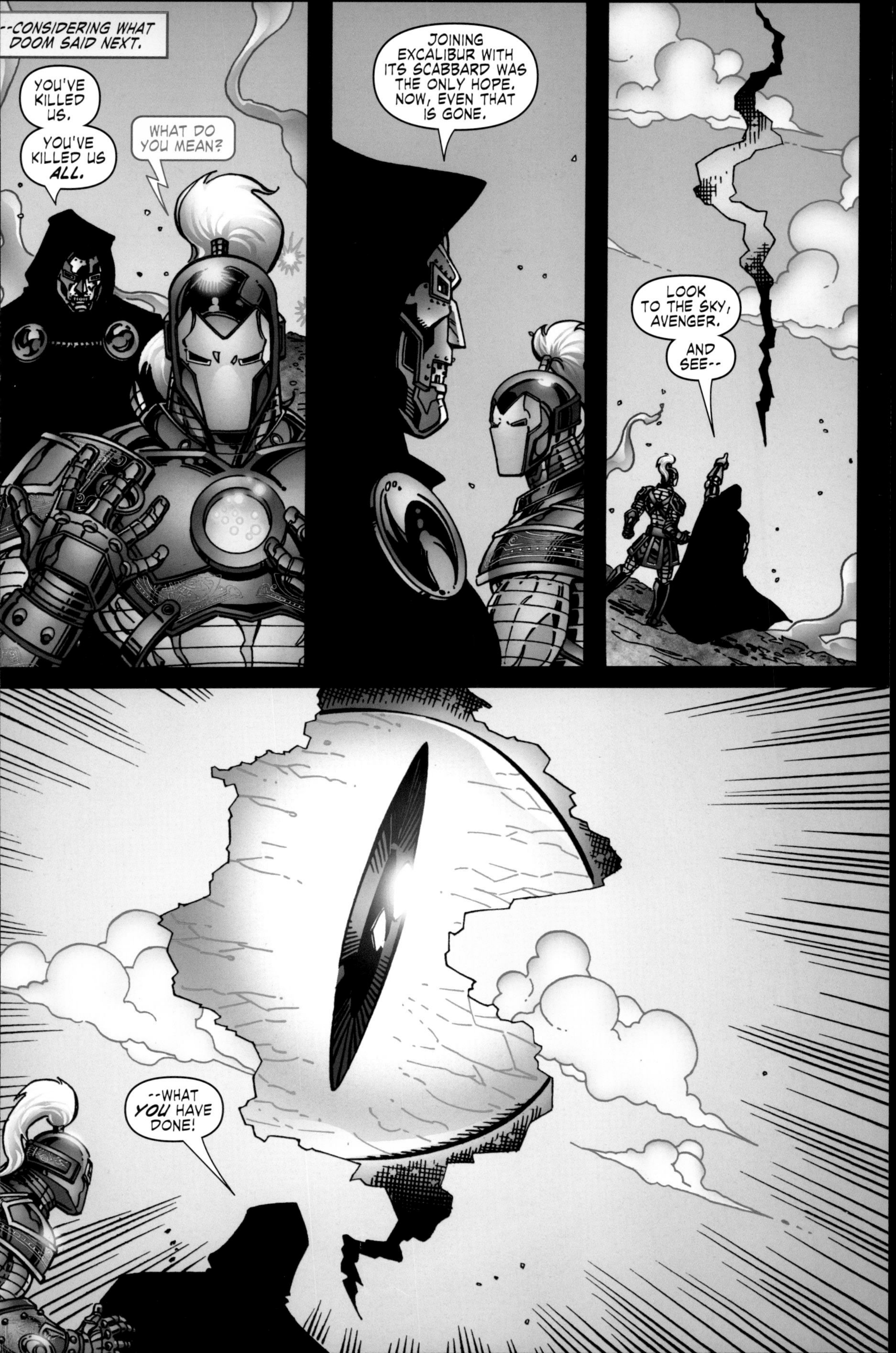
--CONSIDERING WHAT DOOM SAID NEXT.
YOU'VE KILLED US.
YOU'VE KILLED US ALL.
WHAT DO YOU MEAN?
JOINING EXCALIBUR WITH ITS SCABBARD WAS THE ONLY HOPE. NOW, EVEN THAT IS GONE.
LOOK TO THE SKY, AVENGER.
AND SEE--
--WHAT YOU HAVE DONE!

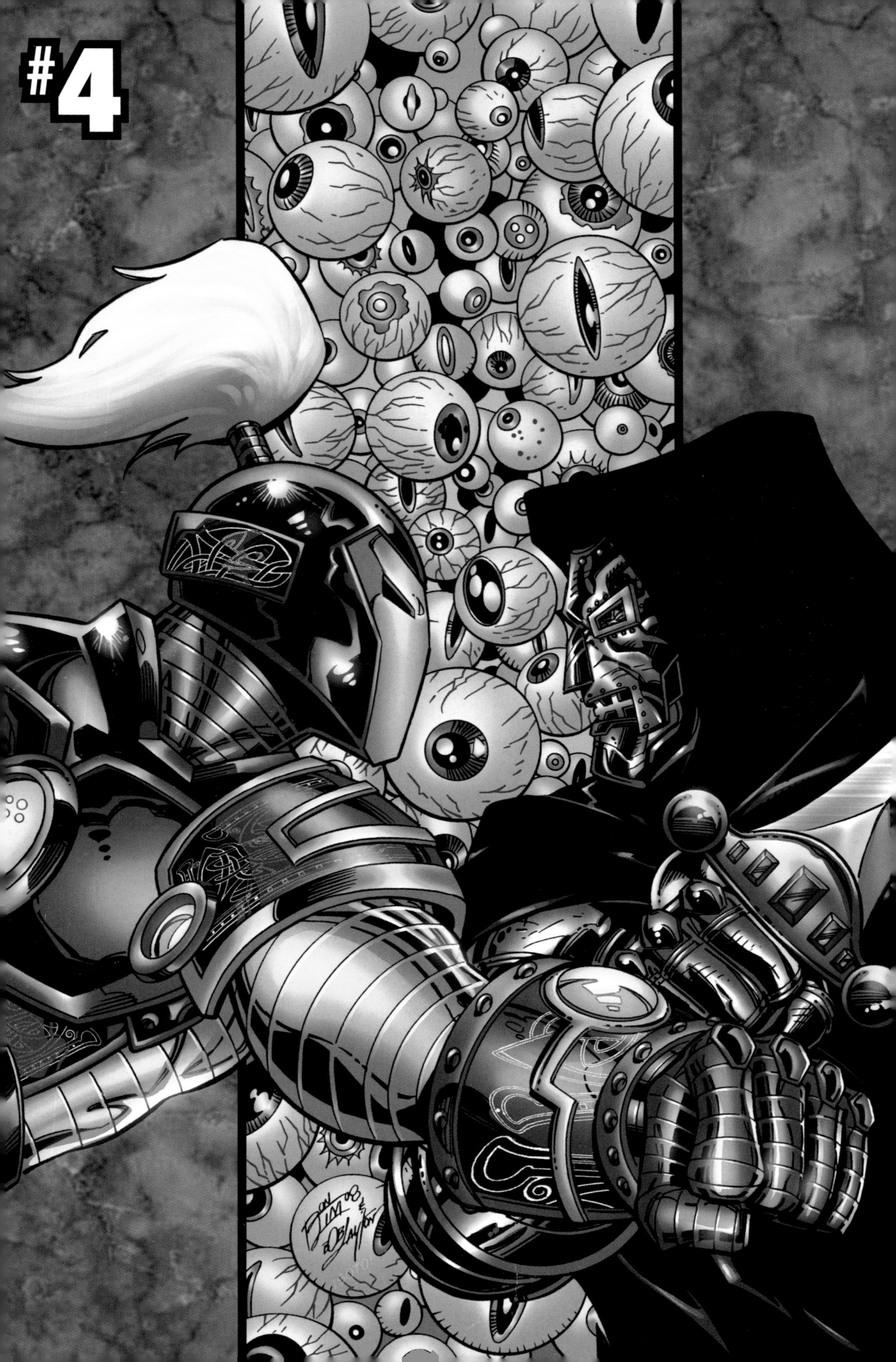
#4

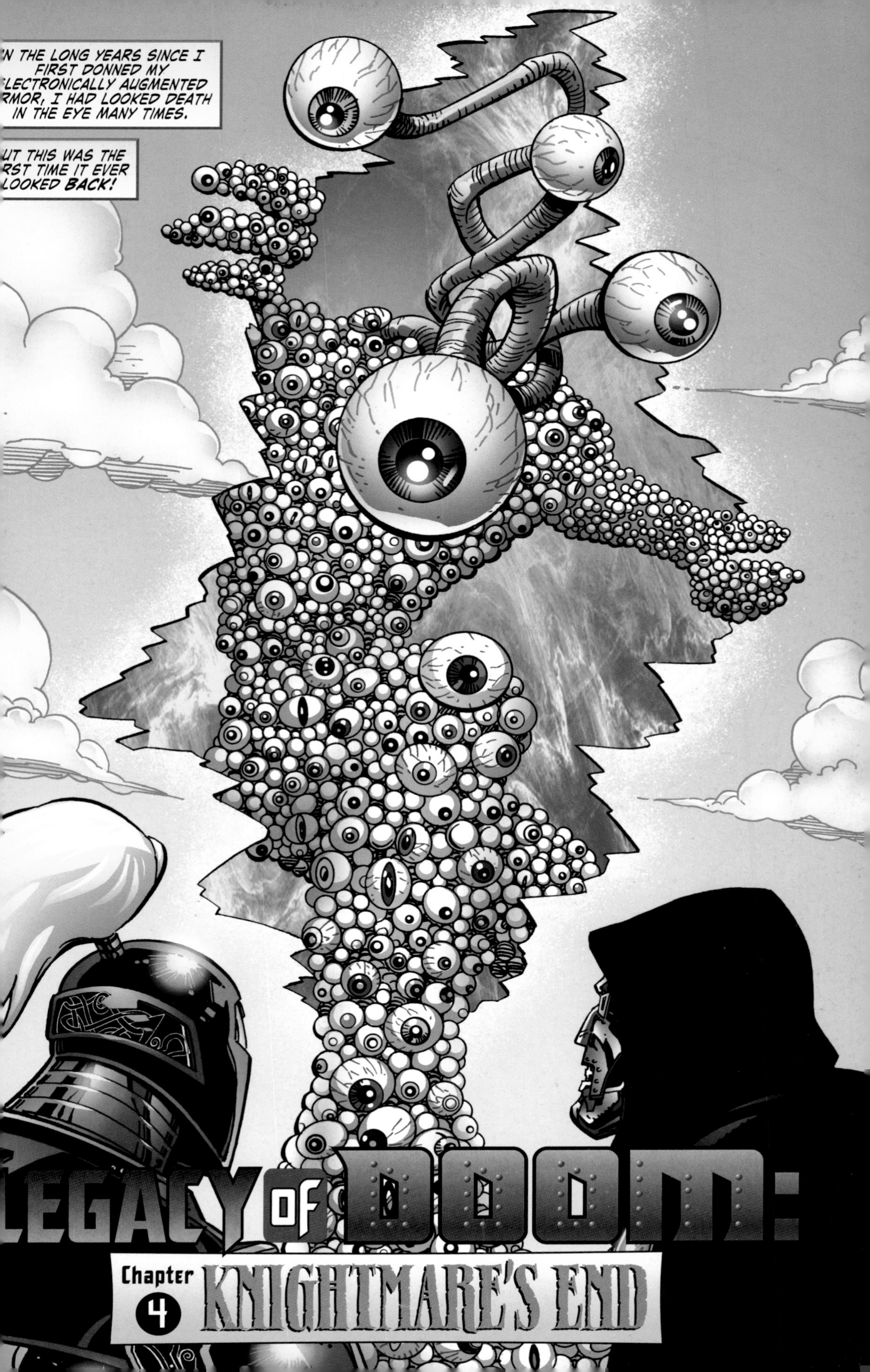

N THE LONG YEARS SINCE I FIRST DONNED MY ELECTRONICALLY AUGMENTED RMOR, I HAD LOOKED DEATH IN THE EYE MANY TIMES.
UT THIS WAS THE RST TIME IT EVER LOOKED BACK!
LEGACY OF DOOM:
Chapter 4 KNIGHTMARE'S END

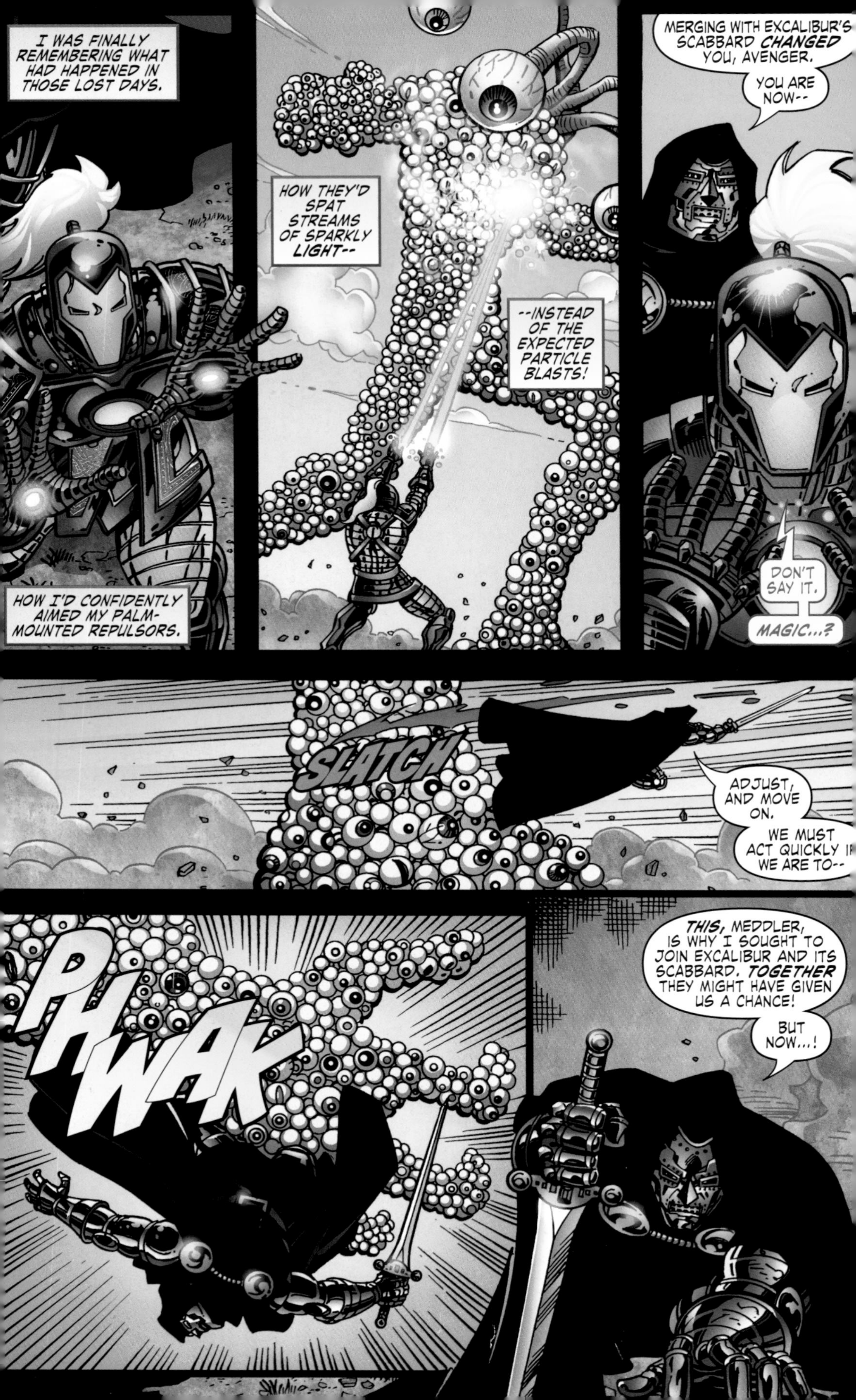
I WAS FINALLY REMEMBERING WHAT HAD HAPPENED IN THOSE LOST DAYS.
HOW I'D CONFIDENTLY AIMED MY PALM-MOUNTED REPULSORS.
HOW THEY'D SPAT STREAMS OF SPARKLY LIGHT--
--INSTEAD OF THE EXPECTED PARTICLE BLASTS!
MERGING WITH EXCALIBUR'S SCABBARD CHANGED YOU, AVENGER.
YOU ARE NOW--
DON'T SAY IT.
MAGIC...?
SLATCH
ADJUST, AND MOVE ON.
WE MUST ACT QUICKLY IF WE ARE TO--
PHWAK
THIS, MEDDLER, IS WHY I SOUGHT TO JOIN EXCALIBUR AND ITS SCABBARD. TOGETHER THEY MIGHT HAVE GIVEN US A CHANCE!
BUT NOW...!

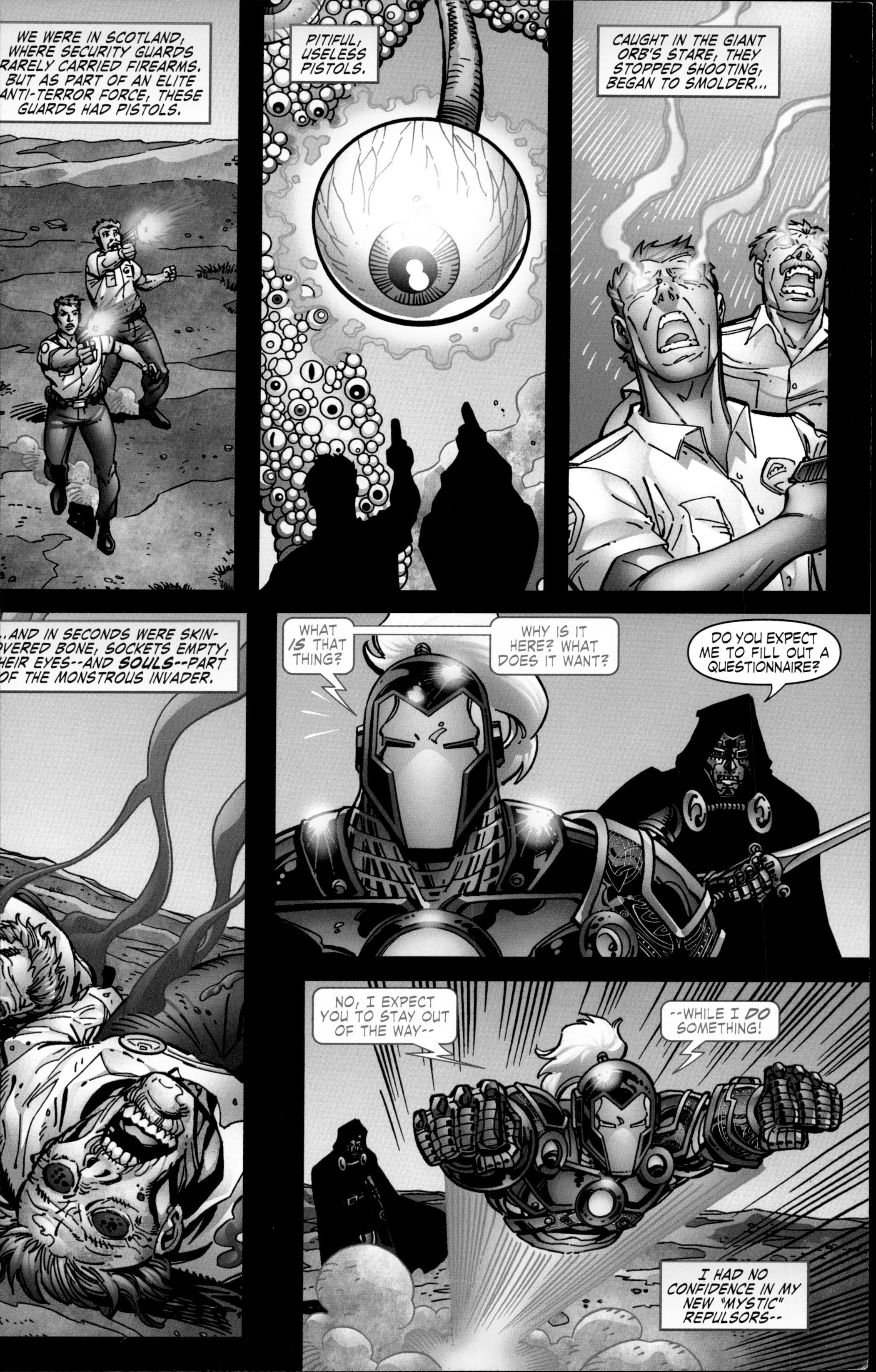
WE WERE IN SCOTLAND, WHERE SECURITY GUARDS RARELY CARRIED FIREARMS. BUT AS PART OF AN ELITE ANTI-TERROR FORCE, THESE GUARDS HAD PISTOLS.
PITIFUL, USELESS PISTOLS.
CAUGHT IN THE GIANT ORB'S STARE, THEY STOPPED SHOOTING, BEGAN TO SMOLDER...
...AND IN SECONDS WERE SKIN-COVERED BONE, SOCKETS EMPTY, THEIR EYES--AND SOULS--PART OF THE MONSTROUS INVADER.
WHAT IS THAT THING?
WHY IS IT HERE? WHAT DOES IT WANT?
DO YOU EXPECT ME TO FILL OUT A QUESTIONNAIRE?
NO, I EXPECT YOU TO STAY OUT OF THE WAY--
--WHILE I DO SOMETHING!
I HAD NO CONFIDENCE IN MY NEW "MYSTIC" REPULSORS--

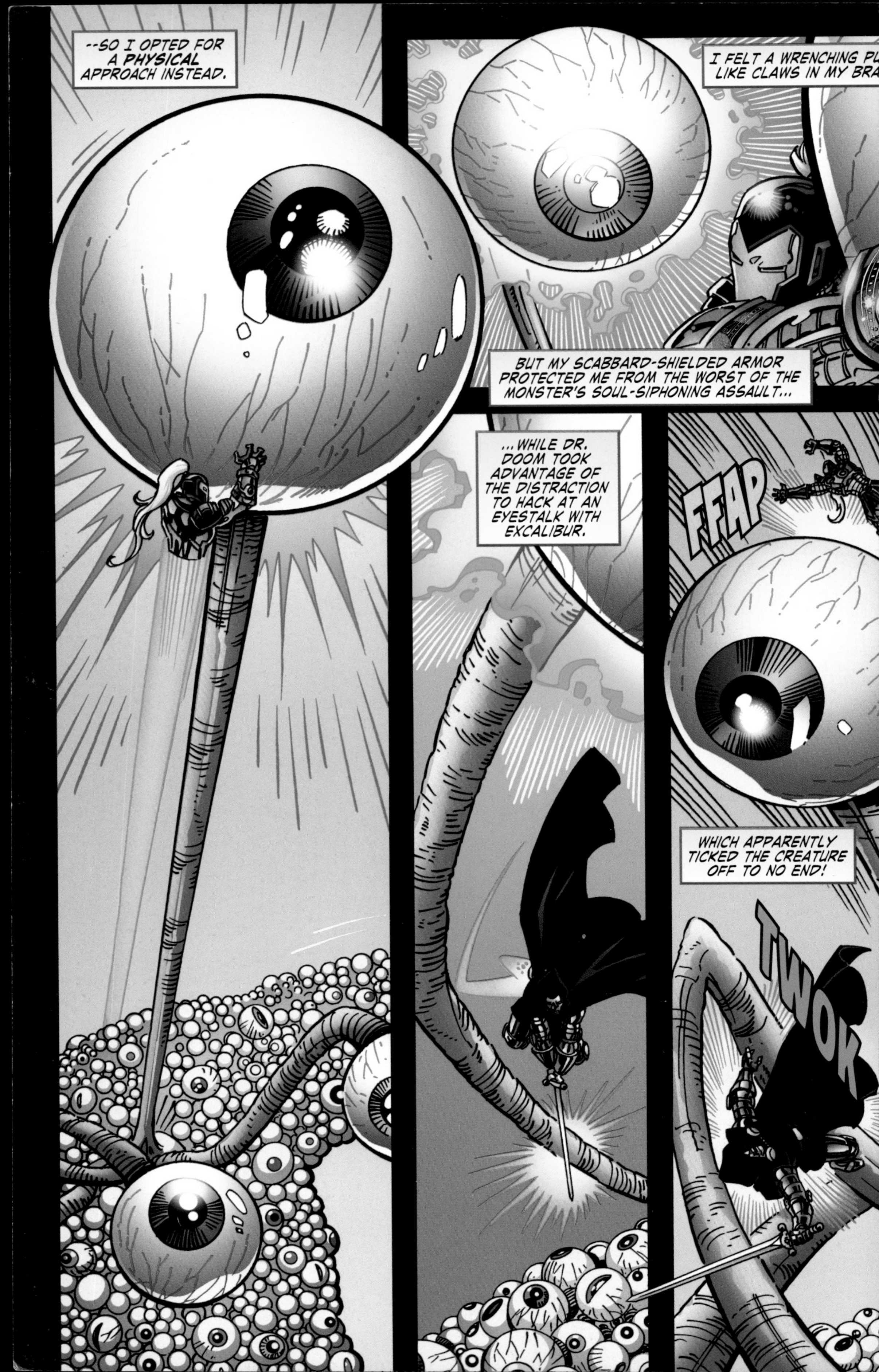
--SO I OPTED FOR A PHYSICAL APPROACH INSTEAD.
I FELT A WRENCHING PU LIKE CLAWS IN MY BRA
BUT MY SCABBARD-SHIELDED ARMOR PROTECTED ME FROM THE WORST OF THE MONSTER'S SOUL-SIPHONING ASSAULT...
...WHILE DR. DOOM TOOK ADVANTAGE OF THE DISTRACTION TO HACK AT AN EYESTALK WITH EXCALIBUR.
FFAP
WHICH APPARENTLY TICKED THE CREATURE OFF TO NO END!
TWOK

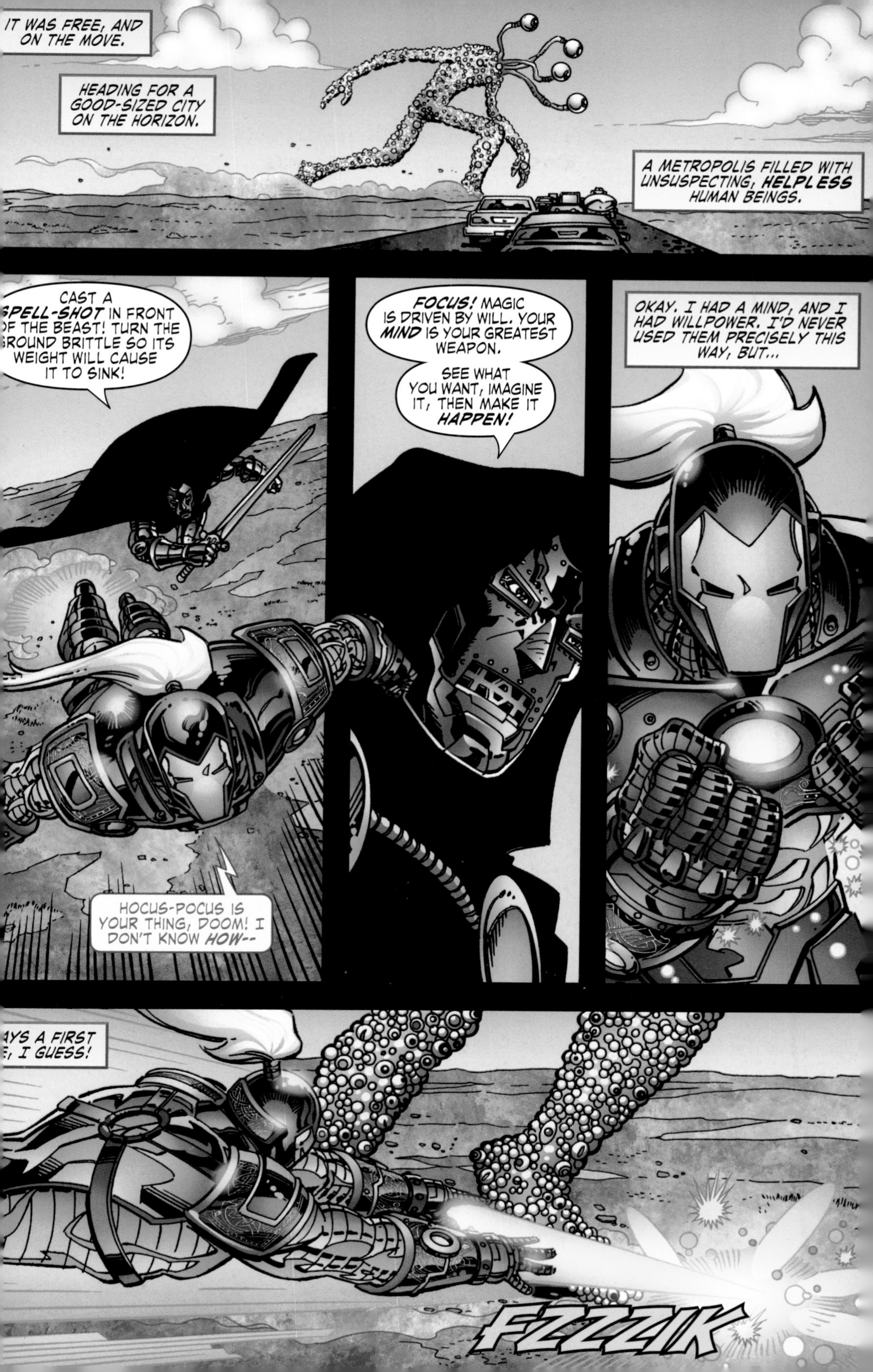

IT WAS FREE, AND ON THE MOVE.
HEADING FOR A GOOD-SIZED CITY ON THE HORIZON.
A METROPOLIS FILLED WITH UNSUSPECTING, HELPLESS HUMAN BEINGS.
CAST A SPELL-SHOT IN FRONT OF THE BEAST! TURN THE GROUND BRITTLE SO ITS WEIGHT WILL CAUSE IT TO SINK!
HOCUS-POCUS IS YOUR THING, DOOM! I DON'T KNOW HOW--
FOCUS! MAGIC IS DRIVEN BY WILL. YOUR MIND IS YOUR GREATEST WEAPON.
SEE WHAT YOU WANT, IMAGINE IT, THEN MAKE IT HAPPEN!
OKAY. I HAD A MIND, AND I HAD WILLPOWER. I'D NEVER USED THEM PRECISELY THIS WAY, BUT...
AYS A FIRST E, I GUESS!
FZZZIK

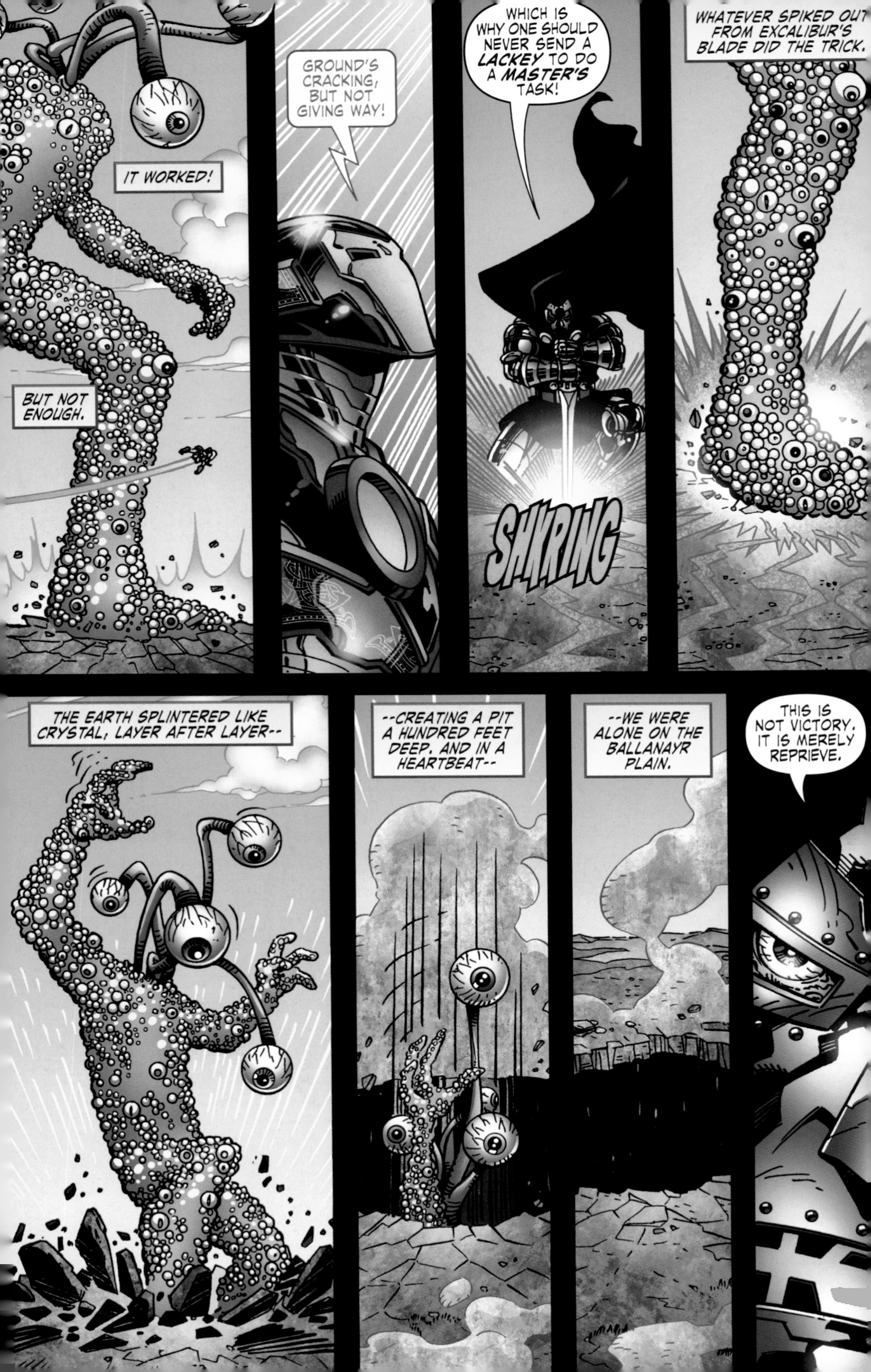

IT WORKED!
BUT NOT ENOUGH.
GROUND'S CRACKING, BUT NOT GIVING WAY!
WHICH IS WHY ONE SHOULD NEVER SEND A LACKEY TO DO A MASTER'S TASK!
SHKRING
WHATEVER SPIKED OUT FROM EXCALIBUR'S BLADE DID THE TRICK.
THE EARTH SPLINTERED LIKE CRYSTAL, LAYER AFTER LAYER--
--CREATING A PIT A HUNDRED FEET DEEP. AND IN A HEARTBEAT--
--WE WERE ALONE ON THE BALLANAYR PLAIN.
THIS IS NOT VICTORY. IT IS MERELY REPRIEVE.

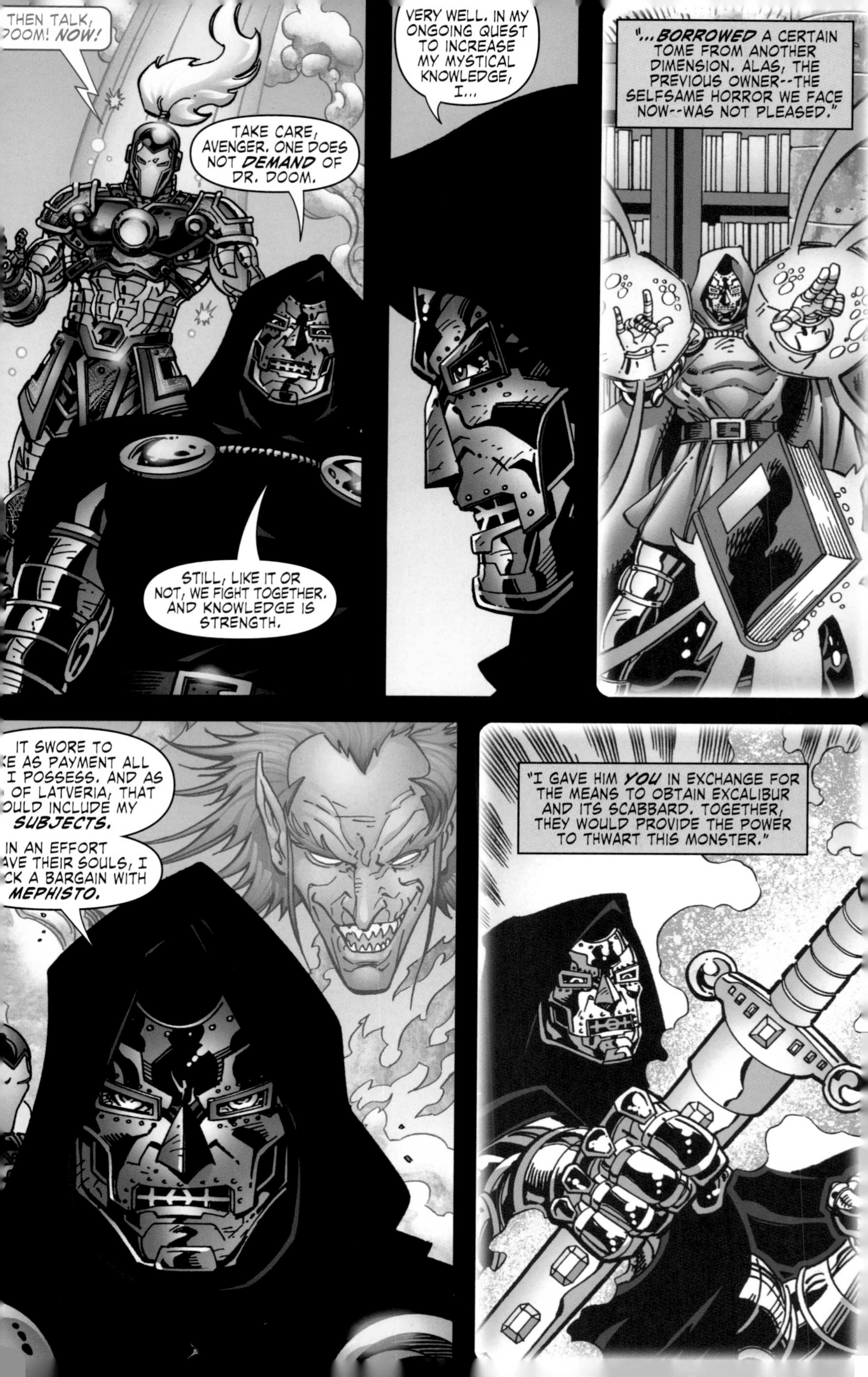
THEN TALK, DOOM! NOW!
TAKE CARE, AVENGER. ONE DOES NOT DEMAND OF DR. DOOM.
STILL, LIKE IT OR NOT, WE FIGHT TOGETHER. AND KNOWLEDGE IS STRENGTH.
VERY WELL. IN MY ONGOING QUEST TO INCREASE MY MYSTICAL KNOWLEDGE, I...
"...BORROWED A CERTAIN TOME FROM ANOTHER DIMENSION. ALAS, THE PREVIOUS OWNER--THE SELFSAME HORROR WE FACE NOW--WAS NOT PLEASED."
IT SWORE TO E AS PAYMENT ALL I POSSESS. AND AS OF LATVERIA, THAT OULD INCLUDE MY SUBJECTS.
IN AN EFFORT AVE THEIR SOULS, I CK A BARGAIN WITH MEPHISTO.
"I GAVE HIM YOU IN EXCHANGE FOR THE MEANS TO OBTAIN EXCALIBUR AND ITS SCABBARD. TOGETHER, THEY WOULD PROVIDE THE POWER TO THWART THIS MONSTER."

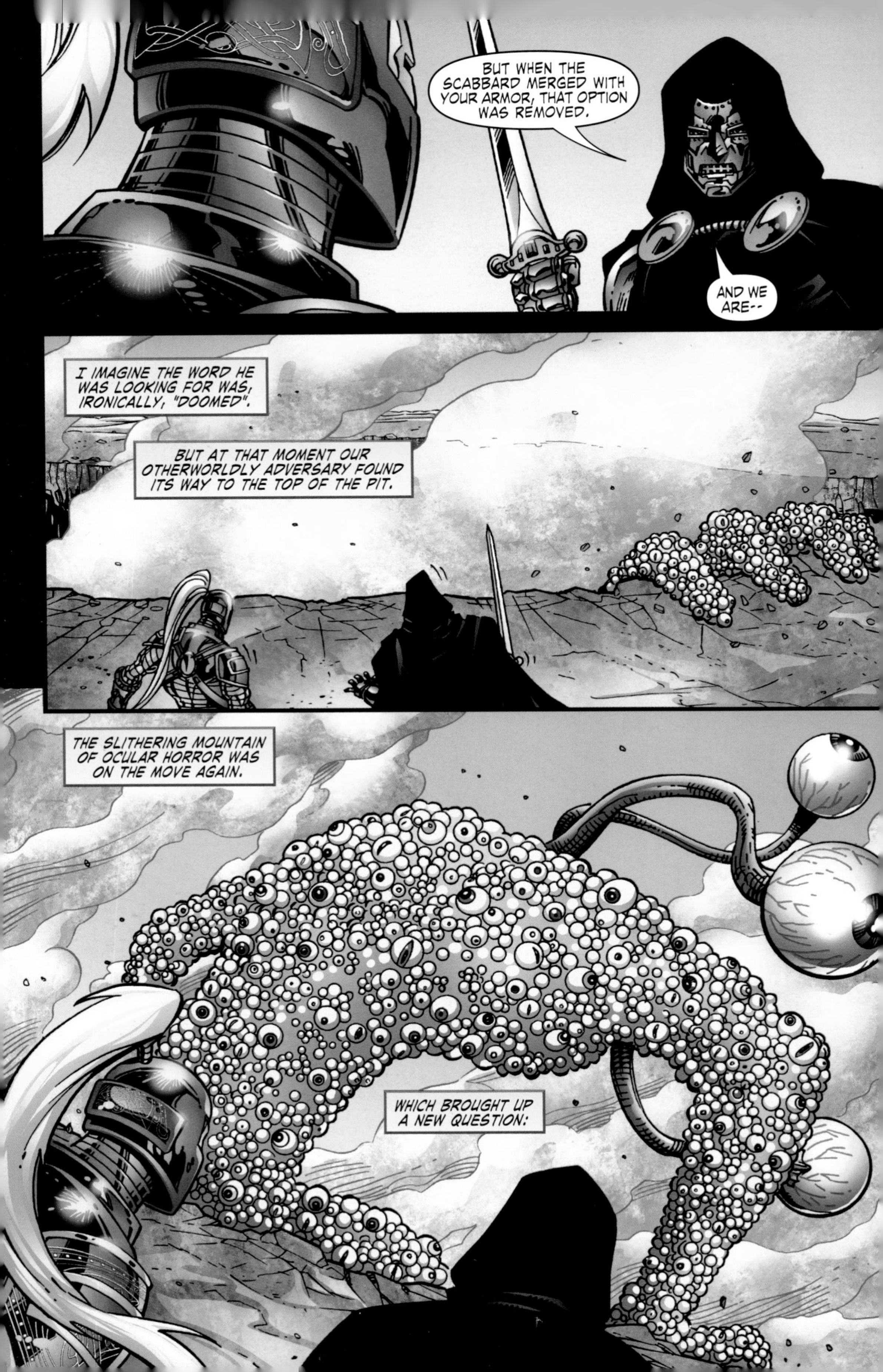
BUT WHEN THE SCABBARD MERGED WITH YOUR ARMOR, THAT OPTION WAS REMOVED.
AND WE ARE--
I IMAGINE THE WORD HE WAS LOOKING FOR WAS, IRONICALLY, "DOOMED".
BUT AT THAT MOMENT OUR OTHERWORLDLY ADVERSARY FOUND ITS WAY TO THE TOP OF THE PIT.
THE SLITHERING MOUNTAIN OF OCULAR HORROR WAS ON THE MOVE AGAIN.
WHICH BROUGHT UP A NEW QUESTION:

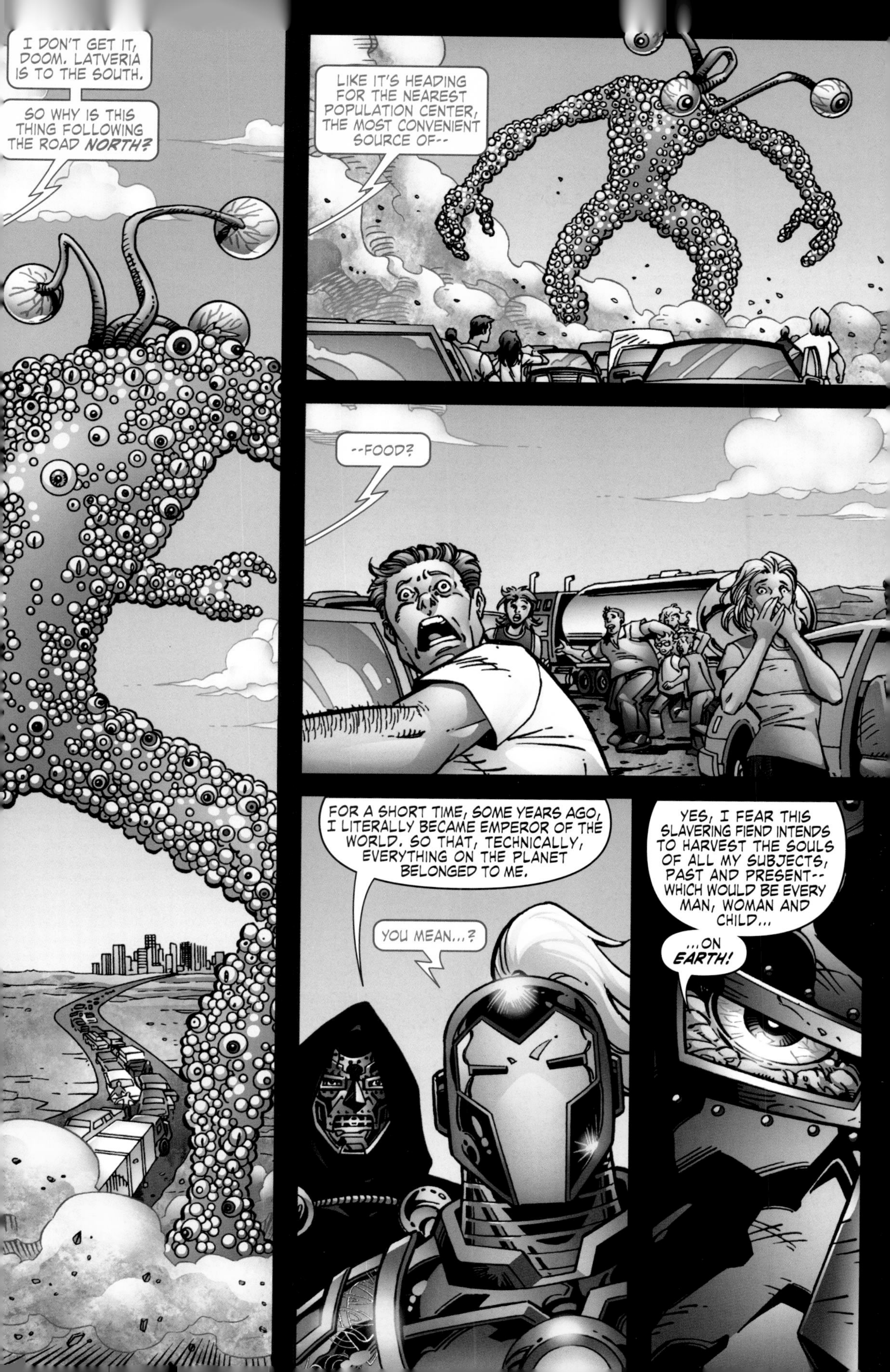
I DON'T GET IT, DOOM. LATVERIA IS TO THE SOUTH.
SO WHY IS THIS THING FOLLOWING THE ROAD *NORTH?*
LIKE IT'S HEADING FOR THE NEAREST POPULATION CENTER, THE MOST CONVENIENT SOURCE OF--
--FOOD?
FOR A SHORT TIME, SOME YEARS AGO, I LITERALLY BECAME EMPEROR OF THE WORLD. SO THAT, TECHNICALLY, EVERYTHING ON THE PLANET BELONGED TO ME.
YOU MEAN...?
YES, I FEAR THIS SLAVERING FIEND INTENDS TO HARVEST THE SOULS OF ALL MY SUBJECTS, PAST AND PRESENT-- WHICH WOULD BE EVERY MAN, WOMAN AND CHILD...
...ON *EARTH!*

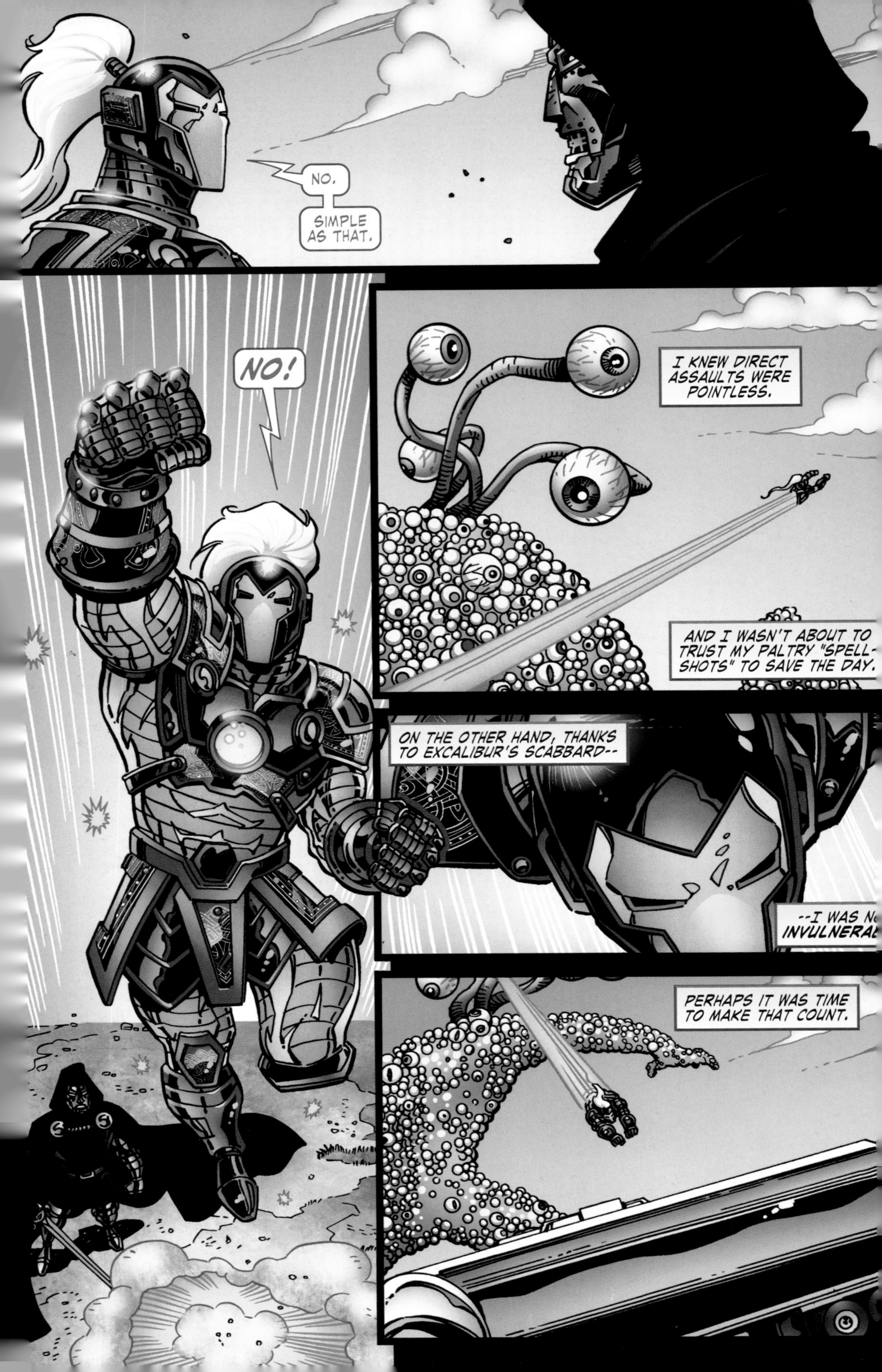
NO.
SIMPLE AS THAT.
NO!
I KNEW DIRECT ASSAULTS WERE POINTLESS.
AND I WASN'T ABOUT TO TRUST MY PALTRY "SPELL-SHOTS" TO SAVE THE DAY.
ON THE OTHER HAND, THANKS TO EXCALIBUR'S SCABBARD--
PERHAPS IT WAS TIME TO MAKE THAT COUNT.

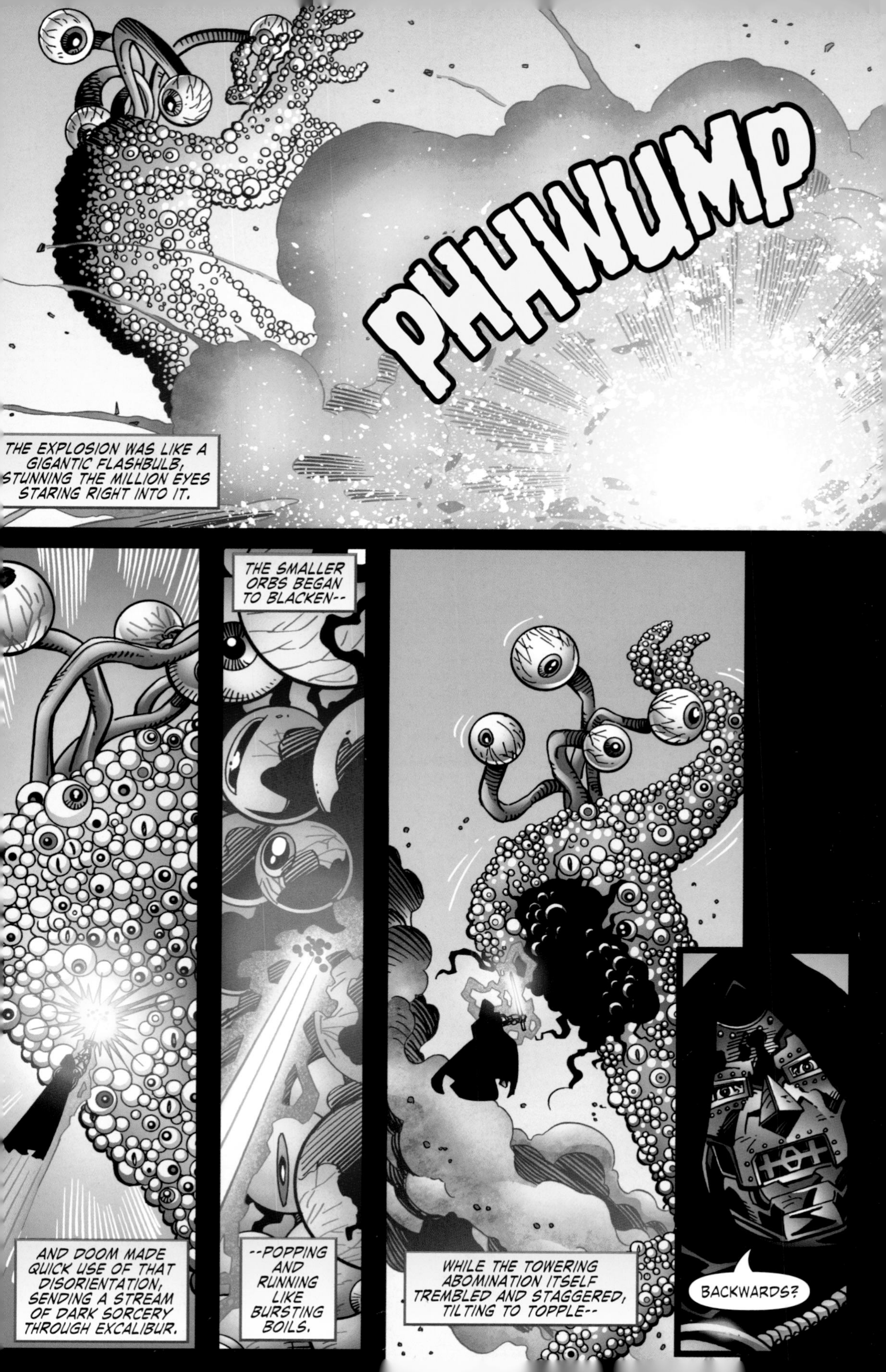
PHHWUMP
THE EXPLOSION WAS LIKE A GIGANTIC FLASHBULB, STUNNING THE MILLION EYES STARING RIGHT INTO IT.
AND DOOM MADE QUICK USE OF THAT DISORIENTATION, SENDING A STREAM OF DARK SORCERY THROUGH EXCALIBUR.
THE SMALLER ORBS BEGAN TO BLACKEN--
--POPPING AND RUNNING LIKE BURSTING BOILS.
WHILE THE TOWERING ABOMINATION ITSELF TREMBLED AND STAGGERED, TILTING TO TOPPLE--
BACKWARDS?

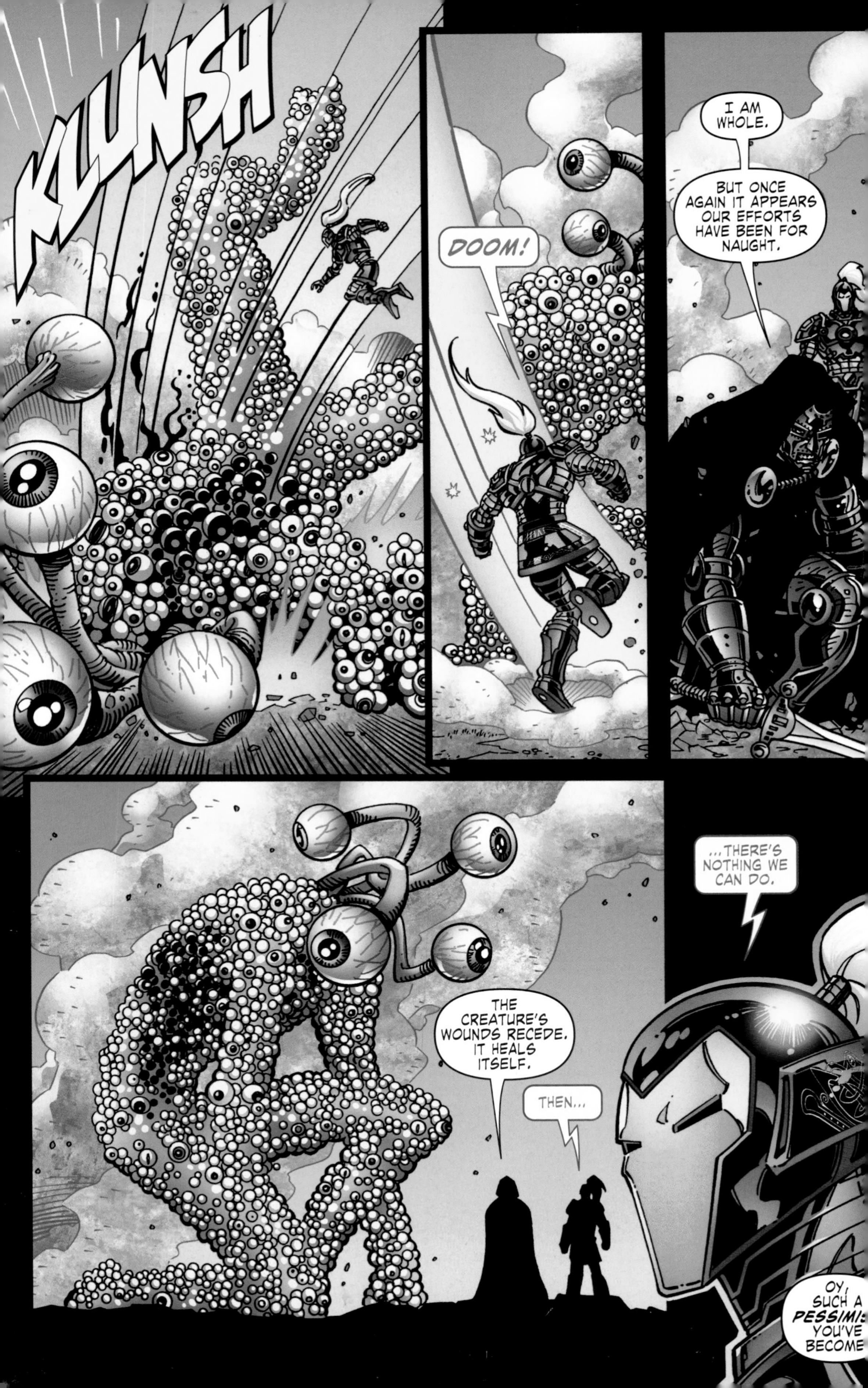
KLUNSH
DOOM!
I AM WHOLE.
BUT ONCE AGAIN IT APPEARS OUR EFFORTS HAVE BEEN FOR NAUGHT.
THE CREATURE'S WOUNDS RECEDE. IT HEALS ITSELF.
THEN...
...THERE'S NOTHING WE CAN DO.
OY, SUCH A PESSIMI YOU'VE BECOME

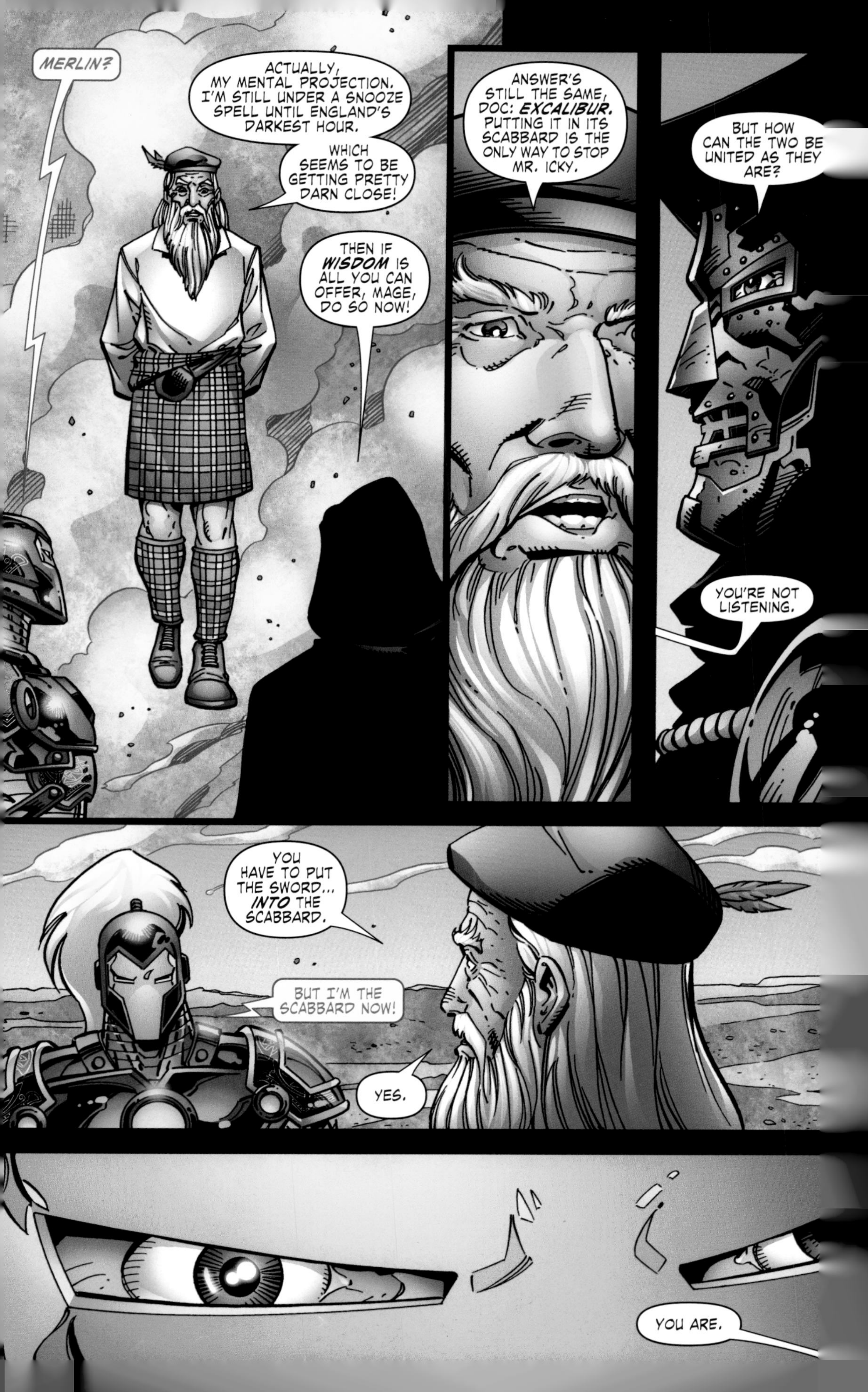
MERLIN?
ACTUALLY, MY MENTAL PROJECTION. I'M STILL UNDER A SNOOZE SPELL UNTIL ENGLAND'S DARKEST HOUR.
WHICH SEEMS TO BE GETTING PRETTY DARN CLOSE!
THEN IF WISDOM IS ALL YOU CAN OFFER, MAGE, DO SO NOW!
ANSWER'S STILL THE SAME, DOC: EXCALIBUR. PUTTING IT IN ITS SCABBARD IS THE ONLY WAY TO STOP MR. ICKY.
BUT HOW CAN THE TWO BE UNITED AS THEY ARE?
YOU'RE NOT LISTENING.
YOU HAVE TO PUT THE SWORD... INTO THE SCABBARD.
BUT I'M THE SCABBARD NOW!
YES.
YOU ARE.

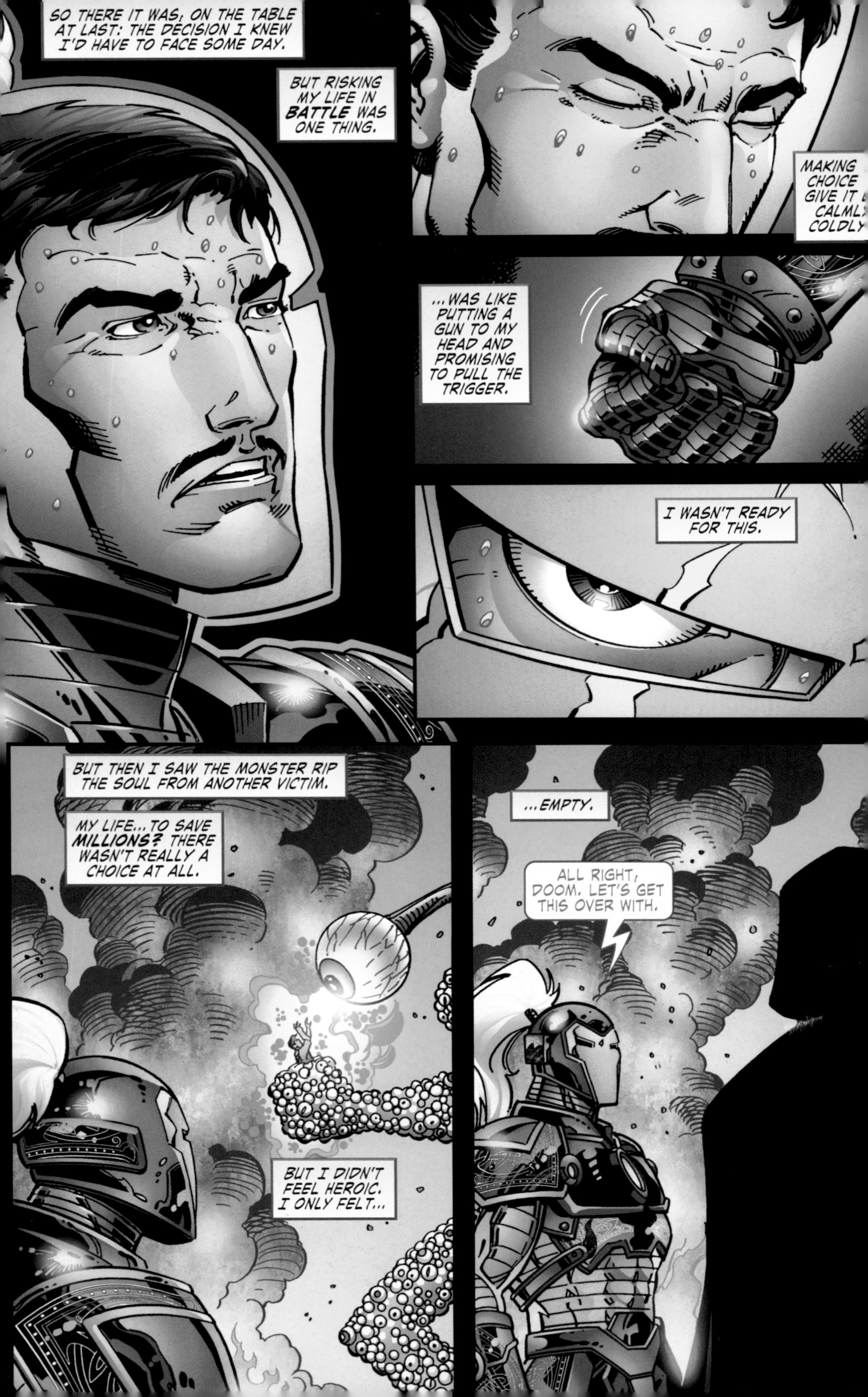
SO THERE IT WAS, ON THE TABLE AT LAST: THE DECISION I KNEW I'D HAVE TO FACE SOME DAY.
BUT RISKING MY LIFE IN BATTLE WAS ONE THING.
MAKING CHOICE GIVE IT CALML COLDLY
...WAS LIKE PUTTING A GUN TO MY HEAD AND PROMISING TO PULL THE TRIGGER.
I WASN'T READY FOR THIS.
BUT THEN I SAW THE MONSTER RIP THE SOUL FROM ANOTHER VICTIM.
MY LIFE...TO SAVE MILLIONS? THERE WASN'T REALLY A CHOICE AT ALL.
BUT I DIDN'T FEEL HEROIC. I ONLY FELT...
...EMPTY.
ALL RIGHT, DOOM. LET'S GET THIS OVER WITH.

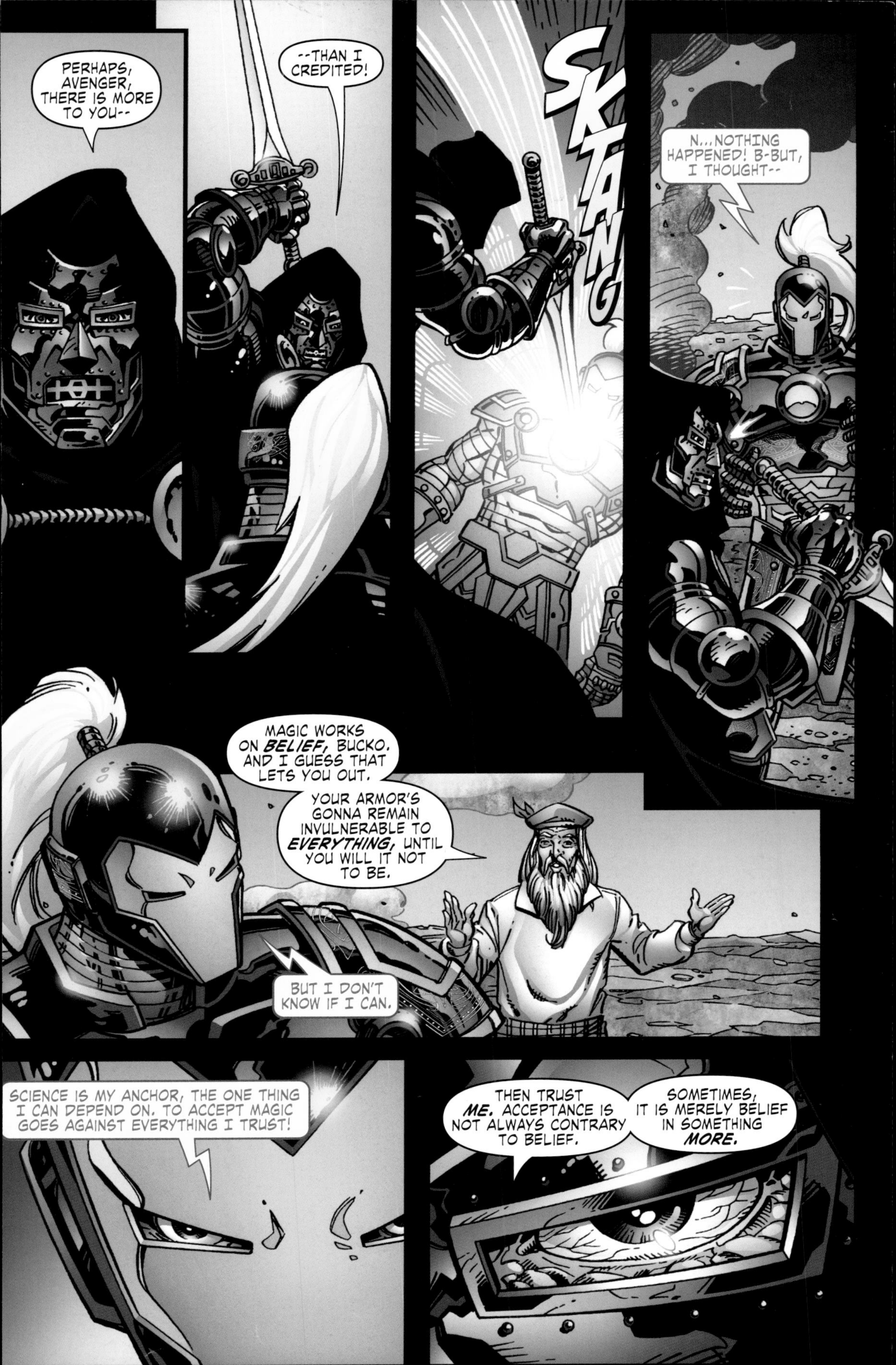

PERHAPS, AVENGER, THERE IS MORE TO YOU--
--THAN I CREDITED!
SKTANG
N...NOTHING HAPPENED! B-BUT, I THOUGHT--
MAGIC WORKS ON BELIEF, BUCKO. AND I GUESS THAT LETS YOU OUT.
YOUR ARMOR'S GONNA REMAIN INVULNERABLE TO EVERYTHING, UNTIL YOU WILL IT NOT TO BE.
BUT I DON'T KNOW IF I CAN.
SCIENCE IS MY ANCHOR, THE ONE THING I CAN DEPEND ON. TO ACCEPT MAGIC GOES AGAINST EVERYTHING I TRUST!
THEN TRUST ME. ACCEPTANCE IS NOT ALWAYS CONTRARY TO BELIEF.
SOMETIMES, IT IS MERELY BELIEF IN SOMETHING MORE.

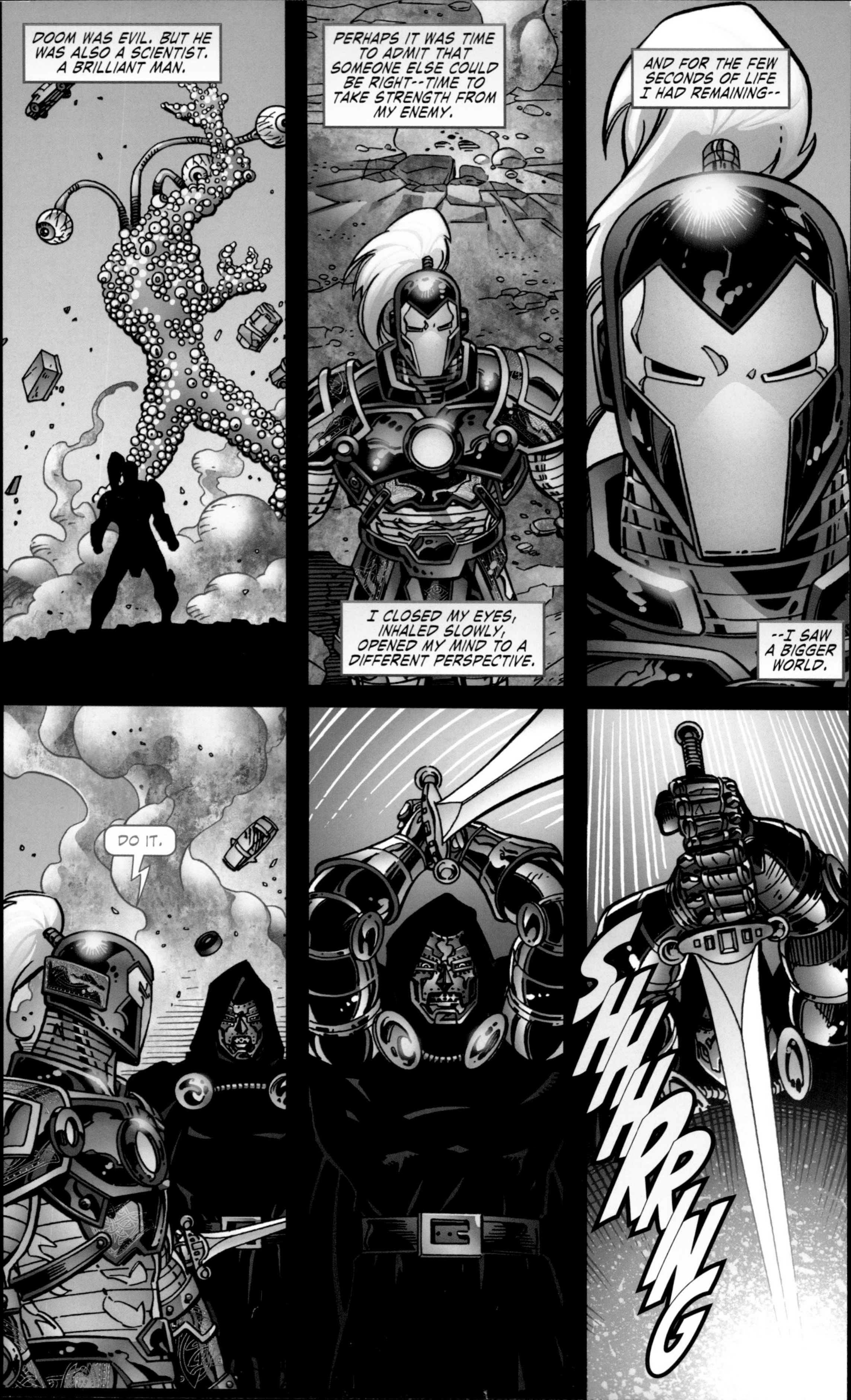
DOOM WAS EVIL. BUT HE WAS ALSO A SCIENTIST. A BRILLIANT MAN.
PERHAPS IT WAS TIME TO ADMIT THAT SOMEONE ELSE COULD BE RIGHT--TIME TO TAKE STRENGTH FROM MY ENEMY.
I CLOSED MY EYES, INHALED SLOWLY, OPENED MY MIND TO A DIFFERENT PERSPECTIVE.
AND FOR THE FEW SECONDS OF LIFE I HAD REMAINING--
--I SAW A BIGGER WORLD.
DO IT.
SHHRRING

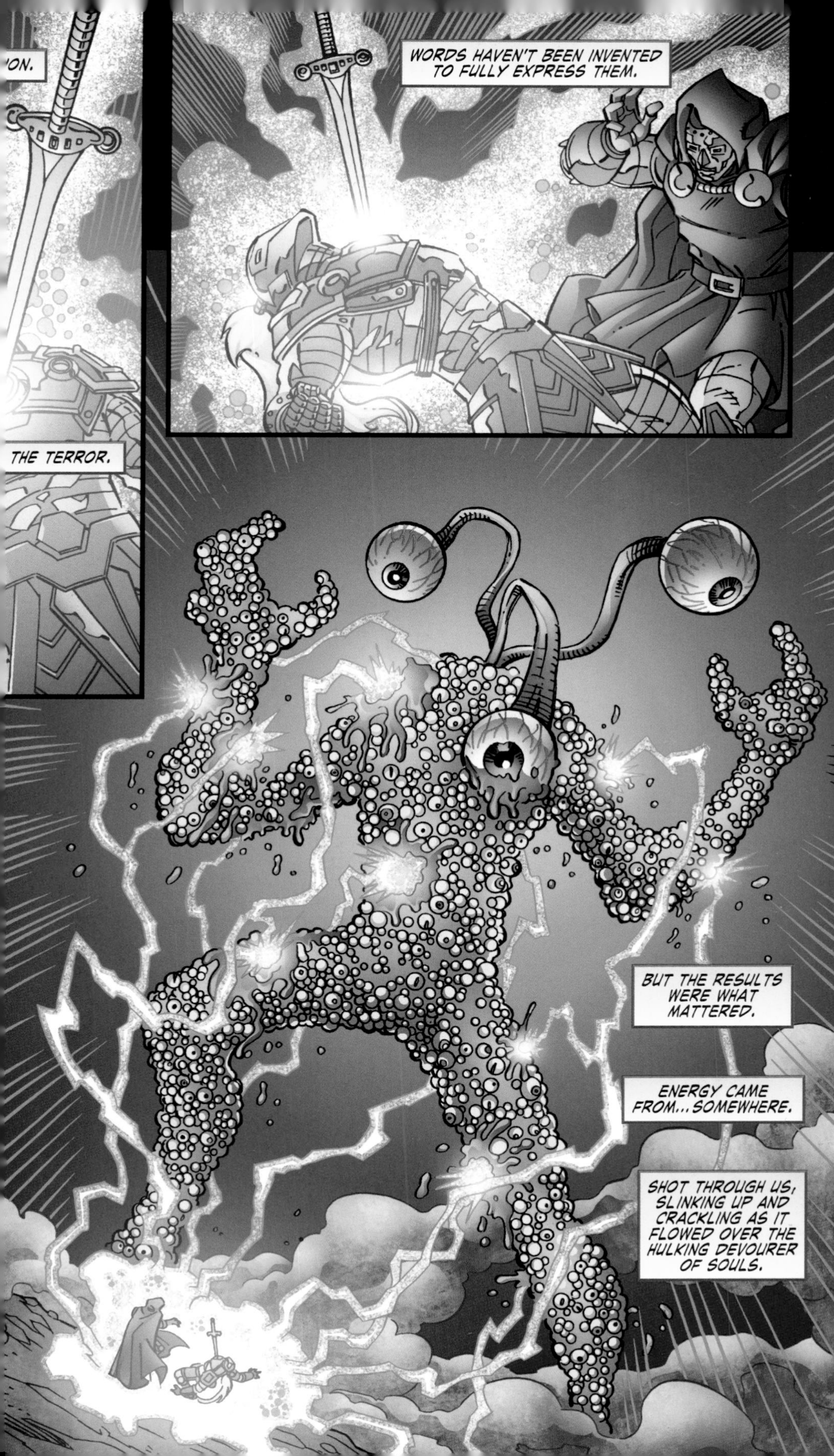
THE TERROR.
WORDS HAVEN'T BEEN INVENTED TO FULLY EXPRESS THEM.
BUT THE RESULTS WERE WHAT MATTERED.
ENERGY CAME FROM...SOMEWHERE.
SHOT THROUGH US, SLINKING UP AND CRACKLING AS IT FLOWED OVER THE HULKING DEVOURER OF SOULS.

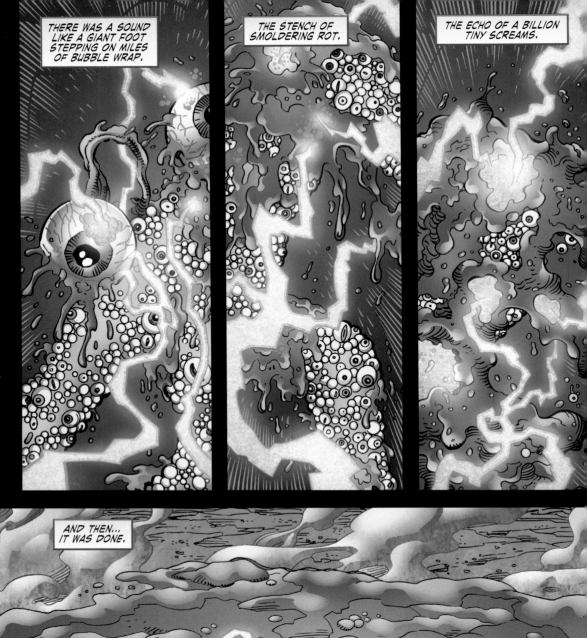

THERE WAS A SOUND LIKE A GIANT FOOT STEPPING ON MILES OF BUBBLE WRAP.

THE STENCH OF SMOLDERING ROT.

THE ECHO OF A BILLION TINY SCREAMS.

AND THEN... IT WAS DONE.

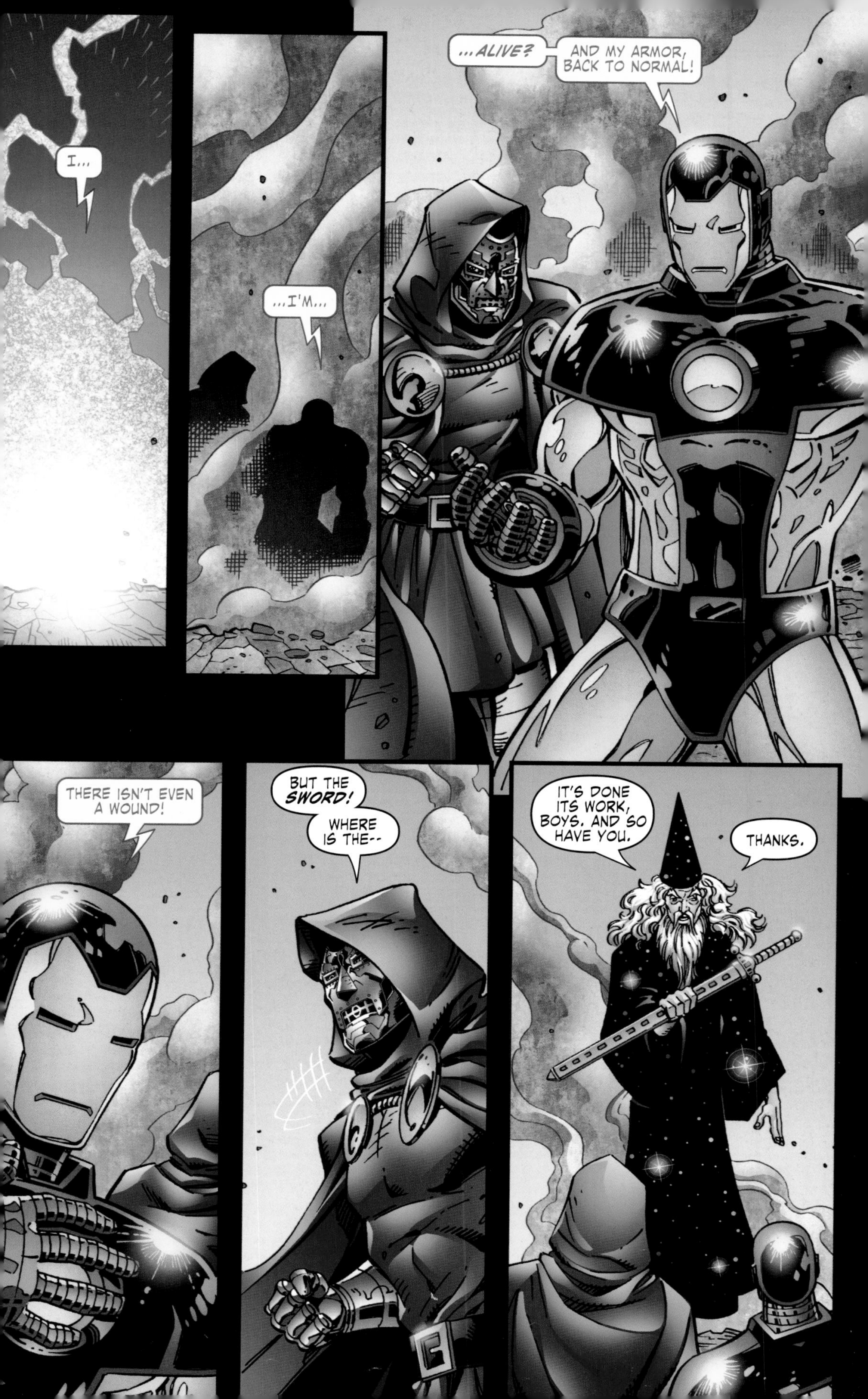
I...
...I'M...
...ALIVE?
AND MY ARMOR, BACK TO NORMAL!
THERE ISN'T EVEN A WOUND!
BUT THE SWORD!
WHERE IS THE--
IT'S DONE ITS WORK, BOYS. AND SO HAVE YOU.
THANKS.

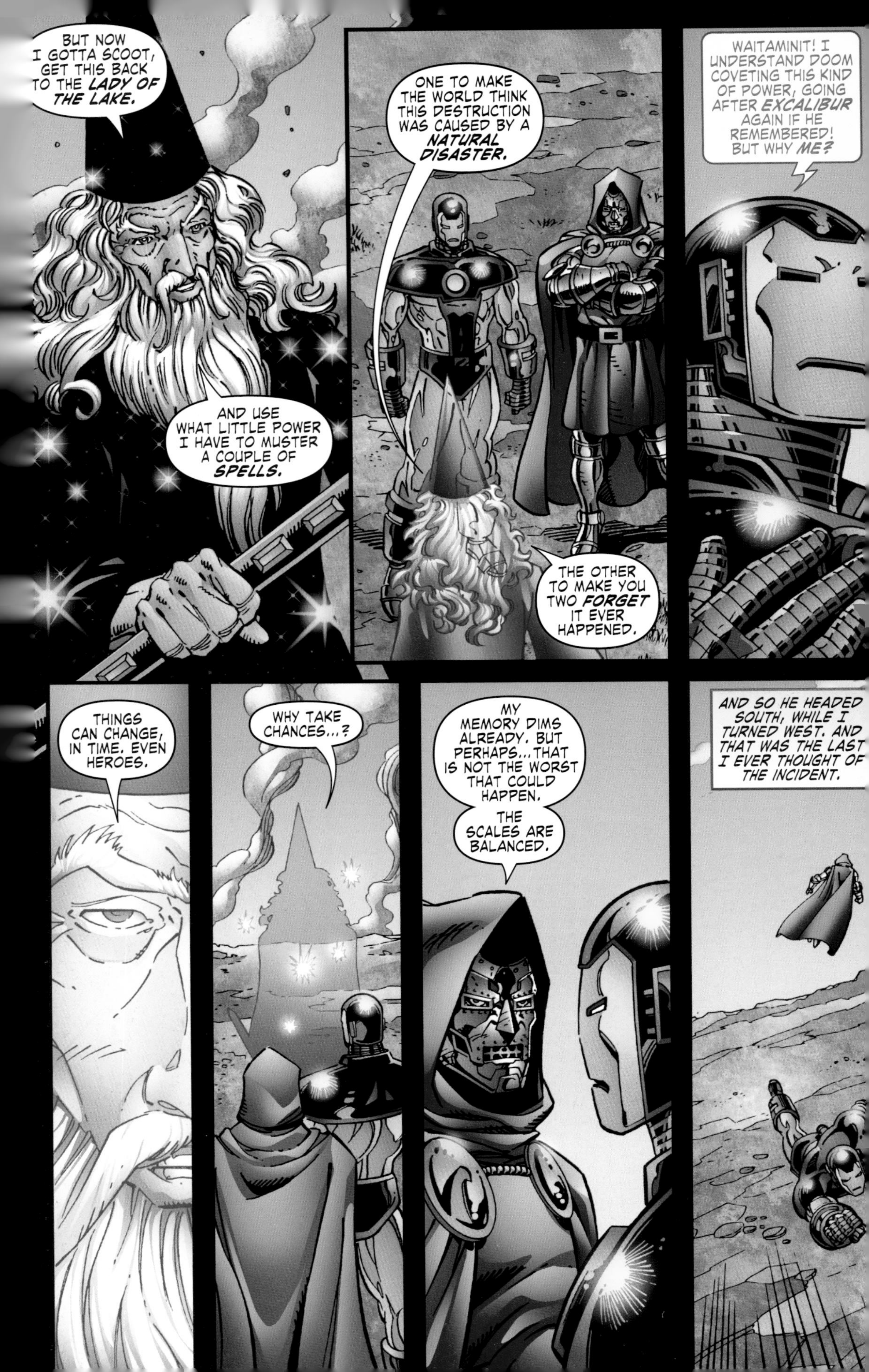
BUT NOW I GOTTA SCOOT, GET THIS BACK TO THE LADY OF THE LAKE.
AND USE WHAT LITTLE POWER I HAVE TO MUSTER A COUPLE OF SPELLS.
ONE TO MAKE THE WORLD THINK THIS DESTRUCTION WAS CAUSED BY A NATURAL DISASTER.
THE OTHER TO MAKE YOU TWO FORGET IT EVER HAPPENED.
WAITAMINIT! I UNDERSTAND DOOM COVETING THIS KIND OF POWER, GOING AFTER EXCALIBUR AGAIN IF HE REMEMBERED! BUT WHY ME?
THINGS CAN CHANGE, IN TIME. EVEN HEROES.
WHY TAKE CHANCES...?
MY MEMORY DIMS ALREADY. BUT PERHAPS...THAT IS NOT THE WORST THAT COULD HAPPEN.
THE SCALES ARE BALANCED.
AND SO HE HEADED SOUTH, WHILE I TURNED WEST. AND THAT WAS THE LAST I EVER THOUGHT OF THE INCIDENT.

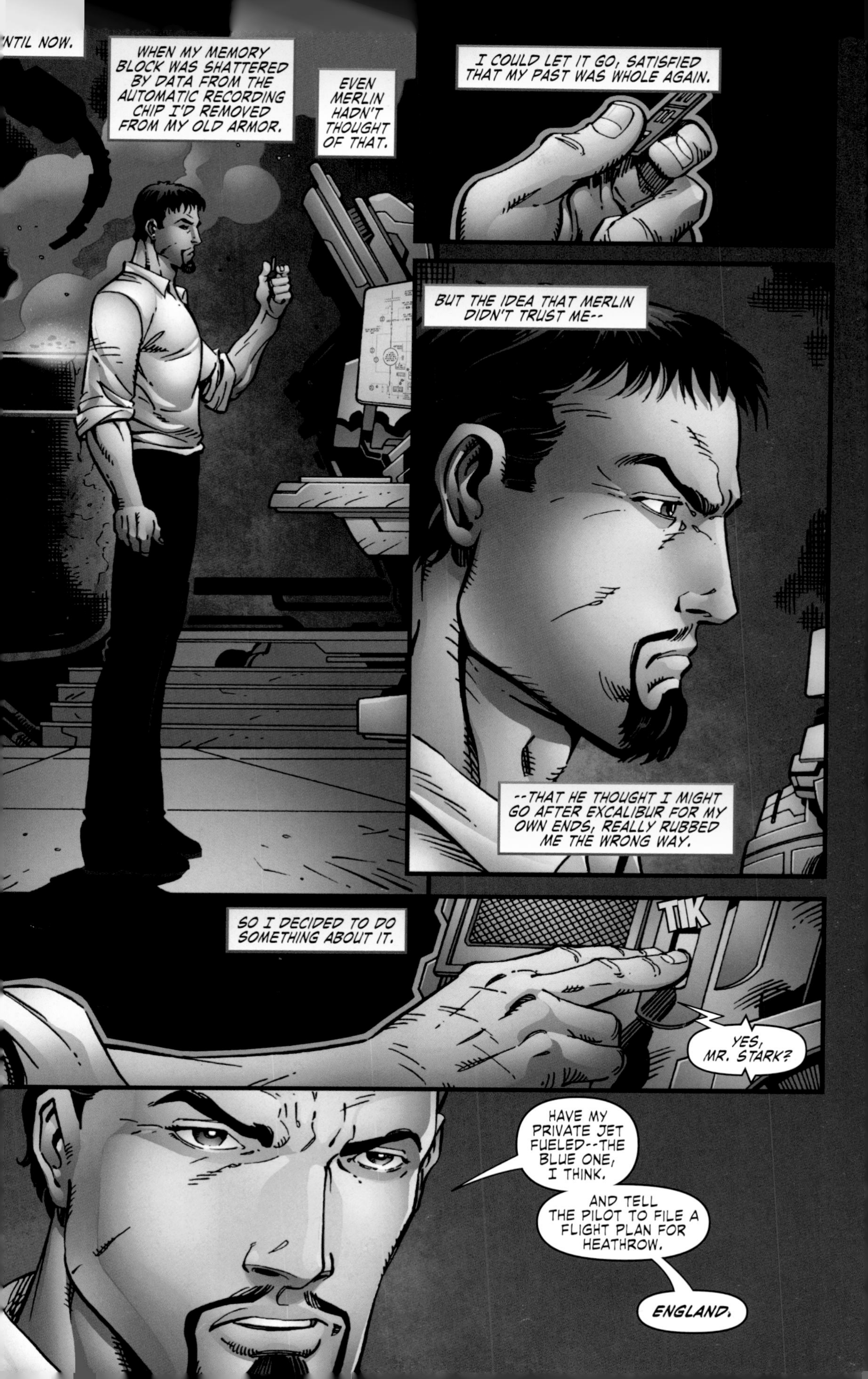

NTIL NOW.
WHEN MY MEMORY BLOCK WAS SHATTERED BY DATA FROM THE AUTOMATIC RECORDING CHIP I'D REMOVED FROM MY OLD ARMOR.
EVEN MERLIN HADN'T THOUGHT OF THAT.
I COULD LET IT GO, SATISFIED THAT MY PAST WAS WHOLE AGAIN.
BUT THE IDEA THAT MERLIN DIDN'T TRUST ME--
--THAT HE THOUGHT I MIGHT GO AFTER EXCALIBUR FOR MY OWN ENDS, REALLY RUBBED ME THE WRONG WAY.
SO I DECIDED TO DO SOMETHING ABOUT IT.
TIK
YES, MR. STARK?
HAVE MY PRIVATE JET FUELED--THE BLUE ONE, I THINK.
AND TELL THE PILOT TO FILE A FLIGHT PLAN FOR HEATHROW.
ENGLAND.

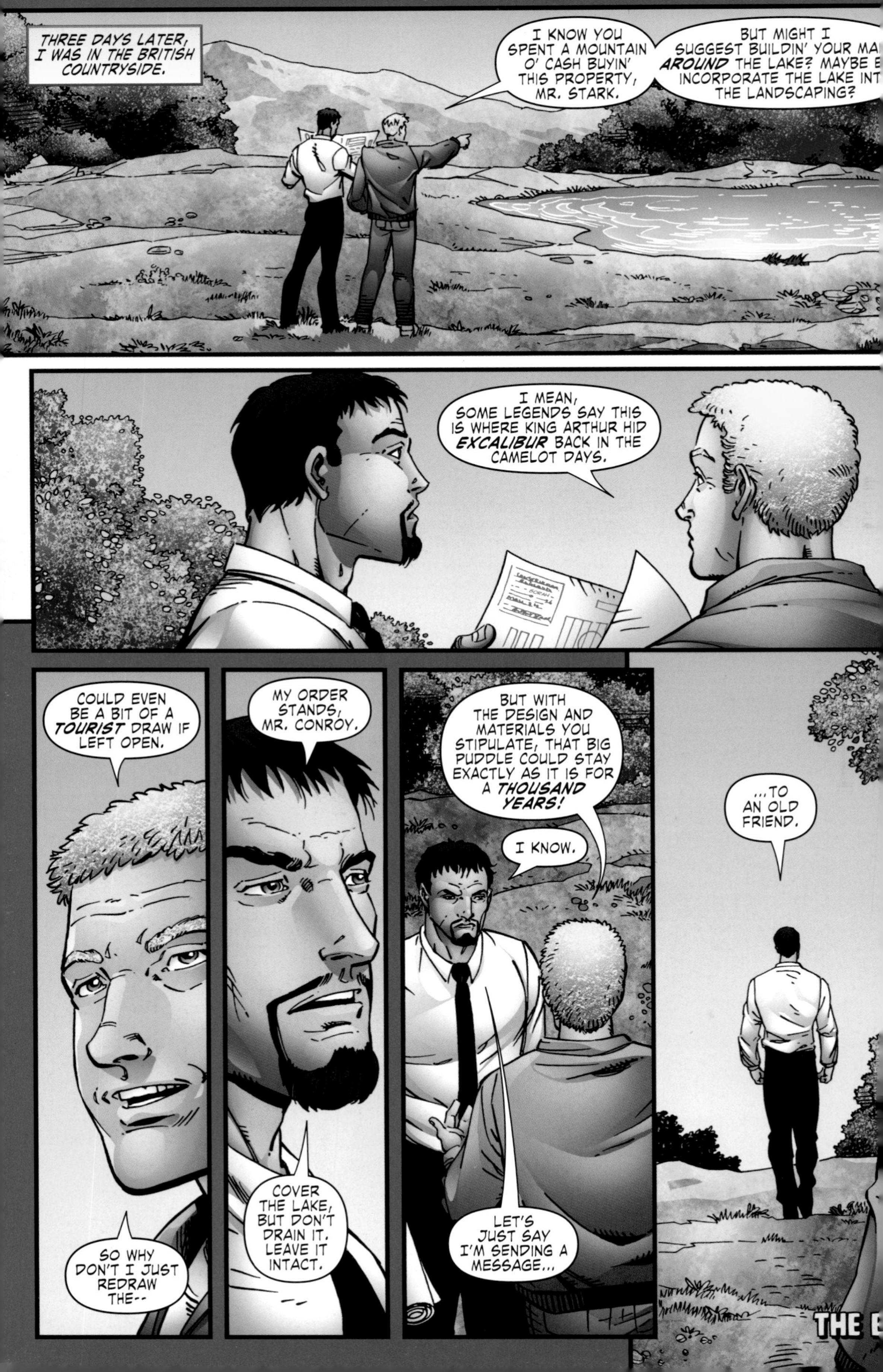
THREE DAYS LATER, I WAS IN THE BRITISH COUNTRYSIDE.
I KNOW YOU SPENT A MOUNTAIN O' CASH BUYIN' THIS PROPERTY, MR. STARK.
BUT MIGHT I SUGGEST BUILDIN' YOUR MA **AROUND** THE LAKE? MAYBE E INCORPORATE THE LAKE INT THE LANDSCAPING?
I MEAN, SOME LEGENDS SAY THIS IS WHERE KING ARTHUR HID **EXCALIBUR** BACK IN THE CAMELOT DAYS.
COULD EVEN BE A BIT OF A **TOURIST** DRAW IF LEFT OPEN.
SO WHY DON'T I JUST REDRAW THE--
MY ORDER STANDS, MR. CONROY.
COVER THE LAKE, BUT DON'T DRAIN IT. LEAVE IT INTACT.
BUT WITH THE DESIGN AND MATERIALS YOU STIPULATE, THAT BIG PUDDLE COULD STAY EXACTLY AS IT IS FOR A **THOUSAND YEARS!**
I KNOW.
LET'S JUST SAY I'M SENDING A MESSAGE...
...TO AN OLD FRIEND.
THE E

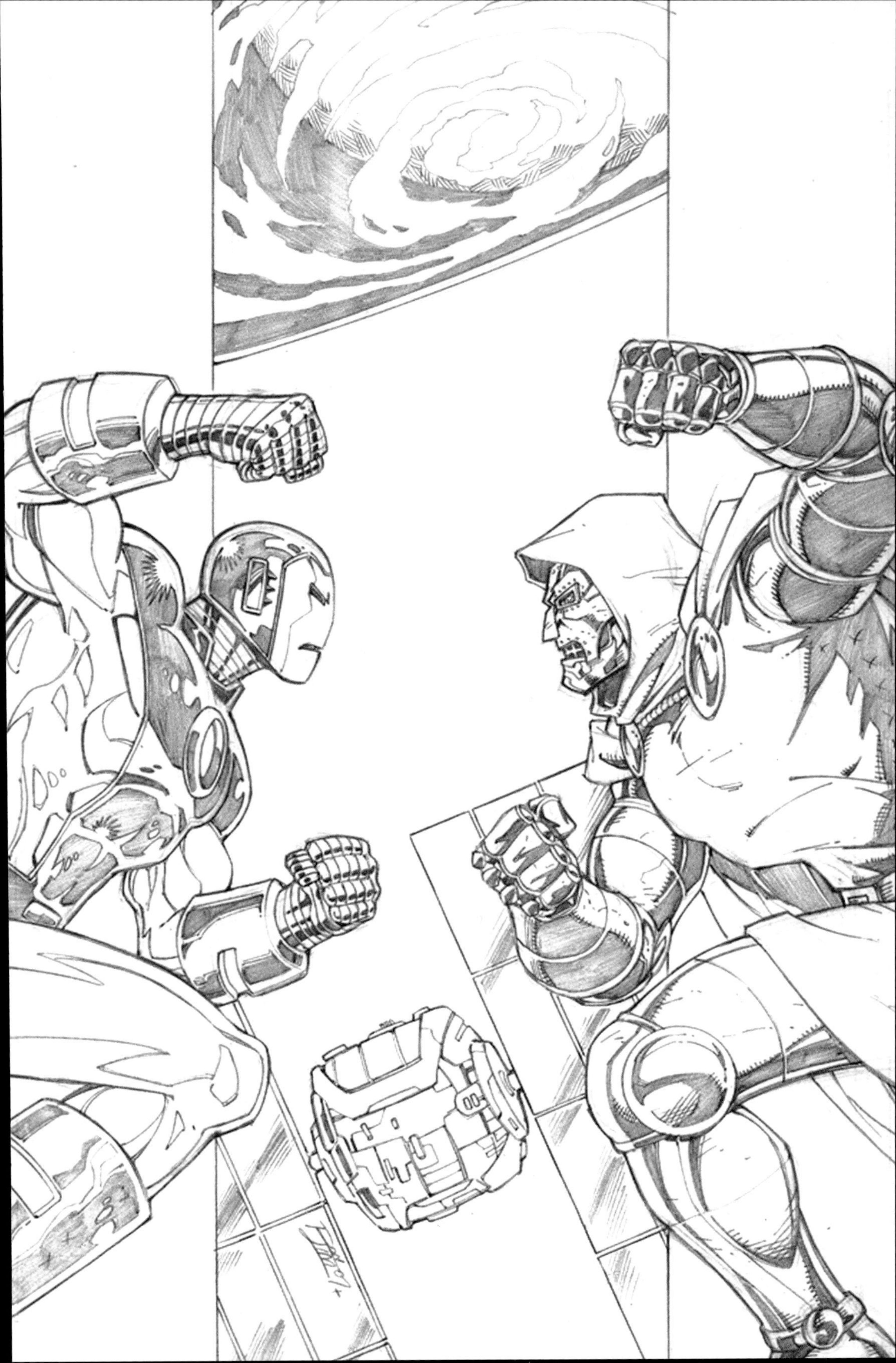

Issue #1 New York Comic Con Exclusive Sketch Variant by Ron Lim

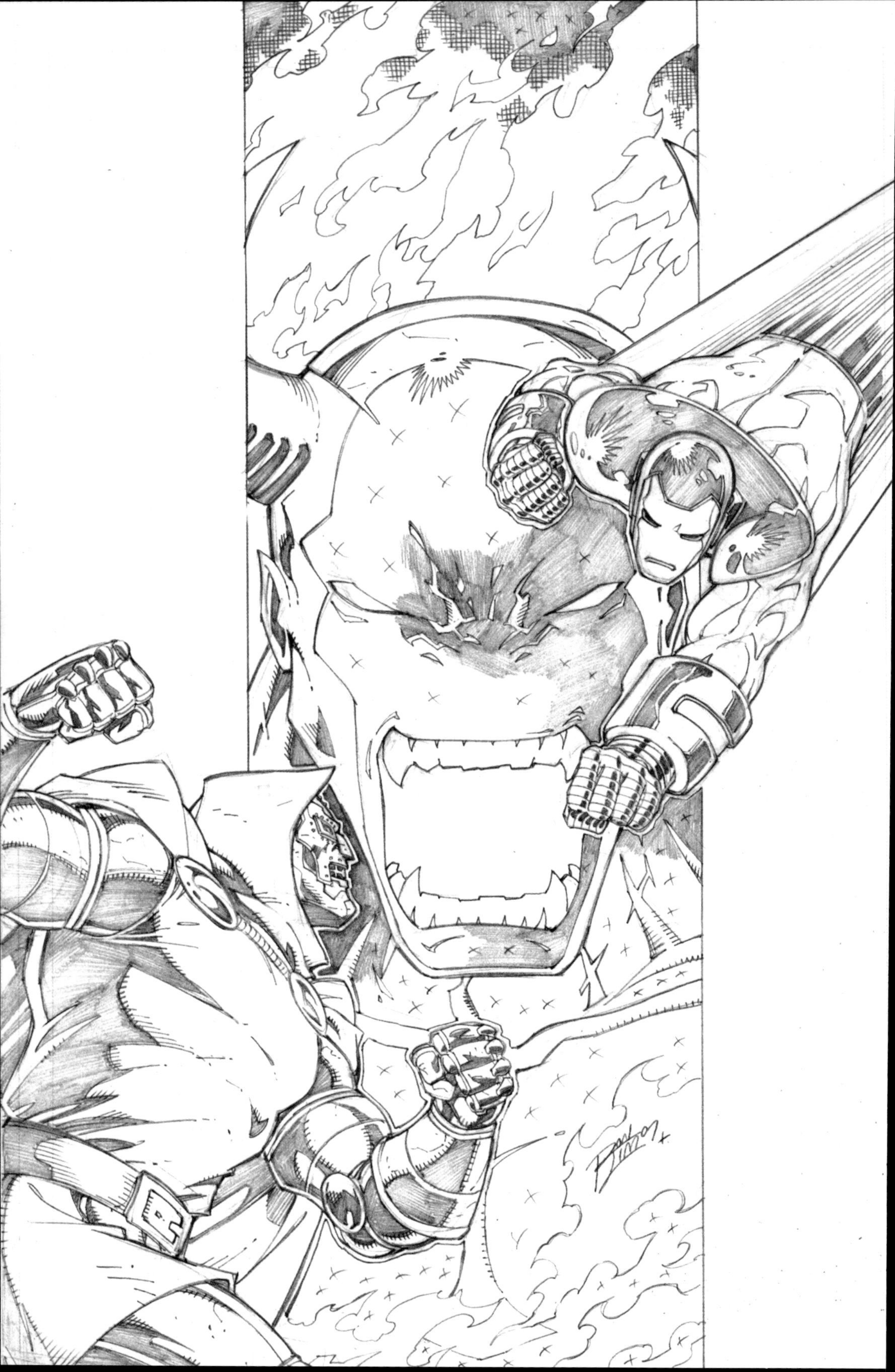

Issue #2 Cover Pencils by Ron Lim

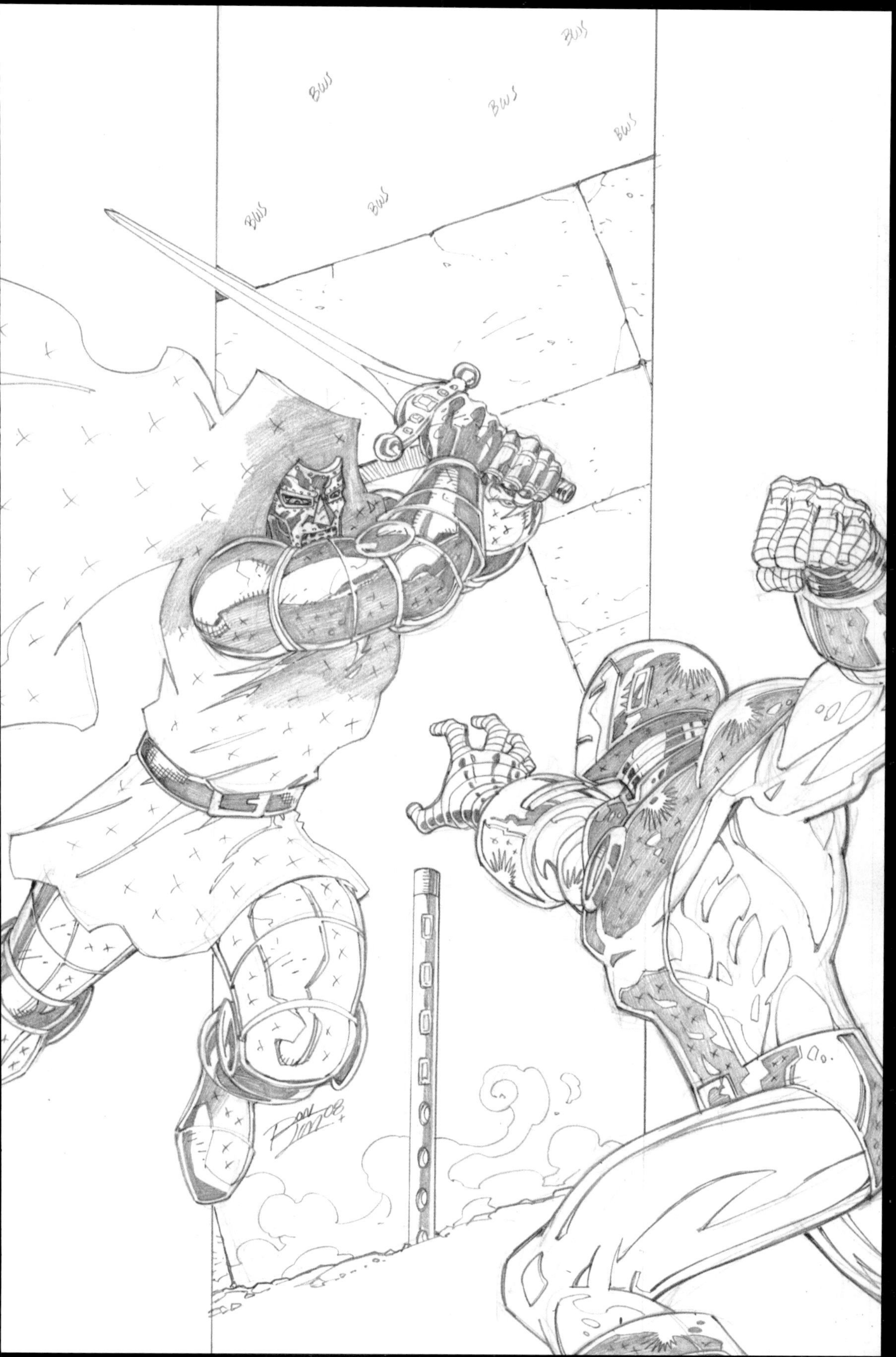
BWS
BWS
BWS
BWS
BWS
BWS
BWS

Issue #3 Cover Pencils by Ron Lim

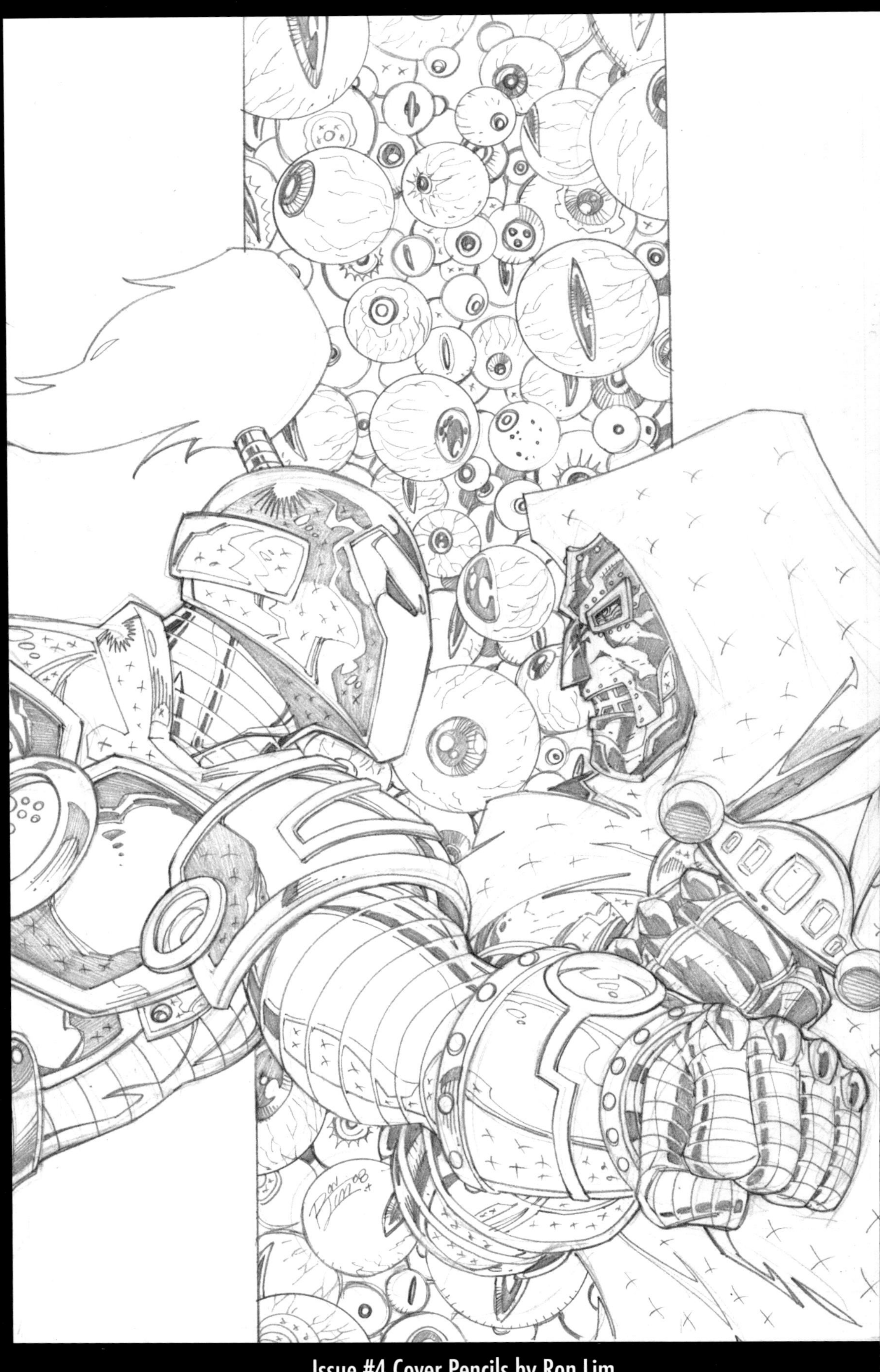

Issue #4 Cover Pencils by Ron Lim

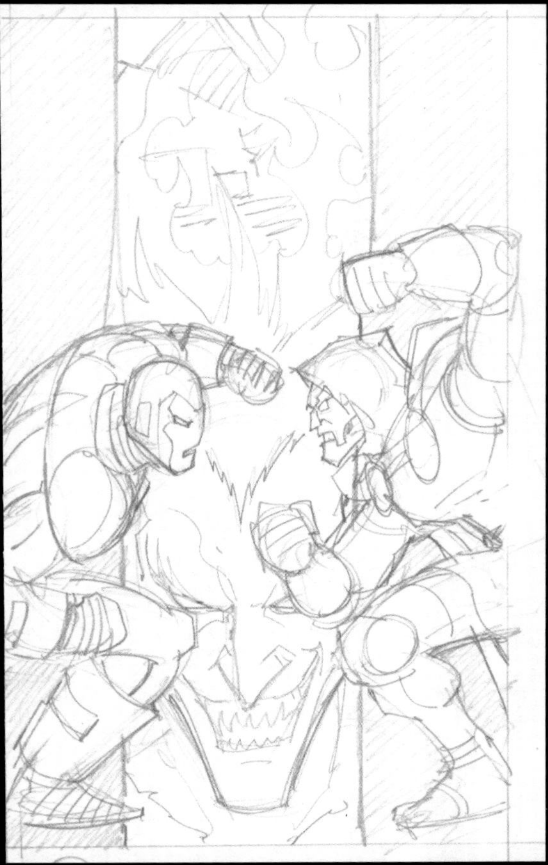

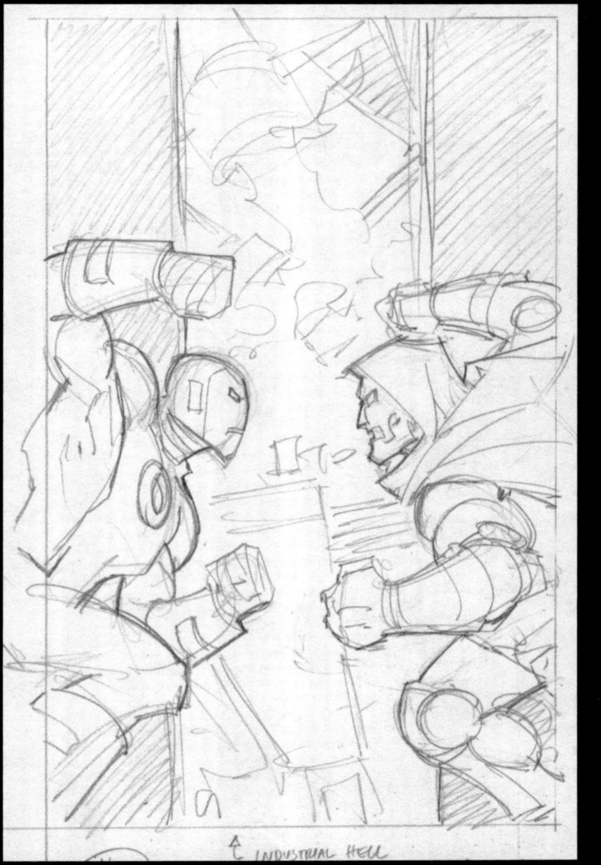
INDUSTRIAL HELL

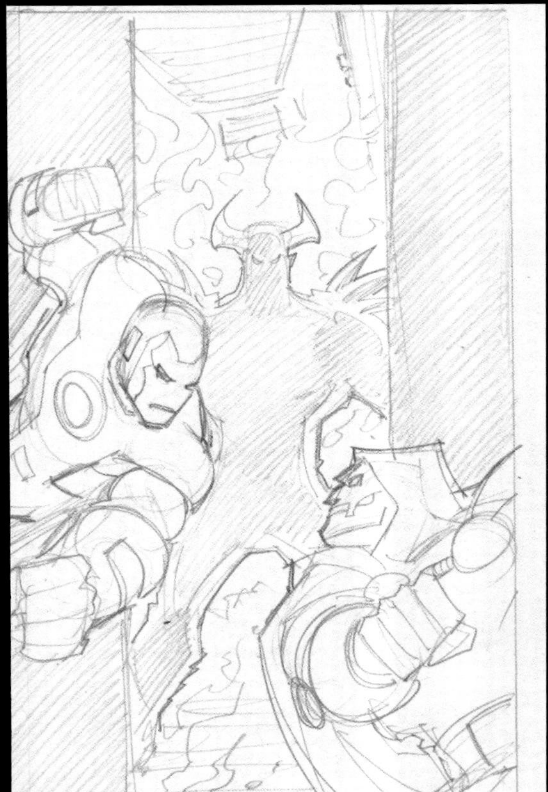

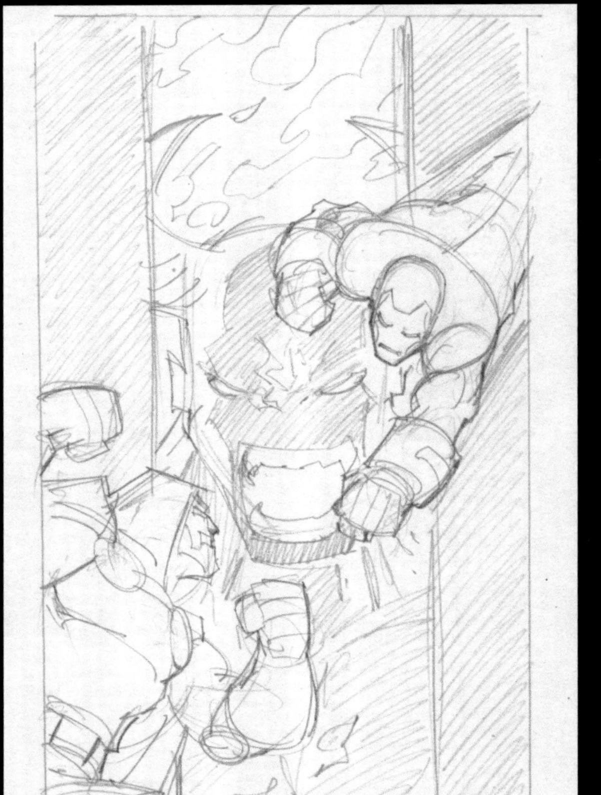
#2

Issues #1 & #2 Cover Sketches by Ron Lim

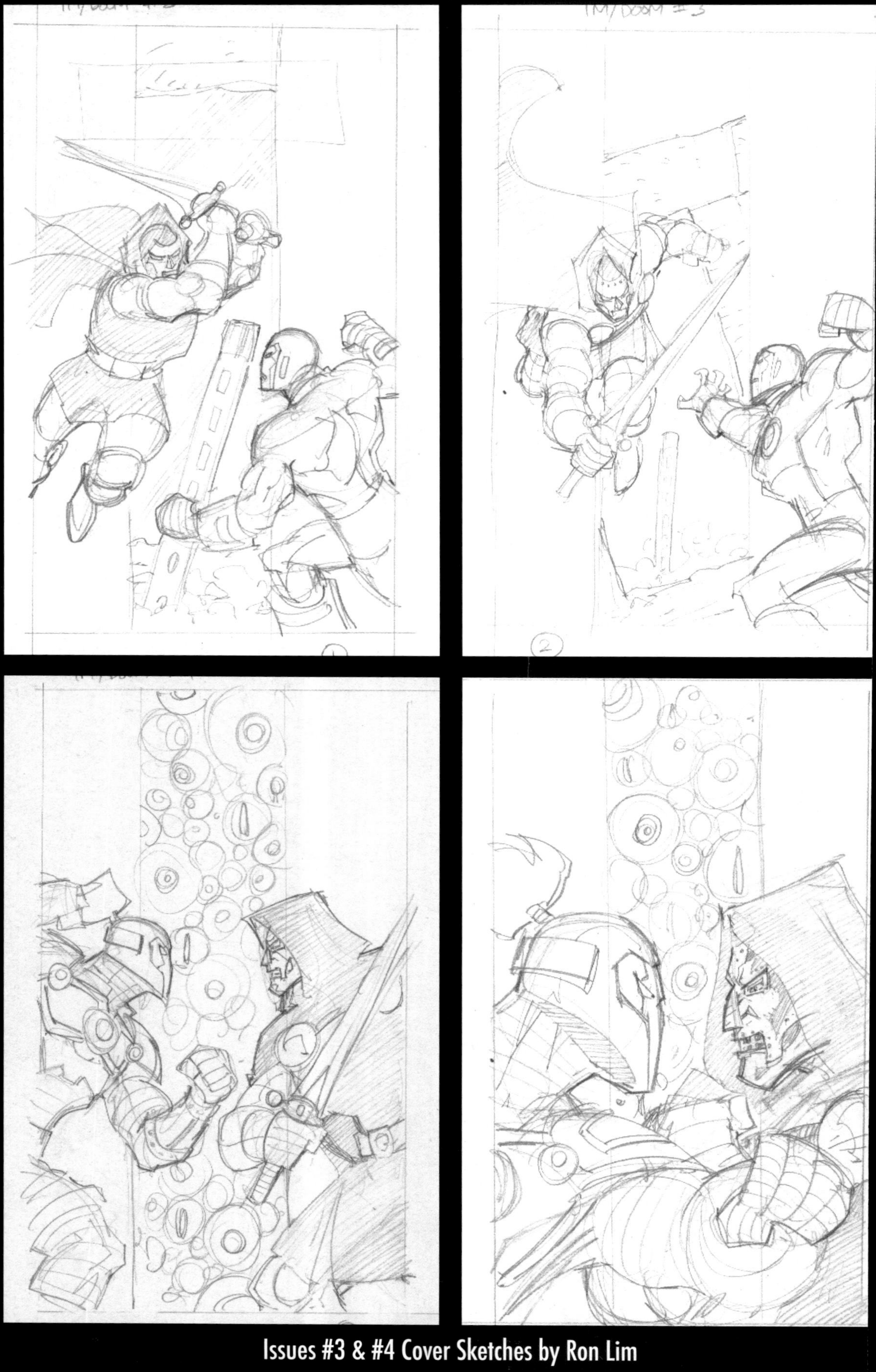
IM/DOOM #3

Issues #3 & #4 Cover Sketches by Ron Lim

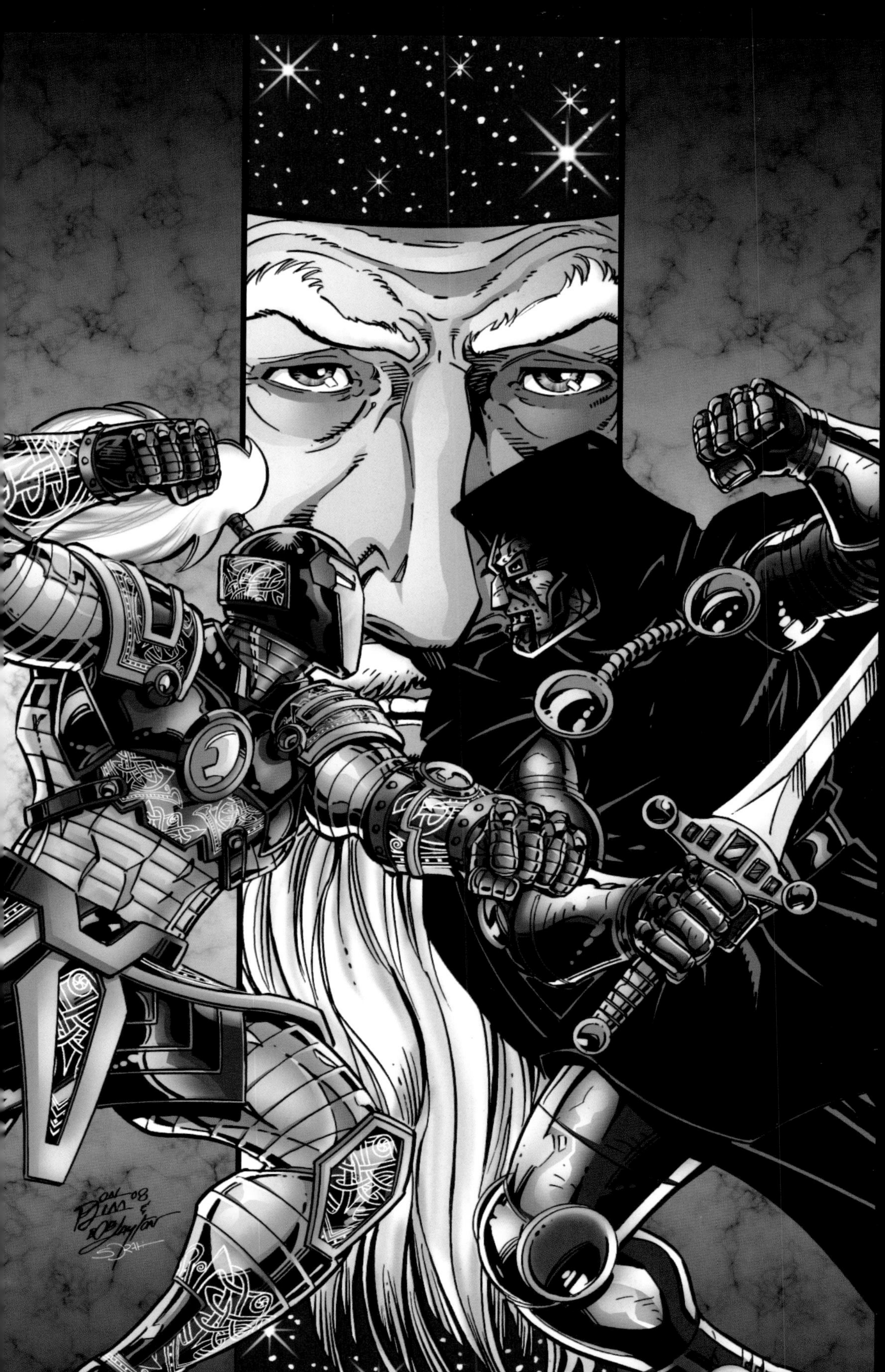

Issue #4 Unused Cover by Ron Lim & Bob Layton

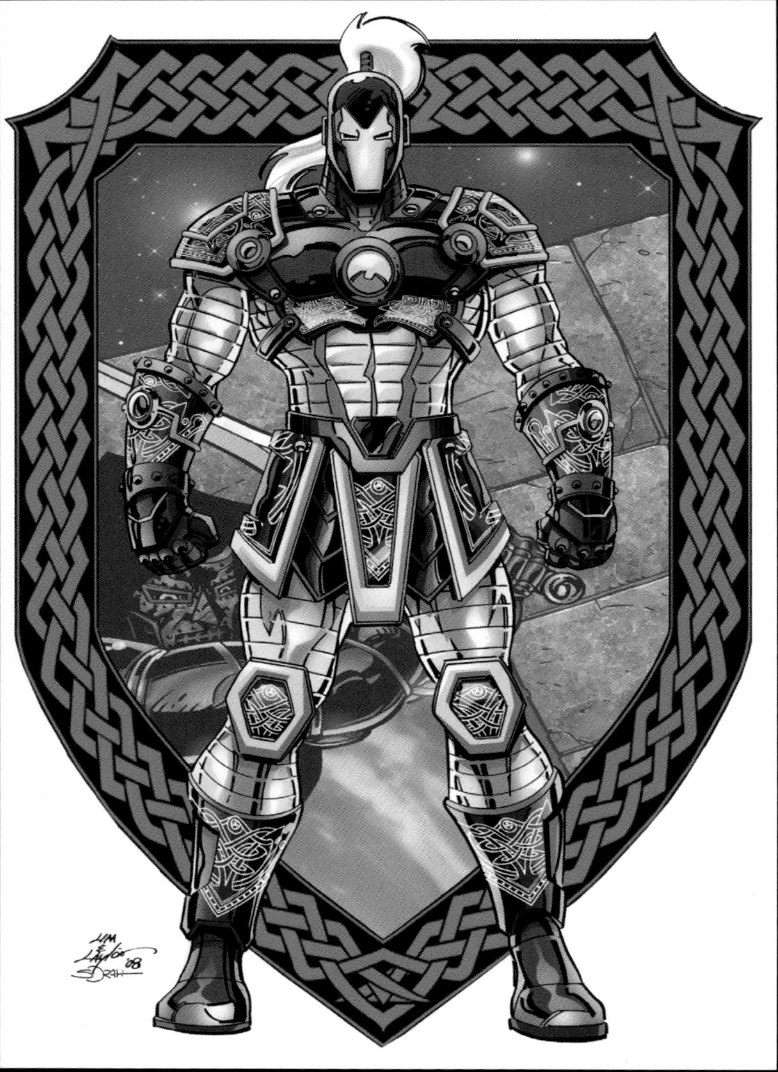

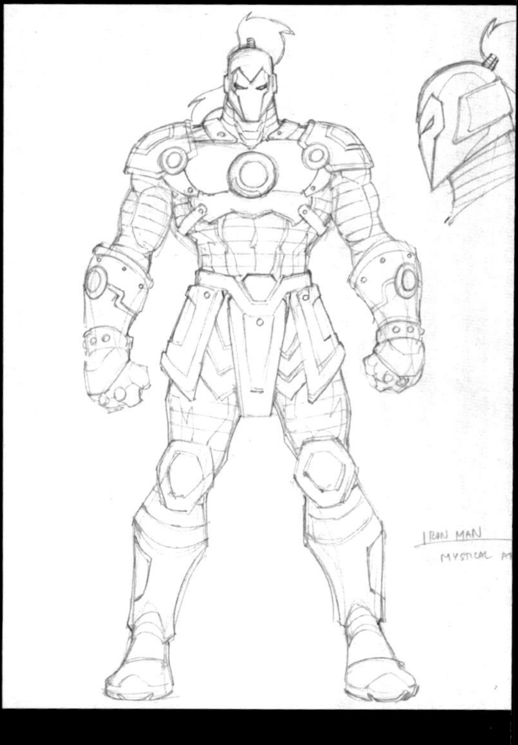
IRON MAN

Mystical Armor Design
by Ron Lim & Bob Layton

IRON MAN: LEGACY OF DOOM
Series Pitch
by David Michelinie

CHAPTER ONE:
"A Knight In Hell"

start with Iron Man in the modified space armor wore in "Bad Blood," working on a satellite in synchronous orbit. The satellite had begun relaying oneous star alignment readings, and he's trying repair it — either because of a contract via Stark utions, or it's his own satellite or whatever. He denly hears an imperious voice in his helmet, turns und and sees DOCTOR DOOM floating in space next the satellite. Acting out of self-preservation instinct, whirls around and lets loose a repulsor blast — which es right through the <u>hologram</u> and smashes part of satellite. (D'oh!) Doom condescendingly orders Iron n to cease his handyman chores and meet him on th, casually mentioning as he fades out that millions ives hang in the balance. Doom's attitude, as always, s Iron Man the wrong way, but the Avenger can't e chances if so many lives may truly be at stake. He urns to Earth, changes to whatever his regular armor t this point, and rendezvous with Doom.

om says that his cabalistic studies have uncovered a dish plot: MEPHISTO has found a way to bring about End Of Days. He's conjuring the Apocalypse before time, before the Forces Of Good can prepare. The ligning of celestial bodies (like those "erroneous" ellite reports) is early evidence of this. Time is of the ence, but Doom has a machine that will send them to I to thwart Mephisto's plan. He explains this

seemingly altruistic behavior as a reaction to Mephisto's gall: he takes it as a personal affront that Mephisto would include him in world destruction. And he explains that he'd selected Iron Man as his "squire" because he might need some lackey-work done, and Iron Man had proven adequate against supernatural threats in the past. Iron Man ain't thrilled, but with the fate of the world in the balance he really can't take chances. Doom then hands Iron Man a small electronic retriever device that will activate Doom's machine and pull them back from Hell when they've finished their mission. Iron Man doesn't have time for a full analysis, but he's not stupid: he demands that Doom hand over his own retrieval device. He scans them both, determines that they're identical, jumbles them up and hands one at random to Doom, figuring that's his assurance that one isn't bogus.

Iron Man and Doctor Doom then travel to Mephisto's realm, where they fight demon guardians to reach Mephisto's chamber. But instead of encountering resistance when they confront Mephisto, that devilish fellow says, "I'm impressed, Doom. Very well...a bargain is a bargain." He then hands Doom what looks to be a small chunk of metal and Doom fades out, using the retrieval device to take him back to Earth. Iron Man triggers his own device, but it doesn't work! Before he fades, Doom explains that both devices are identical, but they only function in conjunction with a catalytic trigger that he had built into his own armor–one that Iron Man doesn't have. As Iron Man is surrounded by demons, Mephisto explains that he'd made a bargain with Doom: trading that metal chip for a major force for Good in the overworld. In other words: Iron Man, who will now remain in Hell...forever!

CHAPTER TWO:
"Hell And Back"

On Earth, Doctor Doom returns to his castle in Latveria, where he casts a spell with the metal chip at its core. As a result, he resurrects MORGANA LE FEY, recently blowed up in an issue of THE AVENGERS. We learn that the metal sliver is the Excalibur chip that Morgana used in IRON MAN #150 to bring the dead back to life, the chip she had taken with her to an unnamed dimension at the end of that story. As we further learn, the dimension she escaped to was Mephisto's realm, and the cost of her sanctuary there was the mystically powered Excalibur chip. Doom holds Morgana in stasis as he reveals his price for engineering her resurrection: he wants her to cast a spell that only she, because of her bloodline, can accomplish. Seeing that her only alternative is a return to death (or limbo), Morgana agrees.

Meanwhile, in Hell, Iron Man resists, and Mephisto raises an army of Iron Man's dead foes to subdue him. After a mighty battle, Iron Man escapes to a visually interesting section of Hell, where he thinks that he'd better give that retrieval device a closer examination.

On Earth, more astronomical observations are becoming skewed; it's almost as if something is pushing stars out of the way!

In Latveria, Morgana casts her spell, and the Excalibur chip attaches to Doom's armor. As part of their agreement, Morgana is then placed in Doom's time cube, to be sent to the future where KING ARTHUR has been reincarnated as a ten-year-old boy (as established

in *IRON MAN #250*); she figures that as a child, he w be easy to slay. But as she starts to disappear, she s that she's instead being sent to the magically sea castle that was her prison in the days of Camelot (ag established in *#150*). As she shrieks her helpless ra Doom calmly explains that he wouldn't be comforta with her in his future, as a potential threat to his o destiny. Besides, she'd run out on him in issue #1 and no one betrays Doom. No one.

In Hell, Iron Man has cannibalized circuits from armor and has attached them to the retrieval dev hoping to duplicate the trigger that Doom had used activate it. As he's located and set upon by Mephist hordes, he powers up the retrieval device, disappe and re-forms in Doom's castle in Latveria. Doom is window, looking out over his kingdom as Iron Man sta towards him, angry. As Doom turns, Iron Man sees he's holding a sword in his hand. Saying that a fa butter knife isn't going to stop him from kicking Doo ass, he raises his hands to zap Doom with a repulsor. Doom swings the sword — and the blade slices thro Iron Man's armor...and his arm! Doom then reveals the sword is the legendary Excalibur, the magical bl that can cut through anything, the Merlin-made wea that makes whoever wields it...invincible!

CHAPTER THREE:
"The Blade Of Destiny"

Iron Man and Doctor Doom go at it one-on-one, and Doc has a distinct advantage. Excalibur deflects repu blasts like a George Lucas dream, and it chops thro anything that Shellhead puts in front of it. Realizing he doesn't stand a chance, Iron Man eventually uses armor's unique abilities to delay Doctor Doom lo enough for him to escape. But now what's he going do now?

e in his castle, Doom thinks us into a flashback that vs Morgana Le Fay's spell working, and explains only King Arthur or those chosen as his champion wield Excalibur. But Morgana, being Arthur's sister of his direct bloodline, was able to conjure a spell enveloped Doom with the Pendragon aura, fooling libur into accepting him as Arthur. Excalibur was plucked from the grasp of The Lady In The Lake transported to Doom. But, Doom thinks as the back ends, this is only half of the power he needs ccomplish his desperate mission. He then holds libur against his forehead and mumbles ritualistic ls. At last he lowers the sword and looks to the h: "Yessssss...!"

hen have a short scene at a N.A.S.A. facility where tists determine that an area of space between Earth Mars is actually...bulging!

ng back on his previous experiences with Excalibur Morgana, Iron Man contacts MERLIN. (I'm thinking makes him more active as a hero than having in contact him, but will remain open-minded. cially since I have no idea how Iron Man could h out and touch a dead magician!) Merlin tells Man of the Excalibur scabbard, how it renders its essor invulnerable; someone possessing both sword scabbard would be literally unstoppable. Iron Man that Doom must be after both, but even to stop histo's deadly plan, would it be wise to let a maniac Doom achieve such power? But then Merlin asks all this Mephisto stuff is about, and Iron Man ulizes the tale Doom had told him. But Merlin just es his head and tells Iron Man that no Apocalyptic gy is flowing from Mephisto's realm. Besides, if e had been such a threat to England, he would have awakened long ago to protect Camelot. Iron Man ssed: Doom lied! But...why? Merlin then reveals

the location of the hidden Excalibur scabbard, and Iron Man takes off, determined to keep Doctor Doom from becoming the most powerful being on Earth.

Iron Man reaches the scabbard's hiding place just as Doom finds it—and another mighty battle ensues. Doom is almost successful, but Iron Man snatches the scabbard from him just in time. The scabbard glows, and fuses with Iron Man's metal mesh, morphing it into a suit of fantastic, kick-ass mystical armor. Doom's shoulders sag: "Combining the sword and scabbard was the only hope. Now, you've killed them all." Iron Man asks what he's talking about, and Doom merely points to the sky: there, the starscape is twisted, warped, and a jagged hole is appearing. Through that hole can be seen giant, slithering, unclean things, nightmares given form, Lovecraftian id-vomit that defies description and belief. Iron Man's jaw drops inside his new mask, as Doom concludes: "This...is what you've done!"

CHAPTER FOUR: "Monsters"

This would basically be an all-action issue. The thing that comes through the tear in reality is the most monstrously evil creature ever seen on Earth. No anthropomorphized Dormammu, this creature is bizarre, original and completely unpredictable, looking like something that would make Stan Winston and the entire crew at ILM drop to their knees and crown us the new creature gods. Doom and Iron Man fight the beast; Excalibur does some damage, but not enough. Iron Man's repulsors are now mystic engines, firing spellshots that also hurt the monster, but do little damage. And while Iron Man can't be hurt in the scabbard-charged armor, he can still be slammed a couple of miles into the crust of the Earth.

At a break in the fighting – perhaps some delaying tactic buys them a few seconds – we learn that Doctor Doom had been seeking answers, or power, and so had conjured an artifact from another dimension. The lord of that dimension (the monster they're fighting now) had become aware of the theft and had sworn to destroy the thief and all he possesses. And because Doom is the king of Latveria, that means that his whole kingdom is his "possession" – and thus his thousands of innocent subjects are at risk. Doom had set out to get Excalibur and the scabbard to fight and destroy the creature he knew was on its way. So, even though he's the cause of the danger, he's actually acting out of nobility, trying to protect his people. He had tricked Iron Man because his arrogance won't allow him to ask for help; and his ego won't let him admit that he may have screwed up. But then Iron Man makes an observation: this monster may be going after Doom, but it seems to be destroying everything <u>else</u> it can reach as well – and they're not in Latveria! This stops Doom cold, and he realizes that he had once actually succeeded in ruling the world (in the EMPEROR DOOM graphic novel). By that standard, the entire planet could be considered his "possession" – and monster's target!

Iron Man and Doctor Doom eventually realize that they have to work together, that the powers of Excalibur and the scabbard must be combined to defeat extradimensional threat. Perhaps, on Merlin's advice they lure the creature to Stonehenge, which legend says Merlin constructed; perhaps it had been built just such an eventuality as this. Maybe the scabbard is drawn from Iron Man's armor (or Iron Man has will the scabbard energy to depart, which would courage since it would leave him completely vulnerable and used to contain the monster. Then Excalibur c power the Stonehenge monument to send the creature back to its own dimension. The scabbard energy c remain in that dimension, to keep the monster dorm which would explain why its fate is never dealt with Arthurian mythology. The process would drain the Ar essence from Doom (or maybe Merlin takes it a now that he's aware of it), and Excalibur is whi back to the Lady Of The Lake, to await Arthur's rel in England's darkest hour. (Or, *IRON MAN #250.*)

Iron Man is left with renewed anger at Doctor D for having been tricked (and left in Hell), but he has a bit more understanding of the man's depth character, of how he does care for his subjects, if only as possessions. And Doctor Doom has reso his oath to pay Iron Man back for issue *#150* – though Shellhead ultimately escaped that revenge. though Iron Man did screw up his plans to defeat other-dimensional monster on his own, the hireling eventually help him prevail. He agrees to allow Man to live – so long as their paths never cross ag (And what are the chances of <u>that</u>????)

HISTORY: Victor von Doom was born to the Zefiro travelers ("Gypsies") Werner and Cynthia in Latveria, a small European country that grew out of Hungary and was ruled by King Vladimir Vassily Gonereo Tristian Mangegi Fortunov, Baron of Sabbat, Baron of Haasen, Baron of Krozi. Victor barely knew his mother, a witch who had invoked the demon Mephisto for power, which raged out of control before she was finally slain by a soldier. Before dying, she asked Werner to protect young Victor from Mephisto. Victor's father, a doctor, was forced to treat King Vladimir's wife. When Werner could not cure her cancer, Vladimir blamed him for his wife's death, and Werner fled with Victor. Werner died from exposure to the cold while protecting his son. Before dying, Werner placed Victor into the care of his best friend, Boris, and tried to warn his son of the fearful life he foresaw him falling into, but he died before he could make Victor understand.

Discovering his mother's mystical artifacts, Victor schooled himself in sorcery. He began an annual contest against the might of Mephisto, attempting to set his mother's soul free. By the time he was a teenager, he had also become a scientific genius and used his inventions to wage a one-man war against the monarchy of Latveria, always a step ahead of them. His genius was heard of even in America, and he was invited to New York's State University on a scholarship. Victor had been in love with Boris' granddaughter Valeria, but he left her behind as his desire to acquire knowledge and the means to seek revenge on others consumed him.

Arriving at State, Doom was greeted by Reed Richards, a fellow student who was interested in rooming with him, but Doom rejected his offer of friendship. Throughout his university days, Doom pursued a petty rivalry with Richards, convinced of his own superior intellect. Doom's greatest invention was a machine designed to rescue his mother's soul from the netherworld. Richards tried to warn him of a flaw in his calculations, but Doom was too proud to listen. He activated the machine, and it literally exploded in his face. Expelled for the explosion, Doom sustained only a few facial scars, but believed his looks had been ruined. Filled with self-loathing, he left America for Tibet, seeking new enlightenment. There, he found the Aged Genghis, one of the enigmatic Immortal Nine; the now senile sorcerer directed him to a long-lost order of monks. Doom made them his servants and had them forge his first suit of armor, designed to hide his features from the world. Doom had them press the mask to his face before it had cooled, ensuring that if his face had not been hideous before, it was now.

Dr. Doom then conquered Latveria, slaying King Vladimir, imprisoning his son Rudolfo, and having a robot duplicate of Rudolfo surrender the Latverian crown to him, after which he renamed the capital city, Haasenstadt, as Doomstadt. He used his genius and technology to transform Latveria into a paradise where no citizen wants, no one is threatened by war, and all praise Doom — or face the consequences. Doom maintained a puppet prime minister; the outside world was largely unaware of Doom's status as ruler, tending to dismiss his existence as a myth. Doom stepped up his scientific prowess, designing a time machine and robotic duplicates of himself (Doombots). In one of his earliest time travels he journeyed back to World War II and considered killing Adolf Hitler for the crimes his Nazi regime had inflicted upon the Zefiro and other travelers, but ultimately decided to leave him to his own fate.

Armed with his genius and the might of Latveria, Victor set for himself three goals: to rescue his mother, to prove his superiority over Reed Richards, and to conquer the world. By this time, Reed and his friends had become the Fantastic Four, so Dr. Doom sought them out and

REAL NAME: Victor von Doom
ALIASES: The Master, Invincible Man, Vincent Vaughn, Hans; has also inhabited the bodies of Daredevil, Norman McArthur and the Fantastic Four
IDENTITY: Publicly known
OCCUPATION: Monarch of Latveria, would-be conqueror
CITIZENSHIP: Latveria
PLACE OF BIRTH: A camp outside Haasenstadt (now Doomstadt), Latveria
KNOWN RELATIVES: Werner von Doom (father, deceased), Cynthia von Doom (mother, deceased); Kang, his counterparts, and offspring (alleged descendants), Victor von Doom II (clone, deceased), Dr. Bob Doom (alleged cousin)
GROUP AFFILIATION: None; formerly Knights of the Atomic Table, Acts of Vengeance prime movers, Legion Accursed, partner of Namor, employer of the Terrible Trio
EDUCATION: College studies in the sciences (expelled before completion of degree); self-educated to graduate level and beyond in most sciences; self-taught knowledge of the mystic arts
FIRST APPEARANCE: Fantastic Four #5 (1962)

abducted the Invisible Girl. He forced the other members to journey back in time to recover the gems of the legendary sorcerer Merlin for him; but Mr. Fantastic tricked him, bringing back a chest full of chains instead. Although the FF survived Doom's attacks, Doom escaped them by using a Doombot as a decoy. Dr. Doom next formed an alliance with the Sub-Mariner, believing that their mutual hatred of the FF made for a natural partnership. Doom nearly cast the Baxter Building into the sun, but the Sub-Mariner turned on him, and Doom was cast adrift into space. He was saved by the alien Ovoids, who taught him how to exchange bodies with others. With this new power, he had Marvel Comics creators Stan Lee and Jack Kirby lure Mr. Fantastic into a trap so that he could take over his body. However, the Fantastic Four saw through Doom's facade and he was forced back into his own body, then accidentally cast into the Microverse.

But the Microverse proved to be merely a new challenge for Dr. Doom's genius rather than a prison. Doom conquered Mirwood, the kingdom of Princess Pearla, and brought the Fantastic Four there as prisoners. Aided by Ant-Man (Hank Pym), the Fantastic Four escaped and followed Doom back to Earth, where they battled him aboard his Flying Fortress, from which he threatened to unleash chaos throughout the globe — when the FF thwarted his plan, he escaped again. Doom soon attempted to reclaim his abandoned Flying Fortress from military custody, but the newly formed Avengers intervened and he was forced to destroy it. Dr. Doom next empowered and sent the Terrible Trio ("Bull" Brogin, Yogi Dakor & Harry Phillips) against the Fantastic Four, but this plot also failed, and ended with Doom cast into space by a Solar Wave, a fate he had meant for the FF. He was rescued by the time traveler Rama-Tut, who was so impressed with Doom that upon his return to his own time, he created for himself the masked identity of Kang the Conqueror. Rama-Tut had suggested to Doom at the time that they might actually be the same person, though this eventually proved false.

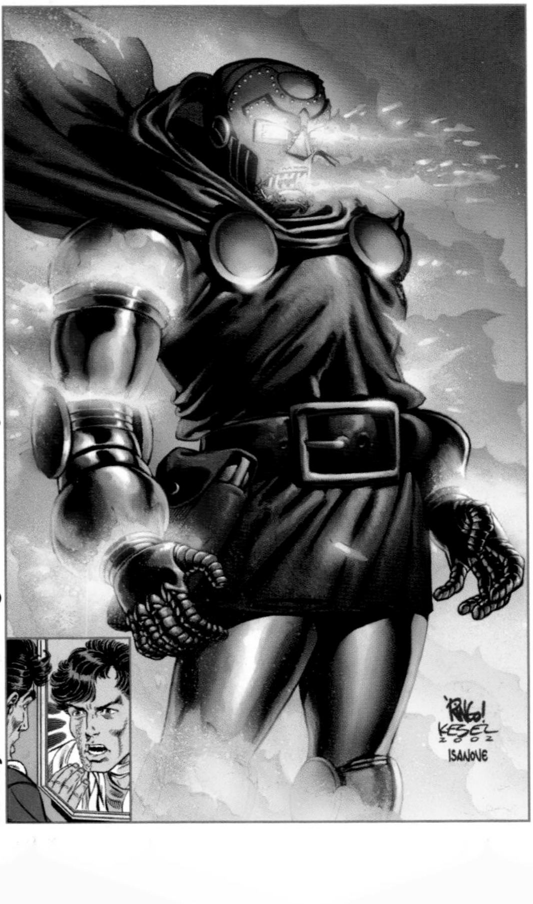
RINGO!
KESEL 2002
ISANOVE

Art by Mike Wieringo with John Byrne (inset)

Dr. Doom next engaged Reed in a mental battle at the Latverian Embassy to determine who had the greater intellect. They employed an encephalo-gun, which would cast the loser into Limbo, and Doom seemed to win the contest; but Reed had actually hypnotized Doom into believing Reed was cast into Limbo. When Doom was freed from the mesmerism by a Latverian hypnotist, he again targeted the Fantastic Four, who had temporarily lost their powers, but was humiliated in the ensuing battle when the Thing regained his powers and, furious that he had been forced to become the Thing to stop Doom, angrily crushed Doom's hands inside his gauntlets then allowed him to slink away. Doom, in turn, never forgot the Thing's actions that day.

When Reed Richards was to wed Sue Storm, a spiteful Doom used an Emotion Charger to send scores of super-villains to the wedding site, but they were defeated by the FF and their super-heroic wedding guests. Reed ultimately undid the assault with a sub-atronic time displacer which sent all of the villains back to before Doom summoned them with no memory of what had occurred. Reed and Sue's wedding took place without further incident. Doom engaged in new schemes, once stealing the Silver Surfer's powers, which he lost by challenging the barrier Galactus had placed around the Earth. He also swapped bodies with Daredevil, but this farce was foiled by the FF. Doom's obsession with the FF once nearly led him to sacrifice an entire Latverian village to kill them. Doom has also played deadly games with his robot, the Prime-Mover, games that have manipulated Nick Fury and Shang-Chi into battling robot duplicates of enemies such as the Yellow Claw and Razor-Fist.

Diablo once tried to force Doom into a partnership by holding his long-lost love Valeria hostage, but Doom used his time machine to cast Diablo into the future. He saved Valeria, but then lost her again — Valeria was ashamed of Doom's petty gloating over Diablo's fate. Doom's throne was threatened by its rightful heir, Prince Rudolfo, who was assisted by the extraterrestrial Faceless One. Doom also had to contend with his rogue creation the Doomsman, and with the Red Skull, who attempted to claim Latveria for himself. The Black Panther, ruler of Wakanda, foiled Doom's attempt to steal Wakanda's Vibranium, but Doom intended to make an ally of T'Challa one day. Doom also accumulated various power objects culminating in his using the Cosmic Cube to usurp Galactus's power, but Reed stole the Cube, reversed its effects, and erased the events from everyone's memory. Doom once fought side-by-side with the FF to save the Earth from the Over-Mind, acknowledging that while he had no love for them, he would not allow anyone to threaten Latveria.

When the Faceless One sponsored another Latverian revolt, Doom hired Luke Cage to spy on them in the United States; however, he then refused to pay Cage for his services, so Cage tracked Doom down in Latveria and fought him to a standstill until Doom finally agreed to pay Cage what he was due. After rejecting Doom's offer of a new alliance, Namor reluctantly sought Doom's aid when the people of Atlantis were rendered comatose and Mr. Fantastic could not revive them. Namor aided Doom against Andro, formerly the Doomsman, who had brought many of Doom's robots under his control through a self-created religion; Doom in turn aided Namor against his enemies Dr. Dorcas, Tiger Shark, Krang and Attuma. Still, Namor could not bring himself to fully trust Doom, so Doom ruined the water rebreather suit Namor needed to survive at that time and threatened to destroy Atlantis unless Namor pledged his allegiance to him. Namor was forced to comply.

Learning of Namor's fate, the FF came to Latveria to aid him, only to discover that the United States had signed a nonaggression pact with Latveria, forcing them to depart. Surviving an assassination attempt by the vigilante Shroud, Doom subsequently mind-controlled the Avengers into fighting Attuma for him. Finally, after receiving Namor's aid against the Red Skull, who had slain Rudolfo and briefly usurped control of Latveria, Doom made good on his bargain restoring the Atlanteans to consciousness; Namor then ended their partnership. Following this, Doom spread a neuro-gas into Earth's atmosphere to bind the entire world's population to his will. His authority was challenged by the mutant Magneto, and they fought, manipulating the Champions of Los Angeles, Avengers and Hulk into fighting for their sides. When Doom was attacked by the Ghost Rider, his mask overheated and he was forced to remove it, inhaling his own neuro-gas; this rendered him unable to control anyone affected by the gas. Via power gained from the Negative Zone, Doom accessed the netherworld, only to be overwhelmed by spirits posing as his parents.

Realizing that his villainous actions had injured Latveria's reputation, Doom planned to abdicate the throne to his "son," actually a clone of himself named Victor von Doom II; but his son's true origins were exposed, and Doom was forced to slay the clone when it turned against him. However, this plot had merely been a ruse for Doom to take mental control of the United Nations using his Solartron Complex. After he was exposed to multiple images of his own face projected by the Solartron, Doom went completely insane and was imprisoned. Prince Zorba, Rudolfo's younger brother, reclaimed his family's throne from Doom, but Doom was freed by Boris and regained his sanity.

Aided by the Puppet Master, Doom had the Fantastic Four's minds placed into miniature synthetic bodies, living a mostly idyllic life in the miniature town of "Liddleville" within his Adirondack castle. Doom hoped this would prevent the FF from interfering with his attempts to regain the throne, but the FF managed to turn the tables on him and he wound up imprisoned within a synthetic body in Liddleville. The Puppet Master, furious at how his stepdaughter Alicia had been treated by Doom's world, led an army against him there. Doom sought aid from the alien Micronauts when they passed through, but was finally rescued when his Doombots activated a contingency plan to return his consciousness to his own body. Learning that Latveria had fallen into anarchy without him, Doom convinced the Fantastic Four to assist him in overthrowing the now-insane Zorba and retaking his throne; Doom himself slew Zorba. A young Latverian boy named Kristoff Vernard was orphaned by Zorba's forces, and Doom took the child under his protection, making him his heir. Another man, Alexander Flynn, claimed to be Doom's true son, but that was later shown to be a falsehood created by the mutant telepath Shadow King.

Unleashing Terrax against the Fantastic Four, Doom was disintegrated when Terrax exploded in a blast of cosmic energy. Using the Ovoid technique, Doom transferred his mind into the body of an onlooker, Norman McArthur, instants before his death. He eventually regained his original body from the Beyonder, who sent him back a short distance in time to participate in the "Secret Wars" on his artificially created Battleworld. There Doom briefly usurped the immense power of not only Galactus, but the Beyonder himself, though he eventually lost all of his stolen power. Back on Earth, Doom once more achieved world domination, using the Purple Man's mind control powers to subjugate the global population. Although Doom was able to solve most of the world's problems by using his work in Latveria as a model, he found the mindless obedience of humanity unsatisfying, and ultimately allowed the Purple Man to slip from his grasp during a conflict with the Avengers and Namor.

After Terrax seemingly killed Doom, his Doombots had activated a contingency plan whereby Doom's past experiences were implanted within Kristoff's mind so that he could assume Doom's role. Kristoff went mad, believing he was Doom trapped in the body of a child. While Kristoff ruled Latveria, one of the Doombots, believing itself to be the true Doom, made a weak attempt at overthrowing him. Finally, the true Dr. Doom returned to Latveria following a time travel adventure, and he retook the throne from Kristoff. Soon after this, he helped cure Ms. Marvel (Sharon Ventura), a new member of the FF who had become a grotesque "She-Thing." Doom used her to spy on the FF, but she eventually gave in to her conscience and turned against him. He transformed her into an even more grotesque creature as punishment.

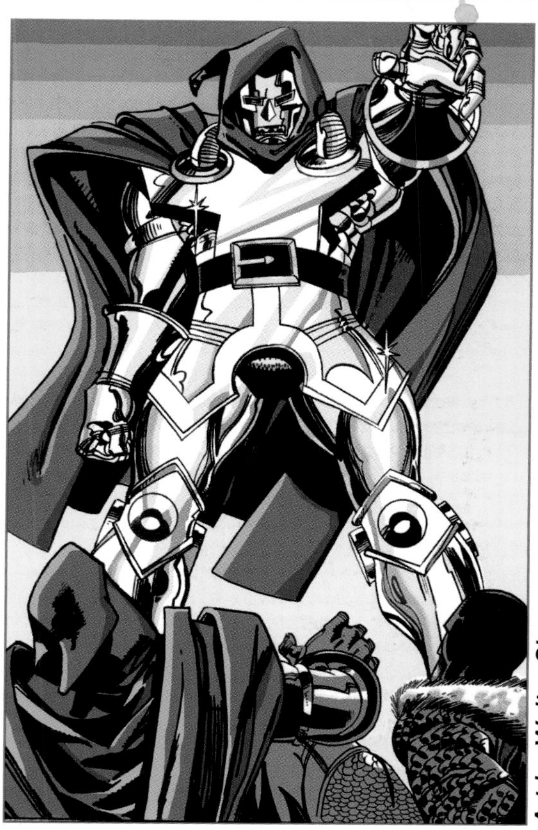
Art by Walter Simonson

Perhaps Doom's most humiliating experience was when Squirrel Girl defeated him by sending her squirrels to chew apart the wiring in his armor. Doom often attributes his many defeats to his Doombots; a Doombot participated in the "Acts of Vengeance," teaming up with the other prime movers — who were unknowingly pawns of the Asgardian trickster-god Loki — against new foes. Other Doombots, such as Mechadoom, have even turned against Doom and pursued their own goals, though such betrayal rarely long survives Doom's discovery. Doom has seen to it that Latveria's history is constantly revised to suit his needs, employing the mysterious Editor to affect all such changes. Doom tends to blame failures on underlings — such as Gustav and Gert Hauptmann — who seldom live to fail again. Doom claims to have a contingency plan for every situation, and regards the FF's victories over him as mere setbacks. Doom's greatest victory came when, after years of combating Mephisto, he and Dr. Strange finally rescued the soul of Cynthia von Doom from Hell, allowing her to pass on to a better afterlife.

After briefly usurping the cosmic energies of Aron the Watcher, Doom was severely wounded while seeking the power of the alien Hunger. Doom attempted to take Reed with him and the pair were seemingly disintegrated in a powerful energy blast; however, the immensely powerful Hyperstorm had teleported them away. Long believed dead, Doom was freed from his extradimensional prison by the Fantastic Four and Kristoff, and aided them against Hyperstorm. Returning to Earth, Doom seemingly died yet again, this time alongside Earth's heroes battling Onslaught; but Doom and the others were preserved in the new Counter-Earth, created by Franklin Richards, and Doom lived out a new life in which he was an old friend of Bruce Banner, Reed Richards and Tony Stark, who had all been members of a fraternity called "Knights of the Atomic Table."

But history repeated itself, and Doom became a villain on this Earth as well. When the heroes regained their memories, Doom helped them return to their own Earth via the Negative Zone, but when he attempted to abscond with Franklin, Doom was assaulted by Thor and cast back to Counter-Earth. With no super heroes to oppose him, Doom soon became ruler of Counter-Earth. He recruited Divinity, Dorma, Lancer, Shakti and Technarx as lieutenants, and won a decisive victory over the powerful Dreaming Celestial, which had attempted to claim Counter-Earth for itself. For a while, Doom ruled both Counter-Earth and Latveria simultaneously by projecting holograms back to Earth, but he ultimately found that Counter-Earth could never equal the utopia of his Latveria, so he returned to Earth to resume his duties in Latveria, leaving Lancer to rule Counter-Earth in his stead. Doom has shown an infatuation with the X-Men's Storm (Ororo Munroe). Via the powers of a defective Cosmic Cube, Doom once merged two realities, creating one in which he ruled Earth as emperor, with Storm as his queen. Like all of such efforts to achieve supreme power, however, the power was eventually usurped from him and normal reality restored.

When Thor led an unauthorized invasion of Slokovia, a country neighboring Latveria, Doom aided the Avengers in fighting their rogue ally — manipulating events so that when Slokovia's government collapsed, Doom moved in and annexed the country, adding it to Latveria. Dr. Doom assisted in the birth of Reed and Susan's daughter Valeria Richards, who was named after Doom's childhood love, but Doom only performed this act of kindness as part of a grander scheme. Having recognized that it was in magic — in which he had been trained by the likes of Radu and Cagliostro — that he was truly Reed's superior, Doom forged an alliance with the demon Haazareth, and sacrificed to them his greatest love, Valeria. The Haazareth increased his mystical might to the point where he was a threat to even Dr. Strange. Dr. Doom fashioned for himself new armor from his former lover's body and made Valeria Richards his familiar. He wielded his new mystical power against the Fantastic Four, attempting to break them as he never had before, sending Franklin Richards to Hell and torturing the FF. Once again, Reed defeated him by both mastering some magic himself and turning Doom's own pride against him by having him claim to acknowledge no superior in front of the Haazareth. The Haazareth took Doom into Hell with them, but he left "parting gifts" — a traumatized Franklin and a scar down the left side of Reed's face.

Art by Mike Wieringo

LEATHER ARMOR

Determined to devise a final solution to Doom, Reed created an infinitely large Mobius dimension to serve as Doom's prison, and had all of Doom's backup equipment in Latveria destroyed. Doom briefly escaped the prison by taking mental possession of the FF, but was ultimately forced back into his own body. When the realm of Asgard succumbed to its destruction in Ragnarok, the mystical forces unleashed enabled Doom to escape. Reclaiming the throne of Latveria, he then sought to obtain Thor's hammer from where it had fallen to Earth, but he proved unable to overcome the mallet's worthiness enchantment. Soon after, Doom was targeted by the Avengers when a Latverian satellite containing vicious extra-terrestrial symbiotes was accidentally unleashed on New York City. Doom recruited creatures from Morgan Le Fay to assist him, but the Avengers ultimately beat him and placed him in SHIELD custody.

BEYONDER-EMPOWERED SECRET WARS FORM

HEIGHT: 6'2" (in armor) 6'7"	EYES: Brown
WEIGHT: 225 lbs. (in armor) 415 lbs.	HAIR: Brown

ABILITIES/ACCESSORIES: Doom can exchange minds with others. He possesses some mystical abilities, such as casting bolts of eldritch energy and invoking mystical entities (principalities) for additional support. While empowered by the Haazareth, his mystical powers were on a par with those of Dr. Strange.

Doom is a genius in physics, robotics, cybernetics, genetics, weapons technology, biochemistry, and time travel. He is also self-taught in the mystic arts. Doom is a natural leader, a brilliant strategist, and a sly deceiver.

Doom wears a sophisticated nuclear-powered titanium battlesuit which grants him superhuman strength, contains jets for flight, houses a personal force field, and discharges concussive force blasts; he can also electrify his armor's surface. The armor contains a 4-hour air supply, and can be sealed for travel into outer space or underwater. Special attachments to the armor have included a molecular-expander, which can cause molecules to expand to the size of boulders, and various devices for absorbing the energies of others (such as the Silver Surfer).

Doom's many inventions include a variety of robots, such as robot duplicates of himself (Doombots), Latveria's robot police force (Servo-Guards), an army of unstoppable robots designed only to destroy (Killer Robots), as well as robots designed for slave labor and non-humanoid models used for special posts; his time machine, with which he can travel through space and time; and a shrink ray.

POWER GRID	1	2	3	4	5	6	7
INTELLIGENCE							
STRENGTH							
SPEED							
DURABILITY							
ENERGY PROJECTION							
FIGHTING SKILLS							

Text by Michael Hoskin